LAWRENCE I. BERKOVE

A Prescription *for* Adversity:

THE MORAL ART OF

AMBROSE BIERCE

THE OHIO STATE UNIVERSITY PRESS

Columbus

Library of Congress Cataloging-in-Publication Data

Berkove, Lawrence I.
  A prescription for adversity : the moral art of Ambrose Bierce /
Lawrence I. Berkove
      p. cm.
Includes bibliographical references and index.
  ISBN 0-8142-0894-0 (cloth : alk. paper)—ISBN 0-8142-5091-2 (pbk. : alk. paper)
  1. Bierce, Ambrose, 1842–1914?—Ethics. 2. Didactic literature, American—
History and criticism. 3. Journalism—United States—History. 4. Moral conditions
in literature. 5. Ethics in literature. 6. War in literature. I. Title.
  PS1097.Z5 B47 2002
  813'.4—dc21

                                                              2001006159

Text and jacket design by Diane Gleba Hall.
Type set in Baskerville by Sans Serif, Inc.
Printed by Thomson-Shore, Inc.

The paper used in this publication meets the minimum requirements of the
American National Standard for Information Sciences—Permanence of Paper for
Printed Library Materials. ANSI Z39.48-1992.

9 8 7 6 5 4 3 2 1

⌐ CONTENTS ⌐

⊰ ACKNOWLEDGMENTS ⊱

THIS BOOK has been a long time in the making, but it has not been lonely work. I can honestly say that I have enjoyed every minute I've spent reading and studying Bierce. Among my happiest memories are the many occasions when I have been in the midst of serious scholars at research libraries and archives, and have been the only one who laughed with delight at the wit and skill of the author I was studying. When I began my dissertation, I had the encouragement of M. E. Grenander. After it was completed, Carey McWilliams gave me his considerable support. My students over the years often helped me with ideas and excitement, and colleagues braced me with their judgment.

There has never been a large number of Bierce specialists, but among them S. T. Joshi and David E. Schultz (neither of whom I have yet met in person) have become friends as well as colleagues. In a renewal of the spirit of cooperation I enjoyed with McWilliams and Grenander, I have been able to assist them with some information and counsel, and they have reciprocated most generously with abundant help for me. Their excellent books were literally at my elbow as I wrote this book, and I have been in frequent touch with them. My obligation to their careful work and their willingness to share information from their massive databases is great. I look forward to their edition of Bierce's correspondence, a much-needed work, and am deeply grateful to them for giving me full access to their data and granting me permission to make use of some material even before their own publication of it.

For access to the letters that I quote, I thank the following archives: the Huntington Library of San Marino, California; the Bancroft Library of the University of California, Berkeley; the Alderman Library of the University of Virginia; the Henry W. and Albert A. Berg Collection of the New York Public Library; the University of Cincinnati; and the M. E. Grenander Papers at the State University of New York, Albany.

I also wish to express my appreciation to my school, the University of Michigan–Dearborn, for the financial and released time support it has given me over the years to pursue continuing research; to the National Endowment for the Humanities, for a summer stipend that enabled me to begin a draft of this book; to Joseph Csicsila for his careful proofreading of my manuscript; and to Michele Kargol, various other friends and associates, and my children for repeatedly coming to my rescue when I've been frustrated to the limit by the esoteric and perverse idiosyncrasies of that (to me) most refractory of all necessary tools, the computer. But most of all, I wish to thank my beloved wife, Gail, and my children, Ethan, Naomi, and Daniel, for their gentle and tactful persistence in never letting me forget that this book was still in me, and never letting me give up my resolution to complete it.

⊰ INTRODUCTION ⊱

I T IS DIFFICULT to write about Ambrose Bierce without being caught up in his personality or, rather, an image of his personality. Most of what has been written about Bierce is either a direct or indirect reaction to the semi-legendary personality who wrote shocking stories, coined wickedly clever definitions, and refined literary insult into an art form, but it is my intention to focus this book not so much on Bierce the man as on Bierce the author. No portrait of Bierce, moreover, can be valid that does not accurately represent his ideas and assess his literary importance. However fascinating his life may have been, he is of interest to students of literature primarily for his writings and not for his colorful personality. The character of his writing, let alone the extent of his influence, has yet to be fully established, but it is doubtful that American literature, and perhaps even world literature, would have been the same without him.[1]

I do not deny the importance of biography to an understanding of Bierce, nor will I eschew it, but most biographies of him have overlooked all but a fraction—and usually the same fraction— of his writings. As good as that fraction is, it is not sufficient to supply its own context, and the rest of his writings, many of which are meritorious in their own right and contain valuable autobiographical as well as critical information, have been largely ignored. Almost alone of all significant authors of the late nineteenth century, he is not studied developmentally. Jack London, who died at forty; Frank Norris, who died at thirty-two; and even Stephen Crane, who died at twenty-nine, are acknowledged to have earlier and later periods. Only Bierce's literature is treated as if it had all been written at the same time, as if no growth or changes had taken place within him. As a consequence, incomplete biography has taken precedence over the literature he wrote and has warped literary interpretation.

Attractively alliterative but simplistic tags, "Bitter Bierce" and "Death's Dilettante," have been applied to him, and the romantically mysterious circumstances of his disappearance have absorbed a great deal of attention without yielding any light. The tags and his disappearance are often linked for the purpose of interpreting his admittedly brilliant short stories, and they and the stories are often forced into a closed loop in which they reinforce each other, but at a superficial level. The great stories, however, have backgrounds, depths, and nuances that have been only touched by conventional criticism. It is long overdue for scholarship to break the loop and introduce new information that establishes the signatures of Bierce's art and thought—for students of literature, the essential Bierce—and reveals how the artist evolved.

The questions of when and where and how Bierce died, and why, are topics of legitimate interest, but are of doubtful value to the understanding of his stories, most of which were written a quarter of a century or more earlier. I accept that he is dead and admit that I have no new light to throw on the matter. More important to readers of Bierce, however, than the manner of his death, or even of his life, should be the manner of his writing. He was a professional writer from 1867 to 1909, and his total output is vast. He tried his hand at a number of literary genres: short stories, the novel, fables, epigrams, satires, hoaxes, essays, and poetry, as well as journalism. He was superb at some and at least successful at the rest, but on all he placed the indelible stamp of his original genius, and his oeuvre includes some of the best short stories ever written.

Few American authors so owe their success to their own unaided ability as does Bierce. He is one of those rare authors, like John Donne and William Blake in British literature, or Edgar Allan Poe in American, who survived in the face of almost overwhelming critical misunderstanding and neglect, but who were kept alive and eventually vindicated because devoted readers kept them in circulation. Professional critics, on the other hand, have always had trouble with Bierce. For the most part, their attitudes toward him have been curiously ambivalent. On the one hand, they have had to admit that, like him or not, he was a firmly established author. On the other, most have been shocked or put off by the seemingly flippant sarcasm or macabre quality of his stories. Even in his lifetime, either baffled by his style or diverted by his legend, they could not explain him, so they "discovered" him,[2] inspiring him to compose this ironic couplet, which is still valid: "My! how my fame rings out in every zone— / A thousand critics shouting, 'He's unknown!'" From his time to the early-twenty-first century, his fiction has received essentially the same treatment. His stories are still being "discovered" to be in conformance with one or another of the literary fads of the moment, and writers of literary histories feel compelled to mention him, even though from their brief and sometimes misleading comments it is apparent that they do not sufficiently understand him.[3]

This study of Bierce's short fiction will therefore undertake to define and explain Bierce's intellectual profile—his philosophical inclination—and to show that his struggle with its demands is what made him a literary artist. A significant amount of evidence for this will come from the analysis of texts of representative Bierce tales, including comparisons with their original periodical versions, and from other works seldom if ever studied. Additional evidence will come from the dating of the texts of his works; from biography and presently uncollected correspondence; and also from the most important and extensive source of information that exists about Bierce, the uncollected lifetime record of his journalism. For over forty years, Bierce wrote the history of his own time in his magazine and newspaper contributions, and revealed a great deal about himself in the process. It is difficult to overestimate the importance of this trove, for it catches Bierce in all his moods and all his encounters with the personalities, events, and ideas of his time.

Apart from the excessive influence of inadequate biography on interpretation of his literature, and the neglect of both his journalism and his lesser-known fiction, a major difficulty in understanding Bierce is that the brilliant surface of his fiction has so dazzled most readers that they have not gotten beyond it, let alone recognized its patternings. A good deal of his fiction, for example, is so stunning in its effects that even professional critics have concluded that Bierce is gratuitously shocking, that effect is all and that there is nothing more. But not long ago, the same was thought of Edgar Allan Poe. As long as critics think this way, they do not pay close enough attention to the way Bierce's stories are constructed, and many do not even suspect that there is intellectual and moral depth to his fiction.

It is true that some of his works are of limited literary value, and have no larger purpose than being startling. It is a mistake, however, to thus characterize most of his fiction, for a great deal of it—certainly including most of the stories in his great collection of 1892, *Tales of Soldiers and Civilians,* and some in *Can Such Things Be?* (1893), but also stories written as early as the 1870s and as late as the first decade of the twentieth century—displays a subtle but positive concern for humanity that endows it with an appeal that has always been sensed but never adequately defined. From the very first, stories such as "An Occurrence at Owl Creek Bridge," "Horseman in the Sky," "Chickamauga," and "A Son of the Gods" have had such popular acceptance and critical acclaim as to challenge the adequacy of the most common aspersion of Bierce's stories—that they are merely technical showpieces of stylistic brilliance but have little depth or direction. These few stories have usually been spared the worst animadversions and have been accorded the status of exceptions, assigned to a sort of literary limbo with a few lines of grudging and superficial compliment. Bierce has fared somewhat better with anthologists, who have generally included one or two of his stories—usually "An Occurrence at Owl Creek Bridge"[4]—in their collections, despite their beliefs that he was a bitter individual and that there was some sort of trick at play in the stories.

Arguments to counter these beliefs can be found in the scholarly literature if only critics would make a thorough search of it. Some attempts, for example, to identify the serious intellectual character of Bierce's stories have located him within the literary tradition of ancient and modern classics. It has not been uncommon for critics to note, at least in passing, that Bierce's work bears some resemblance to Swift, Voltaire, La Rochefoucauld, and other famous "shockers" and cynics. Wilson Follett, for example, early said that "in Ambrose Bierce we have a purely American immortal whose claim is variously akin to the claims of Epictetus, Martial, Aesop, LaFontaine, Pascal, and La Rochefoucauld."[5] This listing, it will be shown, is far from being accidental or gratuitous. Even Adolphe de Castro, the most notorious and unreliable of Bierce's biographers, was perceptive enough to recognize in Bierce's writings a strong link to a famous and formidable intellectual tradition, "the tradition of Juvenal, Martial, Cervantes, Swift, and Voltaire,"[6] and more recently Jay Martin reaffirmed Bierce's indebtedness to the classical tradition, nominating additional classical authors to the list.[7] But although earlier critics traced the ultimate basis of Bierce's fiction back to what Harry Lynn Sheller described as "an earnest moral and aesthetic purpose . . . to compel moral behavior"[8] and what Eric Partridge before him found to be a "far-stretching, profound, general, and kindly" humanity,[9] all stopped short of mapping that purpose.

In sum, the most perceptive studies of the first century of Bierce criticism, the work of the minority of critics who found depth in his stories, have repeatedly called attention to two outstanding features of his art: his techniques of compelling his readers' minds, and an ethical quality in his best fiction that reflects a concern for humanity. As the study of how Bierce manipulates readers' minds naturally leads to the question "To what end?" so does the process of studying his central values naturally leads to the question "How does he manifest them?" At this point, an organic relationship of these two features of his writing is suggested and some justification for considering them together made evident.

The primary goal of this book, therefore, is to establish the relationship of Bierce's concern about the use of reason to his concern for mankind by identifying the basic elements of his thought, and by describing the operation of his literary techniques. A secondary goal is to retrieve his literature from the neglect to which it has been assigned by ill-founded, obtuse, and unproductive approaches based on skewed notions of his personality and forced or facile readings of individual stories. Like Swift, whom he admired and imitated and with whom he had much in common, Bierce was a man who hated boldly and well and yet was not a Timonian misanthrope.[10] Just as underlying Swift's satirical attacks are a set of intelligent and moral principles, so also are Bierce's stands founded upon values that, once identified, can be respected. The assumption that Bierce was unfeeling and cynical his whole life long is untenable when the evidence is evaluated. He was far more complicated than such a simplistic view can support. I do not wish to argue the opposite, that Bierce was easy to get along with or that he was a misunderstood philanthropist. Bierce often was irascible and hard, but it was case-hardness, an exterior severity developed to protect something softer within. Once this is demonstrated, it will be possible to arrive at a more satisfactory understanding of Bierce's art and a more accurate estimation of his rightful place in American letters.

The literary oeuvre of Ambrose Bierce is not a small puddle to be easily plumbed and stepped over. The sophistication of his art and thought requires more attention than the majority of his critics have even imagined. His literary canon is much more extensive than that represented by the twelve volumes of the *Collected Works,* which he himself assembled and edited from 1909 to 1912, and which has been the basis for most of the reprintings of his works since then. For it, he barely tapped his first three books, which were published in England; these have consequently been neglected as sources of information about him and his art. Other explicitly literary works that he either forgot about or decided, perhaps whimsically, not to include in the *Collected Works* were ignored. The vast corpus of his journalism he depreciated as subliterary and represented it scantily and in altered form as reconstructed essays. The original journalism, however, is much better than he thought. A great deal of it remains engaging and insightful, and contains much crucial information about him, but it has been bypassed by all but a handful of Bierce scholars.

Only a small and unrepresentative fraction of his correspondence has been utilized in scholarship. True, as of this writing, his entire correspondence has not been collected and published, but it has always been available to researchers. But assiduous Bierce scholars have always been, and remain, a small minority. A disproportionately large amount of what passes for Bierce criticism has been the work of perhaps well-intentioned amateurs who have lit upon some story, or some group of definitions from *The Devil's Dictionary*, for literary analysis but who have overestimated the capabilities of the literary theories they favored, misjudged the complications of what they were analyzing, and underestimated the need for being more well grounded in Bierce's work as a whole, and Bierce scholarship as a whole.

Modern scholarship begins with Carey McWilliams, one of *four* Bierce biographers who all published their books in 1929![11] What distinguishes McWilliams from those others (and all biographers that have followed), besides the breadth of his reading and his thorough and searching interviews with individuals who knew Bierce, is a mind trained to collect and work with evidence and to arrive at conclusions based on a careful examination and judicious weighing of it. For the most part, his predecessors related partial views of Bierce in memoirs or impressions of him and made little attempt to be scholarly. McWilliams's biography, though corrected or augmented in parts by subsequent scholarship,[12] remains so generally valid and perceptive as to be indispensable. Harry Lynn Sheller completed a dissertation on Bierce's satire in 1945 that remains worthwhile, despite its prodigious length and its exhaustive treatment of the origins of satire. Unfortunately, Sheller did not pursue publication and make his findings more easily accessible. M. E. Grenander followed McWilliams and Sheller with a dissertation in 1948 and articles and books afterward. Like McWilliams, she read widely and deeply in Bierce and was an incisive critic.

I consider myself particularly fortunate in having known personally both McWilliams and Grenander and in having been able to call upon their expertise and share information with them. They set a standard for scholarship that I have tried ever since to live up to. This is not to say that I have always agreed with their interpretations. Grenander and I, especially, have sometimes had quite different readings of Bierce and of individual works. But these have been friendly and respectful differences, made within the context of our common conviction that Bierce is one of America's classic authors— a precious part of our cultural heritage, for all his uniqueness—but that he is seriously misjudged and deserves more painstaking, systematic study and more esteem than he has thus far received.

The recognition that Bierce remains widely misjudged and seriously underestimated is almost a distinguishing characteristic of the best scholarship of recent years. This scholarship has resulted in a number of worthwhile articles and books, some of which I have been able to acknowledge in my notes. Easily the most eminent of these works are the excellent editions of important but hard-to-locate Bierce works that have been prepared by S. T. Joshi and David E. Schultz: *A Sole Survivor: Bits of Autobiography* (1998), *Ambrose Bierce: An Annotated Bibliography of Primary Sources* (1999), *The Unabridged Devil's Dictionary* (2000), *Collected Fables* (2000), and *The Fall of the Republic* (2000), their collection of Bierce's political and social satires. The major extension of new Bierce material beyond the limits of the flawed twelve-volume *Collected Works* that these books represent ought to revitalize Bierce scholarship. I cannot imagine any future scholarship of substance that does not build on the foundation they have helped establish.

It is my hope that this book also becomes part of the foundation of future scholarship. It is the outcome of a continuous interest in Bierce dating back even before 1962, when I completed my dissertation on his *Tales of Soldiers and Civilians*. Since then I have been gratified that colleagues and students who become familiar with my ongoing research find it helpful and leading to an increased interest in Bierce. Their reactions have encouraged me to undertake this more extensive study that assimilates my dissertation but goes well beyond it by addressing a fuller range of Bierce's short fiction. My original ideas have been considerably complemented, corrected, and expanded by new insights, and augmented by what I've learned from scholarship. This book is not a complete discussion of every aspect of Bierce nor is it an overview of all of his fiction.[13] It is limited to using a representative sampling of significant works and supporting evidence to establish that there are recurrent and fundamental themes running through Bierce's writings that tie his early, middle, and late work together; that those themes are essential to an understanding of his deepest values; and that his literary genius consists of the techniques he devised to convey those themes. This book, therefore, essays to advocate and support a useful and valid approach to his short fiction, and thereby establish a sound basis for coming to grips with Bierce and appreciating him as a literary artist and a thinker.

I have not usually footnoted information that I included in my dissertation or subsequently developed in the substantial number of papers I have presented over the years at conferences or published as articles—information that has subsequently been rediscovered independently by others or silently assimilated; I have merely reclaimed what was already my own. Nor have I chosen to identify all the instances where something I wrote was taken out of context or misread. I have concentrated on making known what I have learned about Bierce's short stories during the course of my career, and on doing my best to advance scholarship toward that point in time, hopefully not too far in the future, when there will be more of an informed consensus on Bierce than there is now. I have enjoyed writing this book and trust that some of that pleasure comes from a justified conviction in the merits of its thesis and its methodology: the scholarly evidence it uses for support, and the validity and persuasiveness of the reasoning it employs for its critical assessments. It is my fervent wish to continue the critical tradition of McWilliams and Grenander, and to be worthy of their company.

❦ 1 ❧

THE TOPOGRAPHY OF
BIERCE'S CAREER

The Youthful Years: 1842–60

AMBROSE GWINETT BIERCE was born on 24 June 1842, in Horse Cave, Ohio, an unincorporated backwoods settlement that Carey McWilliams says was founded by "very religious and pious emigrants from Connecticut."[1] Ambrose was the tenth of thirteen children born to farmers Marcus Aurelius and Laura Sherwood Bierce.[2] The family later moved to Warsaw, Indiana, where Ambrose grew to young manhood, and then to Elkhart, Indiana. Bierce detested his early rural surroundings and later spoke disparagingly of them. He had little in common with his family, except for his brother Albert, and did not retain close ties with them once he left home. On the other hand, the common belief—probably an inference from the group of his stories known as "The Parenticide Club"—that he despised his parents is contradicted by the evidence of two surviving letters to his mother occasioned by his father's fatal illness. I quote substantially from them because they are not well known and their information is very important. The first is dated 13 February 1876.

My Dear Mother,
Al has shown me your letter of the fourth, and I can not tell you how deeply it has grieved me to learn that my poor

Father is so low. Of course I had long expected some such news, but had, I think, never fully realized how dreadful it would be. There is nothing I can [do] to comfort you, Mother; I need comfort myself. If Father is still living when you receive this I beg you to tell him how deeply I feel for him, how sorry I am for all the sorrow and trouble I have ever caused him, and ask him for forgive me [*sic*] for the sake of the love I have always borne him. Mrs. Bierce [Mollie, the wife of Ambrose] is, I think, almost as much pained as I at the thought of losing one whom she had learned to love, and whom she hoped to meet on this side of the grave.

My poor Mother, I cannot write as I feel; you know what I would say; you know how dreadful is this affliction to me, who have not even the consolaton [*sic*] of having been a good son to so good a father. It is very hard for us all, but there is nothing for us to do but endure whatever it may please a superior power to inflict upon our helpless hearts. Of us all, you, my poor Mother, are the only one to whom the consciousness of having always performed your every duty with unswerving patience, gentleness and grace will come to temper the bitterness of grief.

I can write no more for I am blind with tears.

The second, dated 30 April, was written after learning of his father's death.

I have delayed writing you for so long since receiving your sad account of the great grief which has fallen upon us all, only because I felt it too keenly for me to trust myself to write of it. I had, and have now, no consolation to offer you, and it seems worse than useless to revive a sorrow so great, without some attempt to alleviate it. Be assured that I deeply sympathize with you in [a] loss which is only less to me than to you.[3]

Bierce seldom if ever said what he did not believe, and although it is indisputable that he resented and opposed the strongly religious atmosphere of his home, both of these letters show that he was tenderly devoted to his parents and genuinely regretful of his shortcomings in his relations toward them.

Very little is known of Bierce's formal schooling. McWilliams reports that although his early education was rudimentary, his father was a relatively well-read man and had a good library for the time.[4] A letter Bierce wrote to James Tufts on 27 July 1897 makes clear that he took advantage of it: "You are right about that library. I owe more to my father's books than to any other educational and directive influence." Paul Fatout says that young Ambrose read and admired Dryden, Pope's translation of the *Iliad,* and a romance in the fashion of Anne Radcliffe, and took to heart some moral literature encouraging young workingmen seeking advancement to study and not look for happiness "in what is misnamed pleasure."[5] Bierce also came under the influence of his uncle, General Lucius Verus Bierce, a successful, patriotic, and distinguished citizen of Akron, Ohio, who helped him attend the Kentucky Military Institute when he approached the age of seventeen and who perhaps also served as a role model for his nephew. There, he first became acquainted with, in addition to some military subjects, the discipline of military life, which was to play an extremely important part in his life and thought after, as well as during, the Civil War. But this formal schooling was cut short by the war, and Bierce thenceforth became an autodidact who taught himself the basics of political, social, and economic theory, and classical, modern, and contemporary literature and philosophy. It yet remains for scholars to sift through his voluminous writings and cull from them the many allusions to specific subjects, authors, and works that would enable us to formulate a clear idea of the full range of what he read and studied and stored in the library of his mind. But without a doubt, the greatest single learning experience of Bierce's life was the Civil War. He cannot be properly understood or appreciated without some sense of what the war meant to him.

The War Years: 1861–67

IT IS AN ODD FACT of American literary history that despite the cataclysm of the Civil War that engaged and branded millions of men and their families, North and South, no American author more eminent than Bierce fought in it. Walt Whitman is a possible and qualified exception, for though a noncombatant he at least was close to the battlefronts. As Edmund Wilson shows, most of the authors with firsthand experience of battle are writers either of only topical reputation or of minor classics.[6] Few in any category equal Bierce in his range and depth of experience, and none in literary ability.

He enlisted at the first call to arms and remained in uniform until almost the end of the war. On 19 April 1861, he volunteered as a private soldier for three months' service with the Ninth Indiana Infantry. After one month, his unit saw action at Philippi, one of the first battles of the Civil War. When the three months were up, he reenlisted as a sergeant and was sent to the Cheat River Valley in what is now West Virginia. He became nostalgically fond of this region and used it as a setting for some of his stories and as the subject of some of his autobiographical memoirs, and revisited it and wrote movingly reminiscent letters about it in the last decade of his life.

After his unit was recalled from western Virginia, he fought at Shiloh (a seminal experience in the formation of his personal philosophy) and at Corinth, after which he was commissioned a second lieutenant. He became a topographical engineer, responsible for reconnoitering the grounds of prospective battle sites and preparing maps. This experience left him with unusually clear recollections of military engagements that he put to literary use in his stories and journalism. Bierce subsequently participated in the Nashville campaign of 1862 and in the battle of Stones River, or Murfreesboro, on 31 December 1862. He fought at Chickamauga in the fall of 1863 and at Missionary Ridge in the battle of Chattanooga, in mid-November. In the spring of 1864, he participated in the southern advance of the Army of the Cumberland from Chattanooga to Atlanta, and was engaged in "skirmishes" at Dalton, Resaca, Adairsville, Kennesaw Mountain, Kingston, Cassville, and Pickett's Mill, all in Georgia.

Finally, on 23 June 1864, at Kennesaw Mountain, he received a severe head wound, which put him out of action for several months and caused him to be furloughed home. In his memoirs of the Civil War, Bierce's stern but deeply admired commanding officer, General W. B. Hazen, recorded this incident and commended Bierce as a "brave and gallant fellow."[7] Carey McWilliams wrote that Bierce never forgot his subsequent evacuation to Chattanooga on a hospital train, where he saw how the wounded "were loaded on flatcars, covered with tarpaulin and left alone for hours with only the moon to commiserate their agonies."[8] After Bierce regained some of his strength, he returned to his unit in September of 1864 and fought with it in Tennessee at the battle of Franklin and the siege of Nashville. When the army went into winter quarters at Huntsville, Alabama, in January of 1865, Bierce, still suffering from his wound, applied for, and was granted, a discharge. Although his health largely returned, for the rest of his life Bierce was subject to splitting headaches and violent asthma attacks that incapacitated him for days on end, and sometimes longer, and drove him to seek relief for weeks at a time in villages on the western slope of the Sierra Nevadas.

That Bierce, in addition to being a close observer of many Civil War battles, was also a courageous and efficient soldier who was valued by his superiors and his subordinates has been thoroughly documented.[9] If his tales of the soldiers and civilians in the war and his autobiographical memoirs seem morbid, it should not be laid so much to a perverse and distorted imagination as to a sensitive and retentive memory of much firsthand experience, and a disposition to accuracy. He found the Civil War to be grim, and he refused to apply his considerable literary powers to making it seem romantic.

After his discharge, Bierce worked for some months with the Treasury Department in Alabama as a minor official "engaged in performance of duties exceedingly disagreeable not only to the people of the vicinity, but to myself as well. They consisted in the collection and custody of 'captured and abandoned property.'"[10] Not only was the work hazardous but it also brought him face-to-face with a different kind of bureaucratic inefficiency than he had known in the army and with the corruption that tainted the work of Reconstruction. Therefore, when a letter came from his ex–commanding officer, General Hazen, offering him a civilian position as an engineering attaché on a four-man expedition into the Indian territory, Bierce accepted.

In July 1866, the expedition left Omaha, then a village at the end of the railroad, and traveled through the Dakotas, Montana, Utah, and Nevada, visiting settlements and the Comstock mining town of Virginia City, inspecting new army posts, and making maps of the country. This expedition gave Bierce a broad view of the new Western territory, but it was not a pleasure jaunt. The group traveled through hostile Indian territory and on at least one occasion Bierce had to fight for his life during a nighttime raid. He also had a close-up, and largely disillusioning, view of pioneers and the frontiersmen who protected them.[11] When the expedition reached San Francisco in 1867, Bierce, disappointed by not being offered a captaincy in the Regular Army, left it and settled in town, getting a job there in the branch of the United States Mint.

The Postwar San Francisco Years: 1867–71

THE NEXT SEVERAL YEARS in San Francisco were important in Bierce's life as a time when he took the first steps that led to his writing career. During this period he apparently embarked upon a rigorous and successful program of self-education and read voraciously in literature and philosophy. McWilliams records that one of Bierce's fellow employees at the Mint remembered that he quoted long passages from Gibbon, looked up all new words in the dictionary, and constantly strove for definition and precision.[12] During this time, also, Bierce developed and polished his distinctively epigrammatic and biting style. It may be supposed that this latter achievement involved considerable work, for although the few wartime letters of his that have been preserved are fairly well written, they give no hint of what was to come. Within his first year there, he began to submit short essays, sketches, and humorous pieces to several periodicals in the San Francisco area. One of them, the *San Fran-*

cisco News-Letter and California Advertiser, accepted some of his work, launching his career in journalism, a profession that he would pursue for the rest of his life.

The editor of the *News-Letter,* James Watkins, played a significant part in this phase. Not only did Watkins use much of what Bierce wrote, but when Watkins resigned in December 1868, he persuaded his publisher to make Bierce the new editor.[13] In addition, and more important, he took Bierce in hand, corrected his style, and induced him to read the classics of ancient and modern literature. As long as Watkins remained in San Francisco, Bierce enjoyed a fruitful and instructive friendship with him. When Watkins finally left San Francisco for New York in 1889, Bierce in his "Prattle" column in the *San Francisco Examiner* attested to the influence Watkins had had on him. He referred to Watkins as "my master" (an extremely rare compliment from Bierce) and said of him: "I have known and studied this man for twenty years and it is my sober and matured conviction, upon the verity of which I would wish to found my reputation for literary sense, that in variety of language, definition of thought and charm of style he is among Americans incomparable and supreme. It needs but a few strokes of his pen, rightly timed and circumstanced, to bring all the judicious to that opinion."[14] Watkins introduced Bierce to a wide range of literary models that he could select from and use to develop his own style, which he quickly brought to distinction.

According to McWilliams, Bierce in his later years also acknowledged that he had once read Mark Twain to learn how "to sharpen lethiferous wit against bovine humor."[15] This is one of the few biographical references to Bierce's hitherto unsuspected connection to the impressive and influential group of writers centered in Virginia City, Nevada, known as "The Sagebrush School." At its peak from the 1860s to the 1890s, some of its authors were past masters of the literary hoax and brought that genre to its highest form of development in American letters. Mark Twain is the most outstanding graduate of that school, but among its most distinguished practitioners are William Wright (aka Dan De Quille) and Samuel Post Davis. Bierce definitely read the works of all three of these authors, partly because their writings were well known and highly regarded on the West

Coast; partly because in his role as editor/writer he accepted some of their stories into his periodicals and published his own writings in the same issues; and partly because he was personally familiar with at least Twain and Davis when they lived in California in 1868 and the late 1870s, respectively. Bierce remained a close friend of Davis, possibly visited him in Carson City, and made occasional references to him in "Prattle," and Davis always spoke warmly of him in the Carson City *Appeal*.[16] It cannot be an accident, therefore, that Bierce not only participated in the Sagebrush tradition of the literary hoax but, as will be shown later, became a master of it in his own right.[17]

In addition to editing the *News-Letter*, Bierce wrote for it a regular feature of miscellanea entitled "The Town Crier." He used the feature to expose and excoriate personalities and facets of San Francisco's political and cultural life that seemed to him to merit rebuke. That there was a controlling moral motivation behind his choice of targets was made plain in his statement of resignation from the column in the issue of 9 March 1872: "The only talents that he [the Town Crier] has are a knack at hating hypocrisy, cant, and all sham, and a trick of expressing his hatred. What wider field than San Francisco does God's green earth present?"[18] Except for its limitation here to San Francisco, this comment might well describe a great part of Bierce's journalism over his entire career. Like Jonathan Swift, whom he read perceptively, he hated, and hated well, and what he hated was pretense, deceit, public folly, meanness, and cruelty.

For the most part, his writing at this time was discursive. It usually consisted of brief, iconoclastic, and generally witty paragraphs on topical subjects and local or well-known personages. Even this early, however, Bierce's writing occasionally revealed glimpses of his ability to compact emotion into passages of disturbing power. One of the untitled sketches based on news items included in his 29 April 1871 "Town Crier" column of the *News-Letter* is outstanding in this regard. It is about a young woman who committed suicide because of her tragic gender confusion (see Appendix A).[19] The account can be read as mocking her, but to do so would neglect both its empathetic portrayal of her despair and the question she asks, "Why did not God make me a man?" The question, not asked frivolously, is another indication that his skepticism about religion derives from its failure to supply him with a convincing explanation of the evils he found in the nature of things and, especially, in human nature. Bierce was already beginning to select incidents that shocked him and to transfer their images to readers in detail that would attack their minds and shock them also.

Though Bierce's style matured over the years, he never fully departed from the feuilleton format, except when writing fiction. By 1871, however, he began to experiment with different genres of writing, sending contributions to the *Alta California* and Bret Harte's *Overland Monthly*. Among his early contributions to the *Overland Monthly* is his first full-length short story, "The Haunted Valley."[20] It is not inconsequential. Although it lacks the range and sophistication of the much richer and more profound stories of *Tales of Soldiers and Civilians*, it contributes to an understanding of Bierce's fiction and will be discussed more extensively later. For the time being, it can be described as a local color story showing the distinct influence of Bret Harte.

The English Years: 1872–75

ON 25 DECEMBER 1871, Bierce married Mary Ellen "Mollie" Day, the only daughter of a wealthy local couple. Mollie's mother, Mrs. Day, has not fared well at the hands of Bierce's biographers. Both McWilliams and Fatout, for example, describe her as socially pretentious and meddlesome. She later followed the young couple to England and stayed with them for an extended visit and also lived with them for very long periods of time after they returned to California. Bierce disliked her and resented her long visits and intrusions into his family affairs. As he was high-spirited and proud, such intrusions stimulated his efforts to become independent of the Day family. McWilliams imputes this motivation to Bierce's later ill-starred involvement with a Dakota mining company: "Bierce had not consulted either the Captain [H. N. Day, his father-in-law, a prominent mining engineer] or James Day, his brother-in-law, before accepting the position with the Dakota mining company. Hence when it failed, he had to return to San Francisco in a rather defiant attitude, and he was precluded from asking or accepting assistance from the Days."[21]

Whatever scruples against accepting aid from the Days developed in later years, Bierce was willing in March of 1872 to quit his job on the *News-Letter* to leave for England with his bride on an extended honeymoon trip given to them by her father. Soon after arriving in England, he undertook to support his family by writing for several English periodicals, primarily *Figaro*, edited by James Mortimer, and *Fun*, a journal edited by Thomas Hood the Younger that specialized in humor and satire and was contributed to by such minor luminaries as the British authors George Augustus Sala and Henry Sampson and, later, the Californian Prentice Mulford. Later in his stay, definitely from February through July of 1874, Bierce also contributed to the *London Sketch-Book*, another periodical edited by James Mortimer. While in England, he also associated with other visiting American authors: Mark Twain, Joaquin Miller, and Charles Warren Stoddard.

During his English years, Bierce soaked up English culture as he associated with sophisticated professional writers who had been raised on English literature and who cultivated the dry wit of irony and satire. He had already become a professional author, but his new English colleagues gave him the opportunity to hone his talents to a finer edge than had been possible in California. In 1873, he published two books: *The Fiend's Delight*, which the introduction describes as "a cold collation of diabolism . . . taken mainly from various California journals"; and *Nuggets and Dust*,[22] subtitled "Panned Out in California by Dod Grile / Collected and Loosely Arranged by J. Milton Sloluck," also a reprinting of a number of old articles and paragraphs he had earlier published in California, plus some new material written in England. A third book, *Cobwebs from an Empty Skull*, appeared in 1874. It consists of "The Fables of Zambri the Parsee" and miscellaneous anecdotes and sketches he had written for *Fun*. These three books, admittedly loose collections of uneven quality, have largely been ignored by Bierce scholars, probably because it is quickly apparent that they generally fall well below the quality of *Tales of Soldiers and Civilians*. Although they are inferior to the best of

Bierce, they are not inferior, and they are of considerable value in charting his development. Much can be learned from them as productions of his English years. These books, for example, demonstrate how extravagant is Van Wyck Brooks's assertion that "it was through his association with authors and artists in London . . . that the semi-literate Bierce learned really to write."[23] "Semi-literate" is a grossly mistaken description, as any scanning of his California materials will show, and Brook's estimate of the influence of Bierce's English associates on him is similarly exaggerated. Bierce undoubtedly throve in the stimulating cultural climate of England, but all the credit for this cannot go to the environment. The evidence of these three books shows that while Bierce may have flirted with English ways, he did not marry them nor did he make himself over; he grew from within. That he in fact maintained a certain intellectual independence from the English journalists in his circle is apparent both from the character of his original writings during this period and from a confidential letter to Charles Warren Stoddard in which he warned Stoddard about the journalists: "[Y]ou just 'bet your boots' I know these fellows and their ways. They think they know *me*, but they don't" (28 September 1873).[24]

A good part of Bierce's writing consisted of verbal wit ("beautiful abuse," H. L. Mencken later called it)—brilliantly vivid and mordant scourging of fools and scoundrels—but the power and purpose of later years had not yet matured. Bierce could jolt but he seldom moved his readers. Although his early writing, both in California and in England, is largely characterized by exuberant, almost gleeful satire, some predilections toward his later seriousness can be seen in it. An example occurs in *The Lantern,* a magazine of only two issues, also founded and edited by James Mortimer but entirely written by Bierce in May and July 1874 and which, unknown to him, had been endowed by the Empress Eugénie of France for the express purpose of forestalling the influence of her enemy, Henri Rochefort.[25]

> My future programme will be calm disapproval of human institutions in general, including all forms of government, most laws and customs, and all contemporary literature;

enthusiastic belief in the Darwinian theory . . . intolerance of intolerance, and war upon every man with a mission; confusion to flunkeyism and disesteem for titles of distinction, from Majesty down to esquire; no earnestness, no indignation, no declamation; human suffering and human injustice in all their forms to be contemplated with a merely curious interest, as one looks into an ant hill. . . .

Of course, I have in reality no settled programme, any more than Mr. Disraeli and the rest of them have, but there exists this difference between other augurs and myself, that whilst they carefully conceal their hilarity under an assumed solemnity, I not only laugh at them but at all the world beside. By this calculated sort of cachinnation the world may perhaps be cajoled into the belief that I am not so much a hypocrite as a charlatan.[26]

Bierce's motive in this declaration, if any, is completely disguised by a mask of irreverent mockery. But purposeless sarcasm and moral indifference had no deep or lasting appeal to him. Later, in his journalism and also his stories, he would make his intentions clearer.

Bierce's three "English" books, consisting largely of collected material previously published in America, have been inadequately appreciated partly because it was not known what and how much he wrote in England—and partly because what he wrote has not been accurately assessed. It has generally been assumed that Bierce this early in his career did not yet show evidence of the skills or themes that characterize his best work. This assumption began to crumble after the acquisition of the Proprietor's Copy of *Fun* by the Huntington Library.[27] That volume greatly illuminates our understanding of Bierce's growth and development during his English years because it specifies exactly which pieces Bierce wrote as well as how much he earned for each. This valuable record shows quite clearly that the English period was unexpectedly productive in quality as well as quantity.

According to the Proprietor's Copy, Bierce began to contribute around July 1872 and continued more or less steadily until September 1875. He normally supplied at least one item a week but sometimes as many as ten, ranging from a two- or three-line quip to a fictional sketch. For this Bierce normally earned between one and two pounds a week for his pieces. His low payment was one pound (for the sketch "Jo Dornan and the Ram"), and his high payment was two pounds, ten shillings, sixpence (for five items). The quality of his contributions varies greatly, but three features stand out: he was making progress on formulating what were to become his unique and characteristic themes and techniques, the first signs of his mature talent were beginning to emerge, and his best work was American in character as well as substance.

The significance of this third feature is at odds with the common belief that Bierce became an Anglophile during these years. Even McWilliams claims of him during this period that "[h]e had definitely abandoned America in his own mind."[28] McWilliams bases his judgment on the surviving letters Bierce wrote to personal friends, on travel letters he wrote for the *Alta California* and subsequently abridged for his first book, *Nuggets and Dust* (1873),[29] and on subsequent bits of autobiography he published in the *Argonaut,* the *Wasp,* the *San Francisco Examiner,* and in his *Collected Works.* While Bierce liked his English stay and retained fond memories of England, I do not find that Bierce, then or later, was ever an "Anglophile" in the sense that he blindly admired England and never opposed it. Bierce made his share of mistakes, but automatic, unreasoned opinions ran counter to his philosophy. Later in his career, although he was often sympathetic to England, his sympathies were never unquestioning and he on occasion forcefully took the side of America against England.[30] Even as early as 1873 in a travel letter to the *Alta,* Bierce describes feelingly the wretched poverty that drove a promising fourteen-year-old English boy to suicide,[31] and in the 28 September 1873 letter Bierce wrote to his American friend Charles Stoddard, his warning about being impressed by the "journalistic nobodies" of Fleet Street shows both in content and American vernacular that he did not identify with the English.

Further evidence contradicting McWilliams's contention that

Bierce had abandoned America in his mind is to be found in his contributions to *Fun*. They can be roughly grouped into three categories: those that are distinctly American in style or substance, those that are British in style or substance, and those that do not display nationalist inclinations. The least numerous and least distinguished of these three categories is that in which Bierce adopted an English pose. Typical of this group are squibs that comment on contemporary British politicians such as Disraeli or Gladstone, on topical British issues such as the Corn or Poor Laws, or on such tourist destinations as Bath, Windsor Castle, and Margate, a fashionable seacoast resort. Insofar as Bierce did attempt to assimilate British style, at most this attempt led him into lifelong bad habits of affecting a haughty and condescending attitude and a related mannered pomposity of style, precious and hypercorrect.

But one cannot read through Bierce's contributions to *Fun* without being struck by how numerous and distinctive are those that constitute the distinctively American category. They occur early and late, and it is impossible to imagine that any reader of *Fun* would not have quickly realized that an American, and a Westerner at that, was writing for the magazine. Several dozen of his abominable "Little Johnny" sketches, intended to be comical unedited observations of a little boy, which Bierce took a perverse and inexplicable delight in writing during his entire career, appear in 1874 and 1875. Although now almost unreadable, they are at least undeniably American. Additionally, a high percentage of his short fictional pieces are set in Western locales and make use of Western dialect.

A much more significant contribution to *Fun* was a piece called "The Civil Service in Florida" (14 June 1873), a grimly humorous anecdote obviously American in substance. A few weeks later (10 July) he published "Pernicketty's Fright," an undeservedly neglected item of autobiography, republished in *Cobwebs from an Empty Skull*, that recounts an Indian attack during Bierce's participation in Hazen's 1866 Army mapping expedition from Nebraska to California. One night, around a campfire, some experienced hunters try to frighten Nick, a nervous greenhorn, with tales of how clever Indians are at imitating wolf howls. As if on cue, wolf howls are heard in the distance and

Nick anxiously saddles his mustang, grabs his rifle and pistols, and stands quaking by his horse, ready to flee. One of the hunters assures Nick that it can't be Indians because they also would have used an owl hoot when they got close. Again as if on cue, an owl hoot is suddenly heard. It is too much for Nick. He springs into his saddle, cocks his pistols and shoves them into their holsters, awkwardly cocks his rifle while holding a bowie knife between his teeth, and handles his horse so nervously that he causes it to back into the fire and across the men's blankets. At the sight of this, everyone roars with laughter until

> *Hwissss! pft! swt! Cheew!* Bones of Caesar! The arrows flitted and clipt amongst us like a flight of bats! Dan Golby threw a double-summersault, alighting on his head. Dory Durkee went smashing into the fire. Jerry Hunker was pinned to the sod where he lay asleep. Such dodging and ducking, and clawing about for weapons, I never saw. And such genuine Indian yelling—it chills my marrow to write of it!

> Old Nick vanished like a dream; and long before we could find our tools and get to work we heard the desultory reports of his pistols, exploding in his holsters, as his pony measured off the darkness between us and safety.

> For some fifteen minutes we had tolerably warm work of it, individually, collectively, and miscellaneously; single-handed, and one against a dozen; struggling with painted savages in the firelight, and with one another in the dark; shooting the living, and stabbing the dead; stampeding our horses, and fighting *them;* battling with anything that would battle back, and smashing our gunstocks upon whatever would not!

Although the story is told humorously, apparently focusing on the panicking of the greenhorn Nick, it is not really funny at all; men were killed that night. It is also not an amateur story. It deserves to rank with Bierce's more mature Civil War stories in which he explores the way the self-deceived mind precipitates tragedy. Years later,

Mark Twain similarly buffered with a humorous context an incident of a murderous ambush in "The Private History of a Campaign That Failed" (1885). Very likely, both Bierce and Twain used humor and irony for the same reason: to put distance between themselves and an occurrence in their lives that still disturbed them.

Four more incidents from that mapping expedition followed in the next few months, two involving Jim Beckwourth, the historical African American frontiersman who was adopted into the Crow Indian tribe and became a famous scout. Both "Jim Beckwourth's Pond" (13 September 1873) and "Mr. Jim Beckwourth's Adventure" (3 January 1874) are tales in which the unfamiliar phenomenon of a hot springs geyser unsettles inexperienced hunters and brings about a superstitious reaction. The former is told as a hoax, the latter as a straight narrative. The other two narratives, "Maumee's Mission" (23 August 1873) and "A Remarkable Adventure" (25 October 1873), deal with mirages and the failure of the experienced to fully adjust to them. These tales of course have American settings. In addition, Bierce's use of the hoax, especially the one in "Pernicketty's Fright," is a distinctively Western technique (much like the ones that Twain used in *Roughing It* [1872]), but Bierce also uses his tales of hoaxes to touch on what would become his familiar and distinctive theme of the tricks that our minds play on us.

Two other American stories, "Authenticating a Ghost" (8 November 1873) and "Jo Dornan and the Ram" (15 November 1873), are significant adumbrations of "The Parenticide Club" series in that both seem to turn on a grisly sense of humor. "Jo Dornan," especially, is an early and relatively undeveloped version of "My Favorite Murder" (16 September 1888), written fifteen years later. In fact, substantial sections of text from this sketch are used in the later story, thus incidentally providing concrete evidence that Bierce sometimes used earlier material as a basis for his more mature and sophisticated stories.

Most of the good prose, fiction and nonfiction, that Bierce wrote for *Fun*—almost all of it American in substance and style—was published in either 1873 or early 1874. The bulk of his contributions either neutral or British in manner show talent but give little hint of his genius. His humor in them is thin, especially when he pretends to be a British traveler or a member of a club, and these works are usually not distinguishable from similar pieces in *Fun*. Toward the end of his sojourn in England, his contributions frequently consisted of forgettable short paragraphs or poems and squibs of two or three lines; apparently either his muse was drying up or he was too preoccupied with personal affairs to compose good prose. One exception to this trend is "A Reminiscence" (3 July 1875), an entertaining but fictitious "memoir" of Artemus Ward.[32]

The Proprietor's Copy of *Fun* thus casts some light into a shadowy nook of Bierce's career and enables us to refine our understanding of his development. Whatever Bierce thought he thought about England and acquiring an English identity, not only his muse but also his creative self were already formed, and both were American, and Bierce's best contributions to *Fun* were American in subject matter and style. If it was not apparent to Bierce then, it is certainly obvious now. His formative years had all been American. He had learned the arts of the tall tale and the hoax in America and he had seen their practical origins and applications in America's real world. While still brooding over the meaning of his experiences, he was already well on the way to formulating a philosophy of life and a personal literary style, and nothing that he learned or experienced in England could match what had already shaped him.

Recently discovered contributions by Bierce to the *London Sketch-Book* further support and greatly augment these conclusions.[33] "The Strange Night-Doings at Deadman's," another story set in the West, appeared for the first time in the March 1874 issue, and was later reprinted in the 29 December 1877 issue of the *Argonaut* after Bierce returned to California. This indicates that Bierce was not just reprinting items that he had written in California but was composing Western stories while he was in England. But without a doubt the most American—and the most important—work that Bierce wrote in England was "What I Saw of Shiloh," hitherto believed to have been first written for the 23 December 1881 issue of the *Wasp*, but now established as having been originally published in the April 1874 issue of the *London Sketch-Book*. This splendid and powerful memoir, in a slightly shorter and unrevised version, is even by itself compelling evidence of the grip that his formative years and experiences had on him.

It is not surprising, therefore, that whatever was creative in Bierce kept accessing the deepest and richest material in him, and that material was American. What is surprising in the English years, however, is the evidence of how far his mind had moved toward what were to be the distinctive themes and techniques of his literature. Those years, creatively speaking, were an early spring. It would be another ten years before Bierce once again began to produce fiction whose quality matched the best he wrote in England. He would then deepen and quickly achieve more power and control, but what had begun in *Fun* would culminate in the serious and brilliant stories that comprised his great 1892 anthology, *Tales of Soldiers and Civilians*.[34]

The Magazine Years: 1875–87

B IERCE RETURNED to San Francisco in the fall of 1875 and, after freelancing for over a year, found employment on the literary weekly *Argonaut* in 1877 as writer and editor. His contributions to it consisted of editorials, miscellaneous poems, articles, a few stories, an occasional reprint of one of the *Fun* fables, and a column called "Prattle." In "Prattle," Bierce returned to the format he had originally used in "The Town Crier" of the *News-Letter* and was to use for the rest of his life—a feature column composed of short essays, single paragraphs, epigrams, and an occasional bit of verse. He also returned to the moral campaign he had described in his last "Town Crier" column. In the issue of 13 April 1878, he confesses his preference for "exoteric philosophy," whose purpose it is, he says, "to lash the rascals naked through the world."

The *Argonaut* job lasted until 1880, when Bierce went to the Black Hills to try his luck as superintendent of a gold mining operation at Rockerville, South Dakota. Paul Fatout's informative study of this part of Bierce's life shows him to have been competent, resourceful, honest, and loyal. But the job, which lasted from 1 June to 16 October, was an unhappy four-and-a-half-month experience because Bierce became the victim of deception, betrayal, the decay of friendship, and commercial and judicial corruption.[35] *The Devil's Dictionary* includes at least two definitions that reflect pointedly on how shabbily Bierce felt he had been treated by his company and a friend in the company: "Fidelity, n. A virtue peculiar to those who are about to be betrayed" (1884), and "Friendship, n. A ship big enough to carry two in fair weather, but only one in foul" (1885).

Bierce was especially resentful of the Dakota judicial system, as he learned firsthand that it favored insiders (local residents) against outsiders (the New York company he represented) and that egregious gaps between legality and justice were commonplace. Among the earliest records of the District Court of the First Judicial District of Dakota Territory (now stored in the District Court in Deadwood, South Dakota), are several court cases involving Bierce. He seems to have won none of them, despite the most glaring evidence of wrongdoings by his opponents and the apparent merits of his positions, and one at least dragged on for another year in San Francisco. Bierce believed at this time that justice was blind. He later realized that he had been blind when he expected the legal system to be impartial and fair. In his later literature, he not infrequently satirizes what passes for law. The four stories of the "Parenticide Club" series, for example, portray societies in which law and justice do not overlap at all. Most of his nine fictional dystopian satires published between 1888 and 1906 sardonically depict the perversion of the legal system as both a symptom and a cause of social failure.[36] His skepticism about litigation is evidenced in other definitions in *The Devil's Dictionary.* For example, "Lawful, adj. Compatible with the will of a judge having jurisdiction." "Lawyer, n. One skilled in circumvention of the law" (1887). "Liar, n. A lawyer with a roving commission" (1886). "Litigant, n. A person about to give up his skin for the hope of retaining his bones" (1887). "Court fool, n. The plaintiff" (1881). Bierce's comment on the whole charade he was put through may be found in one central definition: "Justice, n. A commodity which in a more or less adulterated condition the State sells to the citizen as a reward for his allegiance, taxes and personal service" (1886). It is important to note that Bierce denigrates not justice, but the adulteration and commodification of it.

His dismal experience with the legal system, in addition to the disillusionments of Reconstruction and the frequent encounters he had in San Francisco with hypocrisy, cant, and sham, further eroded the idealism that had induced him to volunteer for military service. He returned to San Francisco at the end of the year. The *Argonaut* did not rehire him, but after a short period of freelancing he was hired by the *Wasp,* another San Francisco journal. Bierce made approximately the same contributions to it that he had to the *Argonaut,* including his regular column, "Prattle." In addition, by August 1880 he returned to the activity that he had begun at the end of 1875 of compiling the alphabetically arranged witty and cynical definitions later named *The Devil's Dictionary.*[37]

Along with his wit was a genuine gift for humor. True, the humor was usually accompanied by ironic or sardonic overtones, but it was excellent humor nevertheless, and there is no period of his writing career when it fails to be expressed. Most of his "Prattle" columns contain risible passages, and some of his fiction is delightful. "Jupiter Doke, Brigadier-General," published in the *Wasp* in December 1885, is a prime example of how Bierce's sense of the ludicrous can be inspired by, yet dominate, his normally somber reflections on the Civil War. Apparently based on a true incident in the war, the story consists of an assemblage of letters by, to, and about Jupiter Doke, an inexperienced and unqualified political appointee to his military rank who will do anything for the Union cause except fight. His cowardice is not concealed by his effusions of loyalty and plans of retreat; nevertheless, despite his character defects and the best efforts of his enemies, both Union and Confederate, he becomes a hero.[38] The tale has elements of contemporary political satire in it, as well as a wry reflection on the role of Chance. In the canon of Bierce's stories about war, "Jupiter Doke" is the exception that proves the rule.

A study of the "Prattle" columns in both the *Argonaut* and the *Wasp* shows a steady growth in Bierce's skill, depth, versatility, and force of style. Although he never rid himself completely of a certain amount of purposeless facetiousness, self-indulgent irreverence, and forced irony, these doubtful qualities slowly receded into the background as he increasingly addressed himself to thoughtful topics worthy of his talents. Foreshadowings of his mature thought occur more and more frequently in the venomed personal satire he directed at the corruption and folly of his time and place and also, paradoxically, in the genuinely moving and often tender reflections he wrote in increasing numbers on war and on the tragedy of the human condition.

In December of 1881 he republished in the *Wasp* one of his finest pieces of nonfiction, "What I Saw of Shiloh," an impressionistic eyewitness account of the battle told in a combination of the past and historical present tenses. Its first publication had been in the April and May 1874 issues of the *London Sketch-Book,* but the *Wasp* version is revised and adds the beautiful twelfth section as a new conclusion. It is one of his earliest written recollections of the Civil War. The article has a strong poetic character; it is an "overflow of powerful feelings," but it originates in emotion recollected in turbulence, not tranquility. Its opening is deceptively modest: "This is a simple story of a battle; such a tale as may be told by a soldier who is no writer to a reader who is no soldier." It concludes in one of Bierce's most famous passages: "Ah, Youth, there is no such wizard as thou! Give me but one touch of thine artist hand upon the dull canvas of the Present; gild for but one moment the drear and somber scenes of to-day, and I will willingly surrender an other [*sic*] life than the one I should have thrown away at Shiloh." The use of the first-person in this piece attracts attention and invites application to the person of the writer. This has been done, unfortunately, almost to the exclusion of consideration of the ideas and values in it. Its awareness of the tragic appeal of illusion will be clarified in our examination of the fiction he was soon to write. An additional hint of the intellectual nature of these stories can be found in one of the serious epigrams Bierce composed between 1885 and 1909:

"Who are thou that weepest?"
"Man."
"Nay, thou art Egotism. I am the Scheme of the Universe.
Study me and learn that nothing matters."
"Then how does it matter that I weep?" (CW, VIII, 355 [1909])

Considered by itself, this epigram is resistant to interpretation. That a paradox is involved is obvious, but the way to resolve the paradox is not. Only the word "Scheme," with its disparaging and pathetic connotation of fraud, suggests a humanitarian resentment implicit in the statement of the situation. At this time, then, when Bierce's reflections on man and life were becoming more serious, when his artistic skill was reaching its powerful mature stage, and when his ability to shock the minds as well as the sensibilities of his reading public had come to be his distinguishing characteristic, it needed but a catalyst to fuse these elements into the purposeful genius that produced *Tales of Soldiers and Civilians*. The next five years provided that catalyst.

The Examiner *Years, Part I: 1887–93*

BIERCE LEFT the *Wasp* in 1886 and was unemployed for about a year until

> One day as I lounged in my lodging there was a gentle, hesitating rap at the door and, opening it, I found a young man, the youngest young man, it seemed to me, that I had ever confronted. His appearance, his attitude, his manner, his entire personality suggested extreme diffidence. I did not ask him in, instate [*sic*] him in my better chair (I had but two) and inquire how we could serve each other. If my memory is not at fault I merely said:
>
> "Well," and awaited the result.
> "I am from the *San Francisco Examiner*," he explained in a voice like the fragrance of violets made audible, and backed a little away.
> "O," I said, "you come from Mr. Hearst."
> Then that unearthly child lifted its blue eyes and cooed: "I am Mr. Hearst."[39]

With that droll encounter, Bierce entered the employ of William Randolph Hearst as a feature and editorial writer for the *Examiner.*

Hearst had just taken possession of the newspaper and was attracting the best talent he could find as he prepared to pour money into it and convert it from just another undistinguished San Francisco sheet into the first newspaper in a mighty chain that would revolutionize journalism. Bierce was one of his earliest picks. Bierce brought "Prattle" with him, exacting two conditions from Hearst: that it appear on the editorial page, next to the editorials; and that it appear exactly as written.[40] Bierce later came to detest Hearst, but even after leaving him more than twenty years later, he openly acknowledged that Hearst "did not once direct nor request me to write an opinion that I did not hold, and only two or three times suggested that I refrain for a season from expressing opinions that I did hold, when they were antagonistic to the policy of the paper, as they commonly were" (CW, XII, 306). Within weeks after his first "Prattle" column appeared in the *Examiner*, Bierce was quite at home in his new location, and he satirized stupidity and vice as sharply and as fearlessly as ever. Hearst had given him free rein, he had a steady (and generous) income, and there were excellent prospects that the *Examiner* would grow; Bierce had cause to be happy. He was not happy, however. A seriousness of mind had come upon him and found expression both in his regular "Prattle" column and in the stories he began to write about this time.

Since "The Haunted Valley," he had written a small number of short stories and long autobiographical pieces, and a larger number of short essays either largely fictitious or making only incidental use of material from his life. He had also written frequently on ghosts and the supernatural, and several of his stories have these unearthly subjects as their themes. But beginning about 1887 in place of his "Prattle" columns and continuing until about 1893, occasionally at first, but more and more frequently, Bierce began to substitute short stories and nonfictional pieces on more consequential subjects than he had before, and to develop the vein of seriousness that had been implicit in the so-called ghost stories. Sometimes, beneath humorous surfaces, he explored in fiction the supernatural, and man's perception of it, and he also began to record his considered responses to his life experiences in the Civil War, over which he had constantly brooded ever since. Critics indifferent to the phases of Bierce's development overlook the fact that his great war stories gestated for twenty-five years, and that there was hardly a day in all that time that he did not remember with awful vividness his experiences in the Civil War and seek to make sense of them.

Late in May of 1888, Bierce published another of his long autobiographical narrations about the Civil War, "The Crime at Pickett's Mill." Two months later, "A Son of the Gods" appeared in the *Examiner*. It was a short story, but it was closely based on one of his own experiences that he had written about in the *Wasp*.[41] In late September, "A Tough Tussle" appeared. In November, he published "Four Days in Dixie," another of his autobiographical pieces on the Civil War. In January of 1889 appeared his great story, "Chickamauga." In February, "A Coward" (later retitled "One Officer, One Man") was printed. In April, he wrote another of his best stories, "A Horseman in the Sky." In June, "The Coup de Grâce." In October, "The Affair at Coulter's Notch." One after another, stories that were to be printed in *Tales of Soldiers and Civilians* in 1892 and *Can Such Things Be?* in 1893 were first published in the *Examiner* between 1887 and 1893, and alternated with autobiographical sketches and "Prattle" articles that were closely akin to them in subject and tone.

During these years, also, Bierce had family trouble and knew personal tragedy. A combination of disagreements between him and his wife and his discovery that some man had written love letters to her precipitated their separation in 1888. McWilliams avers that Bierce loved Mollie, and never stopped loving her, but was excessively proud as well as sensitive, and regarded her even receiving such letters as infidelity. McWilliams also maintains that Bierce did not understand the full truth of the situation and leaped to an unfortunate conclusion.[42] This distress was soon followed by another and keener one. In August of 1889, Bierce's brilliant and beloved seventeen-year-old son, Day, was killed in a gunfight resulting from a disappointed love affair. McWilliams's comment on Bierce's state of mind at this time is revelatory: "Bierce was mortally hurt by the death of his boy, the son he always spoke of as 'another Chatterton.' It was one of the greatest shocks of his life when Day's death was announced. But, again let it be remembered, this occurred in 1889. Bierce was then at the height of his fame as a satirist. Like the matter of his separation from his wife, it was exclusively a personal tragedy. It did not make him 'bitter.' It saddened him, made him weak with grief, but it did not mold his thoughts."[43]

I agree with McWilliams, and further deny that these griefs, painful though they were, made him bitter. As Bierce was at the height of his fame as a satirist, so was he also approaching the height of his productive period as a short story writer. The evaluations of life that he had reflected upon for years were too deeply and thoroughly thought out to be supplanted at this time by his reactions to personal tragedies. In fact, it will be shown that those very evaluations posited an indifferent Nature, and accepted tragedy and merciless death as the rule rather than the exception. These new personal tragedies rather confirmed his philosophy of life than molded it, and far from making him bitter, were more likely, by exposing his vulnerability, to have reinforced the core of humanitarianism in the stories of this period.

The Examiner *Years, Part II: 1893–1900*

BIERCE WORKED for Hearst until 1909 but he never again wrote anything as widely successful as the stories that went into *Tales of Soldiers and Civilians.* The stories in that book were reprinted several times in his own lifetime both here and in England, firmly established his fame in the English-speaking world,[44] and made him an author whom editors solicited for contributions. Translations of the stories began within the decade of their publication (a Russian translation was made in 1898) and the book has been drawn upon for anthologies ever since. In 1892 Bierce collaborated with Adolph Danziger (who later changed his name to Adolphe de Castro) in publishing a short Gothic novel, *The Monk and the Hangman's Daughter.* This cannot truly be said to be representative of Bierce, however, as his part in it largely consisted of rewriting Danziger's translation from the German of Richard Voss's *Der Mönch von Berchtesgaden,* and of adding a new final paragraph.[45] After 1893, when *Can Such Things Be?*, another collection of Bierce's short stories, was published, he continued to write occasional new stories, but not with the burst of creative energy that was manifested from 1887 to 1893, and no new collection was put together. For the most part he settled down to what was for him the humdrum journalism of maintaining "Prattle."

He was too good a journalist, however, for Hearst to ignore his talents and allow them to rust unused. Bierce rose to journalistic fame in 1896 when Hearst persuaded him to go to Washington and play an important part in defeating Collis P. Huntington's railroad refunding bill in Congress. Bierce almost immediately began exposing Huntington's lies, bribes, and graft with coruscating irony. "Huntington Lying in His Last Ditch" reads the headline of his first article on 2 February 1896. Bierce threw himself into the task with remarkable energy, attending congressional hearings, checking Huntington's stories, interviewing people associated with the bill, besmirching Huntington's supporters in California and Washington with embarrassing publicity, and hammering away with unabating attacks every few days on Huntington's tricks and deceits. Unintentionally, Bierce became a forerunner of the muckrakers, although that distinction would not have pleased him, for he did not fully approve of their methods.[46]

The advent of the Spanish-American War of 1898 brought Bierce to one last flaming of journalistic genius.[47] As early as 1897, before the sinking of the *Maine*, Bierce vigorously argued against the journalistic campaign to induce America to intervene in Cuba, of which Hearst was a major instigator. Bierce was probably the only journalist in America who would dare to regularly oppose Hearst's policies on the editorial page while remaining in his employ, and one of the extremely few Americans from any walk of life who risked public censure by conspicuously and continuously opposing war with Spain. Hearst, therefore, must be given credit for keeping him on. Hearst seems to have realized that modern newspapers could not afford to be so monolithic in their policies as to allow only one opinion in their pages. Readers of a different opinion could be kept and maybe even attracted to a paper that occasionally voiced their views, and a controversial writer made for more readers. If, for Hearst, allowing Bierce free rein was a matter of good business sense, he nevertheless set a pattern that most newspapers have followed ever since.

Bierce's opposition to the war talk derived directly from his hatred of war. He still vividly remembered the professional incompetence, the foolish passions, and the butchery of the Civil War, and strove to stem the country's well-intentioned but romantic and headlong plunge into another war. He did not see Cuba as a crucial matter for America; and he knew that Spain already had a well-equipped army in Cuba and that America was not ready for war. But the sinking of the *Maine* on the night of 15 February changed Bierce's mind. Believing, along with almost everyone else, that Spain had been behind the sinking, Bierce felt that America's credibility as well as honor was now threatened, and he abruptly reversed position.

Bierce became the Hearst empire's resident war correspondent and probably American journalism's best. Although he remained in San Francisco, Bierce was much more knowledgeable about war than the correspondents who were sent to the front. They were eager to be patriotic; Bierce was coldly professional. They believed military dispatches; Bierce did not. When, for example, American war correspondents waxed eloquent about the tremendous devastation seemingly caused by the naval bombardment of Spanish fortifications at Matanzas, Bierce was the sole doubter. Subsequent information revealed that the only casualty on the Spanish side was a mule. Bierce thenceforth used the phrase "the mule of Matanzas" as his shorthand for something to be skeptical about.

At first, once he was convinced that the deaths of the *Maine*'s sailors had to be avenged, Bierce was stirred by the prospect of the war. He was tired of the chicanery and greed he saw everywhere in American life and he hoped that the war would renew America's idealism and bring about a rededication to its founding principles. On 24 April, the *Examiner* republished his revised memoir of the Civil War battle of Chickamauga. On 1 May, Bierce changed the title of his column from "Prattle" to "War Topics." Two weeks later, however, Bierce's disillusionment with the way the war was being conducted began to show in his columns. He saw that the American military was being successful largely because its ineptitude was exceeded by that of the Spanish forces. His columns became increasingly sarcastic, and he began calling it the "Yanko-Spanko War." He noted acerbically that the war ended the resistance to the annexation of Hawaii that President Grover Cleveland had embodied in 1893, he foresaw that America would be unwilling to give up the Spanish territories that it conquered, and he observed sarcastically that the acquisition of remote Pacific islands as coaling stations was "necessary" to support the even more remote coaling-station islands America had already acquired.

Bierce's objection to the war was not confined to the inept way it was being conducted, but to the very fact of war. In his "Prattle" of 27 November 1898, he defended Jessie Schley, a young woman from Milwaukee who traveled to Madrid on a personal peace mission. The *Examiner* had ridiculed her efforts in an editorial the week before, but now Bierce praised her "motive and purpose" as being "entirely commendable." In further support of her he asserted that if women all over the world pursued "a uniform, unquestioning deprecation of all war and all wars" they "would be right nine times in ten." Underlying this position is his criticism of patriotism as "love of country, as distinguished from love of mankind."

From 1898 to 1901 Bierce continued to serve as a commentator on war topics. There was no shortage of conflicts the world over. The Spanish-American War slid into the Philippine Insurrection; in 1900 America almost went to war with England and Germany over the partition of Samoa and later sent troops to China to fight against the Boxer Rebellion. Bierce also took an interest in the Boer War and the stirring up of sentiment for a trans-isthmian canal. He usually took a minority opinion on these issues. Later critics have tended to consider Bierce's dissents as evidence of his contrary and cantankerous nature, but the fact is that he was a Cassandra. The majority views of his time are now largely discredited or treated as dated political sentiments whereas many of Bierce's stands have been vindicated and are still vital and compelling.

The Last Years: 1901–1914?

THE FOREGOING EVENTS partially excepted, Bierce began to tire, and a survey of "Prattle" shows him discussing the same old topics, from the same point of view, but without the dash and the feeling of immediacy that made his earlier columns so memorable. He was repeating himself and even giving ground, and his writings and correspondence are tinted by a growing somberness quite differ-ent from the combative irreverence of his early years. In 1900 he moved permanently to Washington, D.C., where he continued to write feature articles and an occasional editorial for various Hearst newspapers. In 1905 he began to contribute short stories, book re-views, and short feature articles to Hearst's *Cosmopolitan* magazine. He kept this up until 1909, when he quit to devote his full time to the preparation of his *Collected Works,* which the Neale Publishing Com-pany brought out in twelve volumes between 1909 and 1912.[48]

In 1913, after putting many of his affairs in order and sending let-ters of ominous-sounding finality to family members and several of his friends, he traveled south to El Paso, stopping off along the way for visits to some Civil War battlefield sites (he had taken a previous "sentimental journey" in 1903). He crossed the Mexican border in November or December, and with a final letter from Chihuahua dated 26 December dropped out of sight. The consensus has it that he went to Mexico hoping for a quick and martial death by getting involved in the insurrection that was going on at the time. This view is supported by his frequently quoted letter of 1 October 1913 to his niece Lora Bierce: "[I]f you hear of my being stood up against a Mexican stone wall and shot to rags please know that I think that a pretty good way to depart this life. It beats old age, disease, or falling down the cellar stairs. To be a Gringo in Mexico—ah, that is eu-thanasia."[49] Rumors of his violent death drifted north to the United States, but none of them has ever been substantiated. Bierce disap-peared abruptly and dramatically and left behind a stock of perplex-ing stories and cynical definitions, and a legend. Bierce would probably not be surprised today to learn that his legend has drawn more attention than his writing.

❧ 2 ❧

"GLEAMS LIKE THE FLASHING OF A SHIELD"
The Theme of War

I F ANY ONE THEME of Bierce's writing were to be singled out as characteristic, that theme would be war. Critics both in and out of literary histories are accustomed to describing him as a master of the realistic war story, and it is a fact that the most famous and widely reprinted of his short stories, "An Occurrence at Owl Creek Bridge," "Chickamauga," and "A Horseman in the Sky," all have war settings. Recollections of and reflections on the Civil War occur often in his journalistic output, as well as observations on other wars, current or historical, and we learn from his letters that the subject of warfare was always close to him. For all of these reasons it is not uncommon to ascribe to the Civil War "a determining influence" on both Bierce's character and his work. Far too frequently, however, this influence has been looked at too superficially as critics, certain that Bierce was purely and simply "bitter," "cynical," "misanthropic," or "wicked," have taken it for granted that the war soured his outlook on life and led him to take the nihilistic position that "nothing matters." Bierce exposes the naïveté of this position in his essay "On the Uses of Euthanasia," and, in fact, argues that war experiences can have the opposite effect: "It is an error to suppose that familiarity with death and suffering exhausts the springs of compassion in one

30

born compassionate. Like many other qualities, compassion grows by use: none has more of it than the physician, the nurse, the soldier in war" (CW, IX, 327).

Just as I take issue with the facile pigeonholing of Bierce as "bitter," I must also take issue with a tendency to oversimplify the influence of war, and especially the Civil War, on Bierce's short stories. The kind of war that takes place between armies or opponents does not exhaust the notion of war. Also possible is war between man and nature, and man and himself. The use of the term "war" in these latter senses is not unjustified if, as is the case with armed hostility, the stakes of the conflict are life or death. "War" in its fullest sense is certainly a characteristic theme of Bierce's, but as it is my contention that his response to war was concern for man instead of nihilistic indifference, this chapter will review Bierce's different conceptions of war and their effect upon the development of his philosophy.

Bierce entered the Civil War young and idealistic. In one of his epigrams, he said: "Twice we see Paradise. In youth we name it Life; in age, Youth" (CW, VIII, 378 [1903]). During the early years of the war, at least, he enjoyed his soldiering experience, for he afterwards always spoke wistfully of happy days spent in the "dreamland" of the Cheat River Valley of western Virginia: "The element of enchantment in that forest is supplied by my wandering and dreaming in it forty-one years ago when I was a-soldiering and there were new things under a new sun. . . . Can you guess my feelings when I view this Dreamland—my Realm of Adventure, inhabited by memories that beckon me from every valley?"[1] The Civil War was young, then, and to the inexperienced youths of Bierce's first outfit it was a romantic adventure. In his autobiographical essay "On a Mountain," he recounts the delights of that first assignment to "the flatlanders . . . suckled in another creed" and describes how the frolicsome young men carved trinkets from laurel roots and mailed spruce gum home to their sweethearts. The piece ends, however, with the illusion of the dream shattered. An "affair of outposts" took place one day and some men were killed. The young soldiers looked at the faces of the dead and were shocked at their repulsive features. "We were as patriotic as ever, but we did not wish to be that way."[2] Returning the next day from a defeat, the dispirited youths did not indulge themselves in admiring the still-beautiful scenery or in fantasies of heroism, but their education was not yet complete. To their horror, they discovered that a herd of swine had eaten the faces of the corpses of the day before (CW, I, 225–33).

Bierce's subsequent experiences in the war were deeply felt, for he never stopped remembering them and pondering them. Years later, his daughter recalled that "soldiering in the Civil War, he had seen many shattered bodies, and could not rid himself of the horror of them."[3] In "What I Saw of Shiloh," originally published in the *London Sketch-Book* in 1874, and "The Crime at Pickett's Mill" and "Four Days in Dixie," both published in the *Examiner* in 1888, Bierce provides us with autobiographical recollections of those experiences and with important records of his frame of mind as he was beginning to write his stories. The participant at Shiloh remembered how the flag at headquarters, "hanging limp and lifeless," mysteriously began to stir when the distant artillery was first heard, and how the exhilarating "assembly" of the headquarters bugle was caught and echoed by other bugles until the call became inaudible in the encampments of unseen valleys. He recalls wincing at nearby shell bursts and being reminded by skirmishers dodging from tree to tree of "figures of demons in old allegorical pictures of hell." He recalls a night rainstorm, a new disposition of Union lines in pitch blackness, and a feeling of unreality as the Federals faced an invisible enemy. He recalls the sudden shock of battle: "The forest seemed all at once to flame up and disappear with a crash like that of a great wave upon the beach—a crash that expired in hot hissings, and the sickening 'spat' of lead against flesh. A dozen of the brave fellows tumbled over like ten-pins. Some struggled to their feet only to go down again, and yet again" (CW, I, 256). He remembers the confusion and the frustration of the engagement, the feeling of bitter helplessness at being shelled by Union guns, and the sight of a little ravine in which "by some mad freak of heroic incompetence, a part of an Illinois regiment had been surrounded and, refusing to surrender, was destroyed, as it very well deserved." He still shudders at the recollection of a burnt field of dead men, some killed outright by bullets, but most lying in "postures of agony" indicating that they had been burned to death while still conscious (CW, I, 261–62).[4] And we get a revealing glimpse of Bierce when he tells of his complex reaction to a proposal by one of his men to end with a bayonet thrust the sufferings of a mortally wounded Federal sergeant. "Inexpressibly shocked by the cold-blooded proposal, I told him I thought not; it was unusual, and too many were looking" (CW, I, 255).[5] This situation was used in an altered context in the 1889 story "The Coup de Grâce."

I earlier suggested that Shiloh was a seminal experience for Bierce. With the possible exception of Chickamauga, no other battle he fought in etched itself so deeply into his mind. It was a battle that epitomized military warfare; it was grand, spectacular, and significant. It had everything: strategy, confusion, and blunder; heroism, stupefaction, and cowardice; tragedy and humor, pathos and irony; exhilaration and despair. There was little subsequent battles could add to Bierce's understanding of military warfare. They were variations on a theme. They corroborated and reinforced impressions, but they did not explain them. For an explanation of Shiloh, for an understanding of war, he needed time, study, and reflection. And he was driven to seek an explanation, for in contrast to his remembrance of the high excitement of Shiloh, his later life seemed insipid, yet he suspected his memory of distorting the truth:

> O days when all the world was beautiful and strange; when unfamiliar constellations burned in the Southern midnights, and the mocking-bird poured out his heart in the moon-gilded magnolias; when there was something new under a new sun; will your fine, far memories ever cease to lay contrasting pictures athwart the harsher features of this tamer life? Is it not strange that the phantoms of a blood-stained period have so airy a grace and look with so tender eyes?—that I recall with difficulty the death and horrors of the time, and without effort all that was gracious and picturesque? (CW, I, 269)

In the revised "What I Saw of Shiloh" (1881), then, the man who recorded this moving recollection of one of the great battles of all time was troubled by memories he could not forget but which he did not trust. The experience had not yet been digested. A few more years were necessary for him to reach some conclusions and to teach himself how to use autobiographical experiences without reliving them or becoming too involved. By 1887 he was at last able, after almost a quarter-century, to place enough artistic and emotional distance between himself and his highly charged philosophy of life to begin testing out its components in fiction.

We can see this development by contrasting "What I Saw of Shiloh" with "An Occurrence at Owl Creek Bridge," written in 1890, and whose setting is the region of Shiloh. A real Owl Creek runs through the Shiloh battlefield, which is in southern Tennessee, approximately twenty miles from the Alabama line. In the story, Peyton Farquhar's northern Alabama plantation is located "about thirty miles" from the Owl Creek bridge. But whereas the memoir is saturated with subjectivity and pathos, the story achieves literary poignancy by abstracting the essence of warfare from the extraneous accidents of history and autobiography and starkly understates the incident by allegorizing it as an "occurrence" in which a foolhardy man much like ourselves plays at war and is caught and killed by enemies.[6]

The idealistic young man whose introduction to death occurred at a skirmish in western Virginia soon became a familiar of death. All subsequent battles impressed him with the precariousness of life and the imminence of death, and he reflected deeply on the patterns of thought and action that could accompany the transition of life to death. He was impressed by the awesome role Chance played in war, and the diminutive role of human intelligence.

Bierce, like most soldiers, probably, at first became disillusioned with the ability of most of his commanding officers and then became coldly enraged at evidence of their pettiness, maliciousness, or incompetence. Ultimately, he reasoned, such defects in commanding officers resulted in a criminal squandering of human life and/or a retrograde effect upon a campaign. The "crime" of the autobiographical prose piece, "The Crime at Pickett's Mill," was the obdurate stupidity of the Union generals who ordered suicidal assaults on impregnable Confederate positions near a waterpower mill on a brook called Little Pumpkin Vine Creek. The battle was not a "significant" one, yet Bierce, a member of Hazen's brigade, reports that "the entire loss was about fourteen hundred men, of whom nearly one-half fell killed and wounded in Hazen's brigade in less than thirty minutes of actual fighting" (CW, I, 279–96).[7] Carey McWilliams claims that part of Bierce's cynicism stems from such experiences as Pickett's Mill: "Later Ambrose Bierce came to feel that life was a rather futile enterprise, full of mocking events and absurd ideals. . . . Men fought bravely, and honorably, for an ideal. They were snuffed out in a word to abate the jealousy of an ambitious commander and history forgot their dying."[8] A comical parallel to "The Crime at Pickett's Mill" is told by Bierce in "Four Days in Dixie" (CW, I, 297–314 [1888]). In it, Bierce relates how he once whimsically crossed enemy lines, was captured, and escaped. Though he was not commanding troops at the time, he risked his own life needlessly and, by his own reckoning, would have deserved death, for as he later put it, "the immemorial and immutable principles of strategy cannot be violated with impunity."[9] In war, a good soldier follows the principles of strategy and does not overestimate his capacity; only a bad soldier—or a civilian—exposes himself needlessly or counts upon Chance to operate in his favor.

Still another lesson that war taught the idealistic young Bierce was not to believe too strongly in men or human institutions. When the war broke out, Bierce was a staunch Union patriot. His patriotism died hard, but die it did. In a "Prattle" column of 1890, Bierce recalled: "It was once my fortune to command a company of soldiers— real soldiers. Not professional life-long fighters, the product of European militarism—just plain, ordinary, American volunteer soldiers, who loved their country and fought for it with never a thought of grabbing it for themselves; that is a trick which the survivors were taught later by gentlemen desiring their votes" (17 August 1890, 6). What patriotic sentiment was not finished off in his Reconstruction experience in Alabama died by degrees over the years as he witnessed—and hotly condemned—the narrow and uncharitable chauvinism,[10] and occasionally the rascality, of Union veterans and administrations. As McWilliams puts it: "The fine tension of the Civil War was succeeded by a flood of miscellaneous filth, a debris of ideas, the flotsam and jetsam of a world broken away from its moorings. Who that fought in 1861 would do other than curse when confronted with the spectacle of Grant's administration? He could hardly be expected to smile."[11] On 13 September 1903, when Bierce was in the vicinity of the Cheat River Valley again, he wrote an illuminating finis to his ideal of patriotism in a letter to Myles Walsh: "They found a dead rebel with his rifle down in one of those hazy valleys a little while ago, and I shall go down and beg his pardon."[12] This position, foreshadowed in the stories of a decade earlier, is as much an affirmation of the worth of human life as it is a rejection of the worth of patriotism, on the same grounds Samuel Johnson used in his famous ironic definition of patriotism: "the last refuge of scoundrels." To Bierce, the comedy of a war between the Big-Endians and the Little-Endians was marred by the fact that human beings had been killed in what had turned out to be, for him, an unnecessary squabble—and that he had been duped into becoming a killer.

Against such statements as H. L. Mencken's that Bierce derived a "cynical delight" from war and enjoyed gloating over it as a "spectacle of human cowardice and folly,"[13] I hold that, far from callously "gloating" over the carnage of the Civil War, or being objectively detached from the sufferings of individual soldiers, Bierce actually tended toward the other extreme, toward being extraordinarily sensitive. Although a superficial perusal of his columns in the *Examiner* may sometimes give the impression that his frequent allusions to various battles and incidents that took place during the war were the product of a simple passion for military history, one has but to read those columns to see, even in them, a sincere and essentially moral interest in the events described. In these columns, over the years, he whittled away at the war, remembering in print something that perplexed or disturbed him, and resolving it if possible. In "The Crime at Pickett's Mill," for instance, which originally appeared in the *Examiner* on 27 May 1888, Bierce comments:

> Early in my military experience I used to ask myself how it
> was that brave troops could retreat while still their courage

was high. As long as a man is not disabled he can go forward; can it be anything but fear that makes him stop and finally retire? Are there signs by which he can infallibly know the struggle to be hopeless? In this engagement, as in others, my doubts were answered as to the fact; the explanation is still obscure. (CW, I, 290–91)

In the "Prattle" of 23 December of the same year, Bierce answered his own question:

> Nothing more frightful (and fascinating) than a great battle can be conceived, but it is not frightful in just the way that its historians love to describe it. Men do not fight as heroically as they are said to fight; they are not as brave as they are said to be. If they were, two hostile lines would fight until all of one were down. As long as a man is not disabled he can go forward or stand his ground. When two lines of battle are fighting face to face on even terms and one is "forced back" (which always occurs unless it is ordered back) it is fear that forces it: the men could have stood if they had wanted to.

This pair of quotations provides a valuable insight into the working of Bierce's mind and into his artistic technique, and we should particularly note their preoccupation with fear. Both this quality and its counterpart, heroism, are present in the majority of Bierce's war tales, and play a dominant part in the stories "One Officer, One Man" (originally published, with significant textual differences, under the title "A Coward"), "George Thurston," "Killed at Resaca," "Parker Adderson, Philosopher," and "One of the Missing." These stories represent a searching analysis of the working of fear upon a human being but, importantly, do not mock the men who feel fear. That their fear brings death upon them is cause for thought rather than mirth.[14]

Bierce was endlessly obsessed with war because he was involved in life, and to him life was a war, and conflict of some kind a truer and more natural state than peace. He suggests this in his *Devil's Dictionary* definition of war: "A by-product of peace. . . . The student of history who has not been taught to expect the unexpected may justly boast himself inaccessible to the light. 'In time of peace prepare for war' has a deeper meaning than is commonly discerned; it means, not merely that all things earthly have an end—that change is the one immutable and eternal law—but that the soil of peace is thickly sown with seeds of war and singularly suited to their generation and growth" (CW, VII, 361). Man, in Bierce's reasoning, was "sentenced to life," for "'Nature red in tooth and claw' has made an ambuscade for him" (E, 11 December 1887, 4). Again and again, Bierce pictured Nature as vindictive and ever poised, ready always to maim or destroy the unwary and the unfit (in which category Bierce included the luckless). "If you wish to slay your enemy," runs one of his epigrams, "make haste, O make haste, for already Nature's knife is at his throat and yours" (CW, VIII, 380 [1903]). Overt war, then, was to Bierce a visible and honest representation of the true state of things, and in common with the Stoics of old, Bierce believed *vivere est militare*, that to live is to be a soldier. As a result, though Bierce was permanently gripped by the horror and spectacle of the Civil War, his tales of soldiers transcend the single historical event of the Civil War and rise to the grander but more subtle theme of man in a hostile universe, and there make common cause with his tales of "civilians," life's noncombatants who by their very ineptness at fighting are foredoomed to early death.

In his eulogistic introduction to the Modern Library edition of Bierce's stories, George Sterling defends his friend and mentor against the common charge of morbidity. "The clairvoyance of the Greek dramatist was here," he says, "revealing man as an august yet helpless figure in the clutch of the main tide of destiny."[15] A year earlier, Leroy Nations had arrived at a very similar conclusion: "He caught the vision of the human race, trapped and betrayed in the wilderness of the world; but, whereas most men have the heart to fight and win, Bierce had the heart to fight and lose. The note of futility pervades his writings."[16] With these comments, Sterling and Nations call to our attention Bierce's design of order, and infer that his conception of war was but part of a larger plan, his conception of

life. Their use of such terms as "fate," "destiny," and "futility," however, is more vivid than precise, and can lead to a misconstruction of
his attitude toward man and the emphasis he places on the mind. It
is tempting to group Bierce with the other American nineteenth-
century writers whose childhood Calvinism was transparently
adapted to their mature art, but to do so is to greatly underestimate
how thoroughly Bierce, a fervent antireligionist, replaced inherited
theological doctrines in himself with humanistic convictions. Belknap
Long was close to the mark when he wrote: "Bierce was not a mystic
or symbolist or expressionist: he was a realistic interpreter of life, living in the midst of a crudely materialistic civilization; and he told the
truth about the things that hurt him in the virile language of a Defoe.
He belongs with the author of *Ecclesiastes* and every great skeptical
liberal and humanist from Lucretius to Cervantes, Swift and
Voltaire."[17] It was not Bierce's disposition to substitute one unknown
for another, to ridicule a belief in God but embrace a belief in an
equally hypothetical entity. He prided himself on an empirical turn
of mind and accordingly founded his conclusions about life upon his
observation of it.

The sort of observations that Bierce made after his discharge
from the army is typified in "J. Milton Sloluck's" introduction to
Nuggets and Dust, published in 1873. Pretending to be surprised by
pious imputations of the "death" of the fictitious Dod Grile to divine
retribution, Bierce's equally fictitious editor Sloluck exclaims:

> I cannot conclude without recording my surprise that certain
> persons belonging to the class with which Mr. Grile waged a
> half-whimsical warfare should have lately done so much to
> justify his estimate of them by presenting that as a judgment
> from heaven which, though sudden and shocking, was clearly
> no more supernatural than are a thousand other phenomena
> of equally fatal if less violent effect. While it is true that sud-
> den death may come upon one man while penning an irrever-
> ent book, is it true that the man engaged in annotating the
> Scriptures is wholly exempt? Lightning falls alike upon the
> just and the unjust; and if we are to regard its fatal stroke as

the special act of offended Deity, we shall have to confess that
Divine Indignation is bestowed with a broad and liberal im-
partiality which even the greediest recipient must feel con-
strained to secretly admire.[18]

Implicit in Sloluck's rejection of the notion of divine interference
in the affairs of men is Bierce's idea that natural causes afford a sufficient explanation of phenomena, and probably a final explanation, as well. This idea is echoed in *The Devil's Dictionary* in the
definitions of "accident" ("n. An inevitable occurrence due to the
action of immutable natural laws" [1904]) and "pray" ("v. To ask
that the laws of the universe be annulled in behalf of a single petitioner confessedly unworthy" [1906]) and is expressed more clearly
in one of his epigrams: "If we knew nothing was behind us we
should discern our true relationship to the universe" (CW, VIII, 372
[1904]). Man deceives himself in thinking that the universe is run
for his benefit. Necessity runs the universe, and the wise man is he
who learns the "immutable natural laws" and their actions and
does not disobey them.

This line of thinking appears repeatedly in Bierce's "Prattle" column in his early years at the *Examiner,* and is behind some of his apparently cold-blooded opinions. In 1892, for example, he wrote that
"every year is a year of fire, famine, pestilence, persecution, war, hurricane, flood, and earthquake. And of these the latter four are
foolkillers." He justified this term on the ground that, as the latter
four disasters could be avoided by the use of reason, their victims
were, consequently, people who disregarded reason. He noted that
people persist in living in areas that are known hurricane paths or
that are prone to annual floods, and that they obstinately prefer traditional and dangerous methods of building to earthquake-proof
techniques. He blamed wars on the people, for, he said, were they
wise they would not allow their leaders to lead them into them (E, 24
April 1892, 5). Later that same year he extended this reasoning to his
ridicule of humanitarian efforts to save the Russian peasantry from a
plague of cholera. In his estimation, the Russian moujik was distinguished by his filth, ignorance, superstition, and bloodthirstiness. He

wrote that "unless the Russian peasant is hardly maligned by those who know him, his perpetuation is a sin against nature, an infraction of the law of evolution" (E, 28 August 1892, 6). Nor did Bierce shrink from applying his view of the workings of Necessity to Americans. In 1898, shortly after the Philippines were won, he wrote: "The vulture is cracking his beak expectantly over our soldiers in Manila. It is their turn to die like flies in grease . . . in other words, the Torrid Zone is exacting its immemorial tribute from the Caucasian race; Nature is prosecuting trespassers. . . . In punishment of our ignorance the glory of conquest entails the calamity of retention" (E, 6 November 1898, 23).

Though Bierce's understanding of "the Scheme of the Universe" did not change appreciably after he formed it, his attitude toward "the Scheme" did. In later years, he was able to take some cold comfort from the belief that he understood the law of survival of the fittest, which he saw as the painfully slow and remorseless operation of evolution on civilization as well as man. But most of the apparent overtones of social Darwinism in Bierce's writings derive from the journalism and correspondence of the late 1890s and the first decade of the twentieth century. Prior to the publication of his stories there is very little evidence in either his journalism or his private letters of an interest in social Darwinism, as such. He had long been interested in heredity, and in at least one of his stories, "A Tough Tussle," he mentions it briefly in relation to racial tendencies, but gives it short shrift.[19] With this possible exception, his stories reflect no significant interest in social evolution. There is good reason to doubt that Bierce was very much concerned with social Darwinism until his later years for, as indicated earlier, the issues and questions raised by his experiences in the Civil War increasingly absorbed his mind until the intensely climactic years between 1887 and 1893, when he finally reached some conclusions.

Furthermore, Bierce's turn of mind in these earlier years, as evidenced by his stories, was empirical but not scientific; his judgments about life and man were founded on his own vivid experiences rather than on the results of dispassionate and orderly study. Not until after he had digested his own experiences did he begin speculating on the nature and destiny of society. Although an interest in, and an influence of, social Darwinism is certainly discernible in his later journalism and letters, and he occasionally mentions Darwin and Spencer with some respect, I would hesitate to call Bierce a social Darwinist at any time of his life. Like many other writers and thinkers of his time, he sometimes used the terminology of social Darwinism (e.g., "survival of the fittest" applied to society) and indeed sometimes agreed with some of its conclusions without necessarily accepting its major premises or implications. All in all, it is far more likely that Bierce in his later years grafted what he found congenial in social Darwinism upon his basic philosophy of life than that he "converted" to it and followed it thoroughly or consistently.

Thus, in a 15 March 1902 letter to George Sterling, Bierce asked: "*Can't* you see in the prosperity of the strong and the adversity of the weak a part of that great beneficent law, 'the survival of the fittest'? Don't you see that such evils as inhere in 'the competitive system' are evils only to individuals, but blessings to the race by gradually weeding out the incompetent and their progeny?"[20] As he explains his point, it is apparent that he may owe as much to Alexander Pope's formulation that "partial Evil [is] universal good" ("Essay on Man," Epistle I, line 292) as to Darwin or Spencer. A later letter to Sterling, in 14 August 1908, however, shows a drift to a more contemporary attitude:

> I think "the present system" is not "frightful." It is all right—a natural outgrowth of human needs, limitations and capacities, instinct with possibilities of growth in goodness, elastic, and progressively better. Why don't you study humanity as you do the suns—not from the viewpoint of time, but from that of eternity. The middle ages were yesterday, Rome and Greece the day before. The individual man is nothing. If this earth were to take fire you would smile to think how little it mattered in the scheme of the universe; all the wailing of the egoist mob would not affect you. Then why do you squirm at the minute catastrophe of a few thousands or millions of pismires crushed under the wheels of an evolution.

> Must the new heavens and the new earth of prophecy and
> science come in *your* little instant of life in order that you
> may not go howling and damning with Jack London up and
> down the earth that we happen to have? Nay, nay, read his-
> tory to get the long, large view to learn to think in centuries
> and cycles.[21]

But in the 1880s and early 1890s Bierce was not yet resigned to his
conclusions. In 1888, reflecting on the catastrophe of the explosion of
Krakatoa, he sarcastically wondered if we should not be grateful "for
the infinite tenderness which averted from us this unspeakable
calamity and sent it upon another people." He criticized the clergy
for calling this a good world adapted to the needs of man, in the face
of "the fury and the despair of a race hanging on to life by the tips of
its fingers; doomed from birth all: in the tick of a clock all gone,
slaughtered to the last man!" He concludes his comment: "Let us be
grateful that we live upon such an earth, hold our lives by so precari-
ous a tenure, and have the good luck to pull through until picked off
singly or in paltry thousands by the neighborly ministrations of
malevolences less picturesque than the wreck of matter and crush of
worlds" (E, 9 December 1888, 4).

The note of resentment against his own conclusions apparent in
the foregoing paragraph is an important and recurring theme in his
"Prattle" articles of the late 1880s and early 1890s and in his stories
of this period. The idealist who had been brutally awakened to war
and surprised by the role Chance played in it was equally struck by
the brutality of "normal" life and by the formidable part Chance
played in it, too. The years 1887–93 were years of struggle for Bierce,
and as suggested previously in the discussion of his developing understanding of fear, both his "Prattle" articles and his stories of this
time chronicle a period of his life in which he was gropingly approaching his severe conclusions about life and reluctantly convincing himself of their validity. Item by item, Bierce slowly added to his
stock of impressions and observations, reached tentative conclusions,
tested them against their contradictions, and then rationally settled
upon his final conclusions.

To follow Bierce's changing opinion of Chance is to see this process at work, slowly but inexorably overcoming all unreasonable—and hence to him untenable—positions. In a "Prattle" of 1890, for example, oddly similar to Ahab's dramatic address to the "clear spirit of clear fire" in "The Candles" chapter of *Moby-Dick,* Bierce explores the significance to life of Chance:

> [I]s there in Chance itself a brutal, blind design, like the unconscious malevolence of an idiot? Is "mere coincidence" ever "mere"? Is it not a stammered revelation, in a tongue unknown, of a meaning and a purpose? Shall we ever find the key to the mysterious hieroglyphics which vanish even as they shape themselves to vision, as do words in sympathetic ink? Who will be first to find the Rossetta [*sic*] stone that is to give us the Science of Coincidences? My friends, I do verily believe that in the word "Chance" we have the human name of a malign and soulless Intelligence bestirring himself in earthly affairs with the brute unrest of Enceladus underneath his mountain. I do verily believe that in the word "accident" we but attest some special manifestation of this Monster's power exerted along the line of intention—not always with disaster, but never with good will to man. To this sole supernal power I would bend the knee in placation and supplication if he were but placable and accessible to prayer. In short, I and those who think as I are heretics and heathens in our blindness, and any honest clergyman will tell you so. We are "cranks" and every enlightened lunatic knows it. (E, 31 August 1890, 6)

Bierce's familiar view of life as harsh and implacable is clearly expressed in this passage, but it is colored over by a transient and romantic overestimation of Chance. Within two years, his opinion of Chance was to change radically. Instead of regarding it literally as a "malign and soulless Intelligence," he now regarded it figuratively as a poetic means to interpret life allegorically.

[H]e to whom life is not picturesque, enchanting, terrible, as-
tonishing, is denied the gift and faculty divine, and being no
poet can write no prose. . . . He has not a speaking acquaintance with Nature . . . and can no more find

Her secret meaning in her deeds

Than he or any other strolling idiot can discern and expound
the immutable law underlying coincidence. . . .

Probability? Nothing is so improbable as what is true. It is the
unexpected that occurs; but that is not saying enough; it is
also the unlikely—one might almost say the impossible. . . .

Fiction has nothing to say to probability; the capable writer
gives it not a moment's attention, except to make what is related *seem* probable in the reading—*seem* true. (E, 22 May
1892, 6; also reprinted in CW, X, 247–48)

Bierce further undercut his early opinion of Chance with his definition of "accident" and with a number of subsequent articles, all at-
testing to the unpleasant but perfectly natural character of life. By
1908 he still regarded "normal life" as fraught with peril and pain but
the old warrior had come to feel that with understanding and reason
man could save himself from some of the traps and reconcile himself
to the rest.

No, it is not a good world, but neither is it so bad as it seems
to a delinquent attention, or one unduly concerned with a single detail, the fate of the individual. The whole is superior to
its parts: what should engage our chief interest is not men, but
Man—not the fortunes of human units, but those of the
human race. The ignorance, the vice, the errors, the poverty,
and the sufferings of our fellows in our own day and generation are painful to observe, and hard is the heart that is inaccessible to their pitiful appeal; but let us not forget that they
are nature's ministers of the general welfare. Through all her

works and ways "one increasing purpose runs": to "weed out" the incompetent, the unthrifty, and, alas! the luckless—all the "unfit." Doubtless an omnipotent power could have accomplished the end without the means, but the situation is as we see it, and not otherwise. The method is cruel unthinkably, but the soul in the body of this death is Hope.[22]

This is one of Bierce's last public utterances, and as such is eloquent testimony to the prominence he gave to speculation about life and death and to the firmness of his intellectual adherence to his Spartan and stoic creed. He had found in life the operation of the same inexorable, impersonal, and implacable "foolkilling" forces, no less deadly for being less obvious, that he had first awakened to in war. Harker Brayton, in "The Man and the Snake," was killed by the same enemy—the deception of his mind—that took Jerome Searing in "One of the Missing." The world that Bierce saw—and wrote about in his stories—was one of war. War was thrust upon all men, and whoever did not understand this in its broadest sense and face up to it constantly, though he wore a uniform instead of mufti, was in truth a civilian who would be picked off on the battlefield of life by one of his enemies: war, nature, or himself.

Carey McWilliams acutely observed of Bierce's protracted response to war: "The war was a troubling memory. It never left him; he mused and puzzled about it all his life. He was still thinking about it when, an old man over seventy, he made that last inspection of the old battlefields. Reading his journalism from its inception to the day of its last appearance, one is impressed with the frequency of his references to war, the constant presence in his mind of its images, and the color that it gave his thinking and even his vocabulary."[23] Not to understand this statement in its extended as well as its obvious sense is to miss much of the richness of Bierce's fiction. Vincent Starrett realized this in his comparison of the war stories of Bierce and Stephen Crane: "The horrors of both men sometimes transcend artistic effect; but their works are enduring peace tracts."[24] Though war is perhaps Bierce's most "typical" theme, it is not his grandest. Not only of arms he sang, but of man,

too. And though a soldier, in reaction to war, his values were ultimately humanitarian. "Life is a little plot of light," runs one of his
epigrams. "We enter, clasp a hand or two, and go our several ways
back into the darkness. The mystery is infinitely pathetic and picturesque" (CW, VIII, 375 [1907]).

⊰ 3 ⊱

THE HEART HAS ITS REASONS
Bierce's Successful Failure
at Philosophy

B IERCE'S SHORT STORIES reflect an author who was almost a
philosopher.[1] Indeed, he was sometimes called "philosopher" as
a respectful compliment, but his admirers were nearer the mark than
they knew. To an unusual degree, Bierce strove his whole life long to
discipline himself to reason logically. More than that, he struggled to
create a rational and logically consistent system of values for himself
out of his selective but intense reading in philosophy and his own reflections. "The test of truth is Reason, not Faith; for to the court of
Reason must be submitted even the claims of Faith" (CW, VIII, 361
[1903]). But he failed. Or, rather, he failed to put together a philosophy to which he could assent wholeheartedly, for his deepest values
were not rational but humanitarian. The same Civil War that burned
away his patriotic fervor, his religious faith, and his youthful idealism,
and turned him into a skeptic, also burned into him an ineradicable
compassion for man, whom he saw ever afterward as a victim: of Nature, of war, and of himself. Bierce was never at peace after the Civil
War, for a civil war seesawed within him. His head and heart clashed
for mastery. This inner civil war fused in his psyche with the outer,
and the poignant stories of conflict that he subsequently wrote reflect
these two battlefields.

It is justifiable to intend "philosophy" in its formal sense when speaking of a philosophical dimension to Bierce's writings. He read formal philosophy and frequently referred to it in his newspaper columns. Partly from such external evidence but mostly on the basis of internal and recurrent patterns of thought that closely resemble certain philosophical positions, it is possible to assess the degree of importance particular philosophies have in Bierce's stories. Later, I will discuss his use of these sources in more detail but for the present I will only name them. From classical times: the Cynics, the later Stoics, and the Eleatics. From modern times: the French and English skeptics of the Enlightenment. Undoubtedly, there are other significant philosophical influences in his work—Plato and Aristotle perhaps—but the ones I've mentioned are the most prominent. Though he took these philosophies seriously and responded to them, he did not adopt them. He was too much a man of his times not to be profoundly aware of the limits of human reason and distrustful of the human mind.

Partly as a result of his recoil from the miserable chaos of life as he saw it and from the seemingly haphazard carnage of war, Bierce looked to reason to deliver him—and, by implication, humanity—from bewilderment and needless destruction. A subsequent search for purpose brought him into contact with many writers and systems of thought, but of all of them, he found the Stoic philosophers and the French and English skeptics of the Enlightenment most congenial to his reliance on reason and experience. These individuals struck a responsive chord in him. Although he did not always agree with them, they stimulated him, served as models of example and technique for him, and challenged him as no other thinkers did either to accept their conclusions or to come up with better ones. An intellectual encounter resulted, and out of Bierce's acceptance of the challenge grew his patterns of thought, patterns that often did not gratify him but that he could not intellectually reject in honesty. One course lay open to him that would have freed him from the bleak and austere pale of reason and restore to him the broad and idealistic humanity he innately inclined toward, but that course was sentimentalism. Shunning it as deceptive and contrary to both reason and experience, Bierce found himself caught between the two extremes of reason and feeling.

Although Bierce professed to scorn sentiment, its appeal to him required constant effort to suppress. Examples of sentimental reactions to instances of tragedy or kindness occasionally appear over the years in "Prattle." Letters of consolation to grieving friends and reflections on the death of his son Leigh are also characterized by feeling. In his letter to Herman Scheffauer of 31 March 1908, for example, Bierce addresses the issue explicitly: "Maybe, as you say, my work lacks 'soul,' but my life does not, and a man's life is the man. Personally, I hold that sentiment has a place in this world. . . . And let me tell you that if you are going through life as a mere thinking machine, ignoring the generous promptings of the heart, sacrificing it to the brain, you will have a hard row to hoe, and the outcome, when you survey it from the vantage ground of age, will not please you."[2] Unable to reconcile reason and feeling, yet unable to resign himself to the remorseless operation of nature's processes, and unwilling to extirpate from himself all sense of sympathy and compassion, Bierce pursued skepticism to the point of Pyrrhonism. Thus the desperate situations in which he places his protagonists represent, allegorically, the insoluble dilemmas with which he himself grappled.

Bierce's distrust of the human mind can be found in his ambivalent attitude toward war. He was able to hate it intellectually, but not emotionally. Whenever he recalled the sense of adventure, the unsullied idealism, the heroism, and the pure youthful surge of his war years, a sentimental indulgence came over him and the sharp memories of carnage and tragedy gave way a little to nostalgia. "There steals upon my sense the ghost of an odor from pines that canopy the ambuscade. I feel upon my cheek the morning mist that shrouds the hostile camp unaware of its doom, and my blood stirs at the ringing shot of the solitary sentinel" ("What I Saw of Shiloh," CW, I, 268). There is a remarkable juxtaposition in this passage of two radically different reactions. Bierce was aware of their presence in him and of their contradictory natures. He never managed to reconcile them; he privileged the values of reason and endeavored to suppress those of emotion. "Thought and emotion dwell apart," he later wrote. "When the heart goes into the head there is no dissension; only an eviction" (CW, VIII, 352 [1903]). He called his fond memories of his war years "illusions," and thought much the same of almost every happy memory or pleasurable sensation: youth, life, truth, and love. "I dreamed of a constant love and spoke / In my sleep, they say, of an iron yoke" (E, 31 June 1887; reprinted in CW, VIII, 352). As he grew older, the realm of illusion seemed larger to him, and its moral deception more enraging. Writing about the intellectual prerequisites of a writer, he once said: "And it would be needful that he [a writer] know and have an ever present consciousness that this is a world of fools and rogues, blind with superstition, tormented with envy, consumed with vanity, selfish, false, cruel, cursed with illusions—frothing mad!" (CW, X, 77). From his war years on, Bierce increasingly distrusted not only his emotions but his memory and his senses as well. In his opinion, they were inferior mental faculties that only registered impressions, and panderlike, indulged the "low, enjoying power." "Perception," he observed, "is not the same thing as discernment" (E, 15 May 1887, 4). To discern the truth about life, to know the viciousness with which he felt the world of nature and man to be infused, Bierce relied upon reason. Slowly and painfully, Bierce put together a reasonable philosophy of life to which he tried with all his might to adhere.

Bierce's passion for reason and his subsequent idealization of it grew out of his conclusion that man must adapt himself to life instead of futilely trying to impose himself—and an artificial concept of order—upon it. In both war and peace, he had observed that the laws of strategy and the laws of nature operated remorselessly, but that through reason the wise man might learn them and save himself from at least some of their adverse effects. Reason was a hard taskmaster, but it is plain from the forthright and controversial articles of his early journalistic career that Bierce applied himself assiduously and conscientiously to its lessons.

In these early articles, Bierce is frequently found to be championing unpopular opinions in the name of reason. While on the *Argonaut*, for example, he defended both Chinese and African Americans against their detractors—almost the whole of the San Francisco community—and "reasonably" disputed some of the main charges against them.[3] In 1889, dissenting from the popular feeling that some military action should be taken against Germany for its hostility toward American interests in Samoa, Bierce coolly noted that America was militarily unprepared: "We have a grievance, apparently, but it is not true in military affairs that he is thrice armed who has a just quarrel. To fight without hope is not soldierly; it is the act of a fool. A general who should bring on a decisive engagement with all the advantages on the side of the enemy would be dismissed, and should be shot" (E, 3 February 1889, 9). He proceeds bluntly to the point that by extending its interests into foreign lands, America is asking for trouble. "A nation is like an individual; when angry it is blind to the plainest considerations and most conspicuous facts. It forgets the values and relations of things; its whole intellectual world is suffused with a false light. The wildest and maddest fancies find acceptance, the soberest dictates of common sense are ignored. It is against this condition of things that the American people should be warned." His message: The moral for the country, as for a man, is that it must not allow its heart to go into its head.

In a sometimes misinterpreted passage, Bierce even went so far as to advocate the imitation of Christ, but for intellectual reasons only. He revealed his "ultimate and determining test of right" as the example of Christ. "What, under the circumstances, would Christ have done?" But his explanation of his position reveals a set of values that are rational rather than Christian: "He [Christ] taught nothing new in goodness, for all goodness was ages old before he came; but with an intuition that never failed he applied to life and conduct the entire law of righteousness. I have before described him a lightning moral calculator; to his luminous intelligence the statement of the problem conveyed the solution—he could not hesitate, he could not err" (E, 28 June 1891, 6). The disparity between an orthodox Christian view of Christ and Bierce's is here clearly seen as the difference between a God who makes and represents laws and a human being with an incredibly fast and accurate computer-like mind that applies laws already made. In the long run, therefore, a man who imitates Christ is simply availing himself of ready-made rational decisions.

Further examples of Bierce's admiration of reason can be found in abundance in the journalism of his entire career, but of special interest is the appearance in the *Examiner*s of 1887–93 of the occasional short story or nonfictional item that, by implication, takes the opposite position and deprecates the rule of reason otherwise advocated. One such example occurs in a "Prattle" from 1891. Commenting in disgust on the apparent inability of the federal government to protect foreign nationals in some Southern states,[4] Bierce jestingly outlines the course that he, as a reasonable individual, would take if a war resulted because the home country of those foreigners intervened on behalf of its citizens. Typically, he implies that reason owes no loyalty to stupidity, and worthy of note is his subsequent conjoining of his reasonable course of action with "cowardly" ones:

> That our Ship of State has not hitherto fouled any of her powerful neighbor-craft . . . must be credited rather to good luck than to good seamanship; soon or late, the collision is certain to occur, and then we shall pay roundly for drifting upon the sea of international politics without a captain. When it does occur, and when the other vessel is hulling us with the projectiles of a righteous indignation for our stupidity, I for one shall take to the water and paddle ashore with the rats and the National Guard of California. I don't fear any unaided European power, but I am not going to help fight against God unless I am in the right. (E, 21 May 1891, 6)

What is said in jest in this context, however, is treated in earnest in some stories of this period. As we shall soon see, a number of these stories have plots in which the reasonable and the cowardly courses are one and the same. For Bierce, these situations represented dilemmas that could not be solved by reason alone because in them reason itself was on trial as a standard of value.

From the prominence given to reason in these stories, and from the variety of positions he takes in them on the issue of reason, we can recognize a probing of his own system for loopholes and a covert resentment at his own conclusions. Many of his so-called pronouncements are really hypotheses, well-turned assertions awaiting further and fuller testing. Such a pronouncement is his sardonic epigram "All are lunatics, but he who can analyze his delusion is called a philosopher" (*Cosmopolitan*, February 1907). The idea behind this remark was analyzed at some length in the 1891 story, "Parker Adderson, Philosopher," which deals with the change in outlook of a condemned spy who at first regards his imminent execution with philosophical serenity, but loses it as death approaches. Other statements, such as the following quatrain, also seem turned inward, ironic comments on his struggle to settle his own conflicting thoughts on the ultimate value of reason:

> The sea-bird speeding from the realm of night
> Dashes to death against the beacon-light.
> Learn from its evil fate, ambitious soul,
> The ministry of light is guide, not goal. (CW, VIII, 374 [1907])

Reason for its own sake kills the spirit, Bierce seems to say. It must have a directing purpose. But if one rejects religious revelation, as Bierce certainly did, where does one find purpose?

Bierce looked to Nature for purpose. Not Wordsworth's Nature, but the scientist's Nature. Man must follow the Nature revealed to him by his reason, learn its laws, and obey them. If he is wise enough, Bierce thought, man can learn from observation; if not, he will have to learn from experience. Life itself will tell man what he needs to know and pass judgment on his decisions. When man makes the wrong decision, he suffers and dies. But man, through reason, can learn what is likely to be. If he would be happy, let him desire that end.

Towards this grim-sounding philosophy of life Bierce was pushed by his reason, aided and abetted by a thoughtful reading of a variety of philosophers and writers who inclined toward reason and empiricism. First among these influences were the Cynics. Bierce has often been called a cynic, in the popular, loose sense of the term. This is an exaggeration. But that he was aware of classical Cynicism as a philosophy and respected it, there is no doubt. His famous *Devil's Dictionary* was first published as *The Cynic's Word Book*; in it is the definition of a cynic as "a blackguard whose faulty vision sees things as they are, not as they ought to be" (1881). More to the point, however, is the emphasis of the Cynics upon the exposure of illusion; their distinction between natural and artificial values; their testing of virtuous claims for hidden agendas; their emphasis upon self-discipline and virtuous action; and their readiness to set themselves apart from the community in order to be fearlessly critical of it. Bierce would not have encouraged others to think him a Cynic if there had not been some accuracy to the charge.[5]

Much more influential on his personal philosophy and his literature was Stoicism. It would be an exaggeration to describe him as a Stoic pure and simple, but more than any other single philosophical system it left its mark upon him. Bierce's first contact with Stoicism might date to his boyhood. A book on Stoicism was published in 1855 by his eminent uncle, Lucius Verus Bierce, whom Ambrose knew and admired, and it is possible that he knew about the book. In any case, however, that Bierce read the Stoics, and read them carefully, is a matter of record. Not only have various critics noticed Bierce's resemblance to the Stoics but Bierce himself readily admitted it. In 1893, for example, he wrote: "I am for preserving the ancient, primitive distinction between right and wrong. The virtues of Socrates, the wisdom of Aristotle, the examples of Marcus Aurelius and Jesus Christ are enough to engage my admiration and rebuke my life. From my fog-scourged and plague-smitten morass I lift reverent eyes to the shining summits of eternal truth, where they stand; I strain my senses to catch the law they deliver" (CW, IX, 176–77). Later in his life, he recommended for the training of a writer "the ancients: Plato, Aristotle, Marcus Aurelius, Seneca and the lot—custodians of most of what is worth knowing," and especially praised Epictetus, who teaches "how to be a worthy guest at the table of the gods" (CW, X, 76). In his 8 January 1899 letter of consolation to his friend Percival Pollard, Bierce enlarges on this last statement: "When I'm in trouble and distress I read Epictetus, and can warmly recommend that plan to you. It does not cure, but it helps one's endurance of the ill. I go to Epictetus with my mental malady—and misfortunes themselves are nothing except so far as they affect us mentally. For we of our class do not suffer hunger and cold, and the like, from our failures and mis-chances—only dejection. And dejection is unreasonable."[6]

It is no accident that common to both the later Stoics and Bierce is a positing of a "God" of natural processes and an impersonal and painful universe of which man is definitely not the center; an ascrip-tion to reason of man's hope of survival; and the notion that through the correct use of reason a sort of happiness is possible for man. Yet, although Bierce was pushed toward these conclusions by both his reason and his reading, he balked at embracing them totally. Some idea of his resistance to the inexorable force of his reason can be gained by examining what appears to be a major debt to the Stoic philosophers Epictetus and Marcus Aurelius. For example, in Epicte-tus Bierce would have found this observation: "What disturbs men's minds is not events but their judgments on events. For instance, death is nothing dreadful, or else Socrates would have thought it so. No, the only dreadful thing about it is men's judgment that it is dreadful."[7] It is tempting to conjecture whether this might not have been the nu-cleus of his story "Parker Adderson, Philosopher." In that story, a cu-rious exchange of contradictory opinions takes place. At the beginning, the captured Union spy, Parker Adderson, appears not to be afraid of death while his captor, a Confederate general, says that it is "horrible." By the end of the story, however, the general appears to be at ease about his imminent death whereas Adderson has become panic-stricken. The story, therefore, is ambivalent, and appears to support both Epictetus's position and its opposite.

The resemblance of another reflection of Epictetus to "The Af-fair at Coulter's Notch" is almost too great for coincidence. "Never say of anything, 'I lost it,' but say, 'I gave it back.' Has your child died? It was given back. Has your estate been taken from you? Was not this also given back? But you say, 'He who took it from me is wicked.' What does it matter to you through whom the Giver asked it back? As long as He gives it you, take care of it, but not as your own; treat it as passers-by treat an inn" (Epictetus, no. 11, 470). In the tale, Coulter, a Union artillery officer from the South, is ordered by a vin-dictive general to shell what the general knows to be Coulter's own home. Coulter obeys. Later, with advancing Union officers who bivouac that night in the shattered dwelling, he finds the bodies of his wife and child, killed by his own shelling. The story can be read either as an example of how the lesson of Epictetus can be applied to real life, or as a criticism of how that lesson imposes heartbreakingly superhuman demands upon mere mortals.[8]

The same ambiguous relation exists between the tale "The Mocking-Bird: A Story of a Soldier Who Had a Dream" and one of Marcus Aurelius's meditations: "Return to thy sober senses and call thyself back; and when thou hast roused thyself from sleep and hast perceived that they were only dreams which troubled thee, now in thy waking hours look at these (the things about thee) as thou didst look at those (the dreams)."[9] In this story, Private Grayrock, a Union sentinel, awakens from a dream of losing touch with his brother, only to discover that a Confederate soldier he had fired at earlier—and killed—was his brother. The story reverses the priority of sequence in the meditation.

Strikingly apropos to "An Occurrence at Owl Creek Bridge" is another of Aurelius's meditations: "Death is a cessation of the impressions through the senses, and of the pulling of the strings which move the appetites, and of the discursive movements of the thoughts, and of the service to the flesh" (Marcus Aurelius, no. 28, 530). The most dramatic part of the story arises out of the hallucinations that occur in the unconscious mind of a man who is being hanged, a man who "was as one already dead." Although the process of his death begins, in reality, when the knot of the noose begins to close around his neck and ends a fraction of a second later when it breaks his neck, to his mind—and the reader's—his life continues (speciously) for what seems hours.[10]

The curious thing about all of the foregoing resemblances between the sayings of the Stoics and Bierce's tales is that while the tales seem to dramatize the sayings, they do so as if in protest against them. The sayings of the Stoics appeal mainly to the intellect; Bierce's stories, however, appeal contradictorily both to the emotions and the intellect, and the emotional appeal is the more powerful. If the stories are seeded at the core with the Stoic counsel of resignation, inviolate in its validity and unaffected by the stories' pathos or the reader's passion, this counsel is not what Bierce conveys to the reader. Rather, it is a freshly aroused sympathy for one's fellow man based on a sharpened awareness of man's demonstrated limitations and the invincible and pitiless violence of life. Pure reason, after all, lacks humanity, and Bierce does not lash ignorance where it is excusable—a mortal consequence of being imperfect.

This distinction takes us to the heart of Bierce's stories. In the best of them, he *explores* reason. Is man a rational creature? How effective is man's ability to use reason? How good is reason? Is there a higher standard of value than reason?

Not even in his declining years, when he became slightly more re-signed to life, did he wholly acquiesce to the rule of reason. For to Bierce, the greatest good was a feeling above reason; it was happi-ness. "To local standards of right and wrong he [a writer] should be civilly indifferent. In the virtues, so-called, he should discern only the rough notes of a general expediency; in fixed moral principles only time-saving pre-decisions of cases not yet before the court of con-science. Happiness should disclose itself to his enlarging intelligence as the end and purpose of life; art and love as the only means of hap-piness" (CW, X, 77). Of civilization, which he regarded as the great-est and most enduring product of reason, he said: "It has accomplished everything, but it has not made humanity any happier. Happiness is the only thing worth having."[11] Even in the last year of his life, he restated this belief, albeit somewhat gloomily: "Nothing else is of any value—just happiness. The difference between a good person and a bad one is that one finds happiness in goodness, the other in badness; but, consciously or unconsciously happiness is all they seek, or can seek. Even self-sacrifice is a species of indulgence. And at the end of it all we see is that nothing matters."[12]

An earlier instance of the apparently negative philosophy of "nothing matters" occurs in a 12 September 1903 letter to George Sterling:

> . . . the same malevolence [slanderous criticism] that has sur-
> rounded my life will surround my memory if I am remem-
> bered. Just run over in your mind the names of men who have

told the truth about their unworthy fellows and about human nature "as it was given to them to see it." They are the bogie-men of history. None of them has escaped vilification. Can poor little I hope for anything better? When you strike you are struck. The world is a skunk, but it has its rights; among them that of retaliation.

Yes, you deceive yourself if you think the little fellows of letters "like" you, or rather if you think they will like you when they know how big you are. They will lie awake nights to invent new lies about you and new means of spreading them without detection. But you have your revenge: in a few years they'll all be dead—just the same as if you had killed them. Better yet, you'll be dead yourself. So—you have my entire philosophy in two words: "Nothing matters."[13]

The concision and dramatic sound of "Nothing matters" must have appealed to Bierce, for he used it with some frequency during his later years. De Castro with typical unreliability repeats it as the quintessence of Bierce's philosophy and sees in it the influence of Schopenhauer.[14] When viewed against the affirmative background of Bierce's life and the overwhelming majority of his stories, articles, and poems, however, the negativity of the slogan does not ring true and raises more questions than it answers. McWilliams views the slogan against the background of Bierce's life and works and interprets it in a contextual sense that eliminates many of the problems raised by de Castro's literal acceptance of it:

Bierce often said—insisted would be a better word—that "nothing matters." But he did not mean this in the Schopenhauerian sense. He was so acute at distinguishing appearance from reality that he had rejected most of the values to which his fellow citizens paid lip-service. "Nothing matters" meant: nothing that society worships matters very much. He was not a nihilist or a god-killer: he had simply learned to stand alone. Nor was he a cynic; on the contrary, he was a rather severe moralist. He appeared to be the arch cynic because he turned the values of the day inside out and found, as men will find if they try the same experiment today, that the inside-out version is a fairly good reliable guide to social reality. Hence his greatest appeal, perhaps, will always be to those who have been forced, as he was forced, to learn to stand alone and who feel, therefore, the tonic contagion of his spirit, his wit, his stoicism, and his courage.[15]

The strongest part of McWilliams's rebuttal of de Castro is in his indirect allusion to Stoicism, for "nothing matters" stems from the classical philosophy. The origin of "nothing matters" in Stoic doctrine is revealed in several letters Bierce wrote in the late 1890s. In his 3 October 1897 letter to Ray Frank, Bierce recommends to her a philosophy of indifference as a way of coping with some grievances:

> Dear Ray, you really should habituate yourself to more just and cheerful views of things. The hand of everybody is not against you. The things that rouse your anger are not always significant of unfriendliness, as in my own case I know. I suppose you have had much to embitter you, but adversity, injustice, even wrong, should *not* embitter; they should sweeten and soften. In their tendency to embitter lies all their evil. Deny them the power to do that and you are invulnerable. All else that disaster and malevolence can do to us is a trifle compared with the wreck that they *may* make of our dispositions—our characters.[16]

In addition to showing a warmly humane aspect of Bierce, this letter makes clear the depth of his assimilation of core Stoic teaching. Life may present us with misfortune, but by controlling our reactions to it we can deny it power to harm our most precious possession, our characters. Several months later, in closing his 16 March 1898 letter to Jean Hazen, he makes the connection of "nothing matters" to Stoicism unmistakable: "Don't imagine that this disciple of

Epictetus worries, nor for a moment forgets his brief philosophy—his before Zeno stole it from him—that 'nothing matters.'"[17]

On 31 March 1901 Bierce was devastated by the death of his remaining son, Leigh. It was both an overwhelming personal tragedy and an acid test of his Stoicism. Typically, like Captain Coulter in the story, he maintained an outward show of control while his internal equilibrium was in ruins. Two days later, he confessed to Herman Scheffauer, "My boy died on Sunday morning. I'm a bit broken in body and mind."[18] On 21 July, in a letter to May Elizabeth (Betty) McAlister, a younger woman with whom he might have had an amorous relationship, he made another confession precipitated by his son's death, one that had to have been enormously painful for him: "Sorrow has laid a heavy hand upon me. My mind is, I hope, inaccessible to the malevolence of Fate, but that which would have been helpful to you was a physical quality—an animal vitality that is gone, I fear, forever. I am an old man, Betty, so old that I hardly recognize myself. Between my present and my former self is a gulf so wide that my thought can hardly span it."[19] This letter offers both a refutation of the popular misconception that he was unfeeling and heartless and an insight into the operation of his Stoicism. In the letter, Bierce acknowledges the permanent damage his personal tragedy had on his earthly and vulnerable self, but he falls back on his ultimate line of defense, his mental resignation to the possible malevolences of life so that his character is inaccessible to them. In this respect, "nothing matters" means that nothing has happened or can happen that will dislodge his mind and character from his principles. This position is fundamentally discrepant from either a nihilistic or a pessimistic indifference. In later years, his use of "nothing matters" occasionally suggests that he might have drifted away from this basic sense of the term, but its original meaning should now be clear and also, therefore, the realization that distorted meanings of the phrase cannot accurately be applied retroactively to the works and values of his earlier productive years.

Bierce's longing for happiness, on the other hand, was present even in his earlier years. In the revised "What I Saw of Shiloh" (1881) and the other autobiographical battle memoirs he wrote in the eighties (e.g., "On a Mountain," and "Four Days in Dixie") there is an undisguised nostalgia for the happiness and thrill of his youth. For Bierce, the feeling of happiness was a real fact; that it was induced by illusion or ignorance, another and separate fact. Yet such is life, and such are the respective merits of wisdom and happiness, Bierce would say, that the wise man faced with the choice between the two would choose happiness, though by that choice he forfeited his wisdom. This, at least, is the moral of "Haïta the Shepherd" (1891), originally one of the stories in the first edition of *Tales of Soldiers and Civilians.* In this parable, a pure and pleasant shepherd lad is tantalized and confused by the abrupt appearances and disappearances of a maiden of surpassing beauty. Finally, a holy hermit tells the boy who she is and why she vanishes whenever he tries to become better acquainted or to learn how to keep her:

> "Know, then, that her name, which she would not even permit thee to inquire, is Happiness. Thou saidst the truth to her, that she is capricious for she imposeth conditions that man can not fulfill, and delinquency is punished by desertion. She cometh only when unsought, and will not be questioned. One manifestation of curiosity, one sign of doubt, one expression of misgiving, and she is away! How long didst thou have her at any time before she fled?"

> "Only a single instant," answered Haïta, blushing with shame at the confession. "Each time I drove her away in one moment."

> "Unfortunate youth!" said the holy hermit, "but for thine indiscretion thou mightst have had her for two." (CW, III, 306–7)

In the irony of that single word "indiscretion" is the implication that there is a judiciousness above reason.

Bierce returned to the fictional examination of happiness in one of his last stories, "Beyond the Wall" (1907). This neglected but surprising tale is remarkable for being one of the very few he wrote that can qualify as a love story. Like section 11 ("Twenty-eight young men bathe by the shore") of Walt Whitman's *Song of Myself*, "Beyond the Wall" is also about a protagonist whose aristocratic pride in pedigree keeps him from acting on the love he feels (and that is apparently reciprocated) for a charming and graceful young woman not of his class. She is his chance for happiness in this life but, acting very rationally, the protagonist forfeits it because he does not respond to her attempt to communicate with him. A supernatural element in the tale, however, implies that love is stronger than death and that happiness may yet be achieved "beyond the wall" of earthly existence. Coming as it does at the end of his career and near the end of his life, "Beyond the Wall" is impressive evidence of how much Bierce was aware of his own divided mind, and of the fact that intellectual pride and commitment to reason do not result in happiness and might not even protect against sorrow.

Even with these two works, happiness is not a prominent condition in Bierce's stories. In fact, it is conspicuous by its absence. None of his major protagonists is happy, or seeks for happiness. In Bierce's deadly universe, they fight for sanity or survival; Pyrrhic victories are their utmost achievement; and happiness is a luxury beyond reasonable hope. Bierce's own experiences with happiness convinced him that it was at best unpredictable and ephemeral and not infrequently a prelude to disaster. Moreover, as Haïta discovered, happiness could not be deliberately achieved. Though Bierce personally longed for it, he did not deceive himself about its opposition to reason. With Swift, Bierce might have said that it was *"a perpetual Possession of being well-Deceived"* (*Tale of a Tub* 108). But unlike Swift, Bierce recognized that part of him would have been grateful for the blessing of that deception.

Bierce's early awareness of the futility of hoping for happiness or of expecting pure reason, and his realization that the imperfect creature man was, in truth, imperfectible, led him to be skeptical of reason, happiness, man, and himself. In 1878 he wrote that when he came to California in 1866 he had "a cast-iron conviction about everything from the self-evident to the unknowable, both inclusive."[20]

In 1888, he wrote that he had memorized the following passage from Bacon: "He that has justly considered matters, the causes which bring them about, and the consequences which flow from them, is denied a choice and remains always a skeptic" (E, 4 March 1888, 4). But Bierce did not have to go to Bacon for his skepticism, for years earlier, under the tutelage of the editor James Watkins, he had studied the great skeptics of literature and had incorporated their philosophies into his own.

An important start in the difficult undertaking of identifying and assessing the influence of such writers on Bierce was made by Harry Lynn Sheller in his dissertation on Bierce's satire. Among his findings is that Bierce's debt to the English and French writers of the Enlightenment is quite substantial. He notes that it goes beyond occasional literary allusions and imitations and extends to a basic similarity in ideals, attitude, and philosophy of life between Bierce and some of the leading spirits of the age, chiefly Swift and Voltaire. Sheller claims, however, that "Bierce cannot be accused of imitation." Instead, he finds that Bierce was inspired by the examples and ideas of his predecessors to develop his own thought and satiric patterns in a way consistent with his original genius and his integrity.[21] Thus, in order to fully exploit Sheller's conclusion, it is necessary to go beyond the surface similarities of Bierce to other authors, and examine also that aspect of his satire in particular and his art in general which reacted to stimulus in a wholly original and creative way. I have already indicated such a reaction in my discussion of Bierce's love-hate relationship with the Stoics. To some extent, a similar relationship exists between Bierce and the writers of what is called "the Age of Reason," with this difference: that while he was not completely comfortable with their conclusions, he was at home with their tool of skepticism. This he made his own and henceforth used it distinctively for his own purposes.

The tag name "the Age of Reason" is a misleading label for the eighteenth century because it implies only a favorable attitude toward reason. The major contributions of such writers as Swift, Voltaire, and La Rochefoucauld, however, consist of their attacks on reason, their use of skepticism and empiricism to awaken men from their rosy dreams of what reason might accomplish, and their reminding men of their limitations and of reason's. It was these demonstrations, these authors' use of the analytic power of reason to check the synthetic, that appealed to Bierce. He already had an accelerator; he needed a brake.

As Sheller implies, Bierce was not an eighteenth-century anachronism writing at the end of the nineteenth century; his use of skepticism was masterful, but it was modern.[22] An interesting comparison between Bierce and certain Enlightenment authors might be made, for example, with the theme of how man's love for woman leads him to folly. The most famous eighteenth-century treatment of this theme is probably Pope's mock epic, *The Rape of the Lock*. The humorous opening lines establish the tone of the poem, and immediately alert readers to be skeptical of what they read: "What dire offence from amorous causes springs, / What mighty contests rise from trivial things, / I sing" (canto I, lines 1–3). There is no tragedy in this poem because the subject is too slight for tragedy, because the characters are toylike types that cannot feel or know real sorrow, and because the reader is in on the joke. Throughout the poem Pope protects readers with his skepticism, and gently points out the reasonable moral to them after having saved them from the indignity of laughing foolishness to scorn, only to find out later that they had laughed at themselves.

Earlier, Swift had treated the same subject with sarcastic humor. In his *Tale of a Tub*, violence and warfare are attributed to so slight a cause as a frustrated love affair. A certain prince, Swift writes, was inflamed by the eyes of a female, but "she was removed into an enemy's country" before he could enjoy her. "Having to no purpose used all peaceable Endeavours, the collected part of the *Semen*, raised and enflamed, became adust, converted to Choler, turned head upon the spinal Duct, and ascended to the Brain. The very same Principle that influences a *Bully* to break the Windows of a Whore, who has jilted him, naturally stirs up a Great Prince to raise mighty Armies, and dream of nothing but Sieges, Battles, and Victories" (104). In Swift, skepticism is not invoked to save readers from embarrassment but to jolt them into seeing themselves for what they are: creatures more subject to the rule of passion than they would like to think, even plunging into war because of an excess of a hormone. After reading Swift, one cannot take without a grain of salt the dictum that man is a rational being.

Bierce's treatment of the same theme occurs in his story, "Killed at Resaca" (1887), which considerably anticipates William Dean Howells's rendering of a similar situation in "Editha" (1905). In Bierce's tale, Lt. Herman Brayle distinguishes himself among his comrades in the Union army by his apparent indifference to death. It is widely interpreted as courage. One day, the lieutenant outdoes himself in gallantry, conspicuously galloping across the battlefield in fulfillment of a command, though he had been ordered to take a safer route. He is killed, of course, but not before his example in-spires a hundred Union soldiers to leave their shelters and rush to their needless deaths on the battlefield. A fellow officer finds among his effects "an ordinary love letter," in which Lt. Brayle's sweetheart indirectly insinuates that he is a coward. "These were the words which on that sunny afternoon, in a distant region, had slain a hun-dred men. Is woman weak?"

If the story had ended at this point, it could have been described as an exercise in irony and a lesson in skepticism. Courage in battle is seen to be, in the case of Brayle, a death wish inspired by an amorous cause, a trivial thing when put into perspective. In the case of the foolhardy Union soldiers, their courage was just an indulgence of emotion—a thoughtless sympathy. None of these deaths was neces-sary; in a very real sense, Brayle and the others were victims of their own loss of reason, of obeying their feelings instead of their minds. Thus far, Bierce parallels Swift. But there are significant differences.

For one, Brayle and the others are victims, not the offensive and offending bullies and princes of whom Swift wrote. For another, they do die. Moreover, Brayle is not a stereotype character or a straw man. Handsome, intelligent, and admirable in character, he has been endowed with personality and is believable. In addition to these dif-ferences from Pope and Swift, Bierce adds a further level of com-plexity as he continues the story for a few more paragraphs. Brayle's fellow officer, the narrator, carries the love letter to its sender, a woman of fascinating beauty and charm. She reads it with some embarrassment but no apparent remorse, then casts it into a fire in revulsion when she sees a blood-stain on it. "How did he die?" she asks. The officer turns his glance full on her before answering.

> The light of the burning letter was reflected in her eyes and touched her cheek with a tinge of crimson like the stain upon its page. I had never seen anything as beautiful as this detestable creature.

"He was bitten by a snake," I replied. (CW, II, 104)[23]

With this ending Bierce turns skepticism upon itself and pushes what had been merely irony to a tragic insight. In those last lines, Bierce confirms and intensifies our verdict against the woman and recruits our sympathy for the lieutenant. We put out of mind our first and uncharitable conclusion that Brayle is merely infatuated and revise our opinion of the matter. No longer is Brayle a victim of his immature feelings; he is now a victim of an unworthy and heartless but fatally attractive charmer. By developing character in the sweetheart, by changing her from an abstract woman into a live woman, heartless but of great beauty, Bierce leads us to see her from the narrator's point of view, to apprehend with him her fatal power, and out of compassion for Brayle to reject the lesson just taught us by our skepticism. But this is a trap, for to try to justify Brayle on sentimental instead of reasonable grounds is to imply that had we been in his place, we too might very well have acted unreasonably. And thus Bierce implicates us in the tragedy, for Brayle's tragedy is ours, too; though in theory reason can save us, in practice it is beyond our grasp and we are ruled by our emotions. The story, therefore, does not resolve the issue of love for a woman leading a man to folly. On the contrary, it adds complexity and depth to the issue. And by turning skepticism against itself, Bierce frustrates a hope for an easy and simple solution to the dilemmas of life.

The tool of skepticism put into his hands by writers of the Enlightenment enabled Bierce to analyze not only his memories and impressions but the ideas of those writers as well. Thus reason and skepticism both came under his scrutiny. It is likely that just as he reacted against some of the maxims of the Stoics, so did he react against some of the notions of the French and English skeptics as he put their claims to the test. La Rochefoucauld, for example, whose maxims are acknowledged to have had an indisputable influence on Bierce, would easily have attracted Bierce's attention with such observations as this: "Vanity, a sense of shame, and above all temperament often make up the valour of men and the virtue of women."[24] The pertinence of this maxim to "Killed at Resaca" is self-evident. While it cannot be proved that this maxim, specifically, was the seed of the story, its appropriateness to Bierce's themes of fear, valor, and emotion make it at least worthy of consideration as having seminal value. Another maxim of La Rochefoucauld that possibly influenced Bierce is the following: "Intrepidity is unusual strength of soul which raises it above the troubles, disorders, and emotions that might be stirred up in it by the sight of great danger. This is the fortitude by which heroes keep their inner peace and preserve clear use of their reason in the most terrible and overwhelming crises" (Maxims, no. 217, 62). The striking relevance of this observation to Bierce's war stories, especially "The Affair at Coulter's Notch" and "The Horseman in the Sky," must be noted. Again, however, since the heroes of those stories lose their inner peace *because* of their intrepidity, these same stories might both be taken to be commentaries, not necessarily acquiescent, on this maxim.[25]

This survey of Bierce's philosophical position has aimed at demonstrating that there is a considerable and complex philosophical dimension to Bierce's stories, and what the general outlines of that dimension are. It has not attempted to completely chronicle his intellectual indebtedness, nor has it insisted on claiming direct influences of particular philosophical statements on individual stories. The first would have been overreaching and the second reductionistic. Nevertheless, as I will show shortly, it is essential to be aware of his philosophical orientation in order to interpret his tales, because a biographical approach to Bierce's short stories is inadequate to explain either their genesis or their power. Bierce wrote fiction, and like almost every other literary artist, altered or embellished the facts of his life, or created plots entirely from his imagination, in order to create vehicles for what lay deepest within him. And that was the desire to tell the truth about life or at least to recommend some worthy course of action in the face of its mystery.

Bierce, we have seen, failed to be consistently philosophical. But his bitter struggle to discover order was not fruitless, for out of it came some incomparable stories—a remarkable success of literature. Further, there is a consistency to these stories of conflict; at their next to deepest level they reflect failure. The failure, for one, of human reason to persuade itself that it has found fulfillment and purpose in human existence. The failure of idealism to convince experience that existence is not an illusion, and often a deadly illusion. The failure of skepticism to keep from turning on itself and becoming Pyrrhonism.

But at their deepest level, Bierce's tales hold compassion for either their protagonists or their readers—the one honestly positive value the author had left when philosophy failed. The desperate situations in which Bierce placed his protagonists represent, allegorically, the insoluble dilemmas with which he grappled. Though his problems were philosophical, his concern was man. In his tragic vision that man never won, that death was man's inevitable portion and Pyrrhic victory his utmost reward, Bierce sublimed his compassion for human existence.

⁖ 4 ⁖

BIERCE AS CRAFTSMAN
His Concern with Mind

T HE COMPASSION Bierce had for the humanity symbolized by
   some of his protagonists is almost never openly expressed for
the humanity represented by his readers. Only on a very few occasions in fiction or nonfiction did Bierce ever try to appeal directly to
the reader through the heart. His first full-length short story, "The
Haunted Valley" (1871), was such an attempt. Its affinities with the
Bret Harte type of sentimental local-color story are not accidental,
however; Bret Harte had recently been editor of the *Overland Monthly*,
which published it. "A Baby Tramp" (1891) and "The Applicant"
(1892), both collected in *Can Such Things Be?* in 1893, are two more examples of sentimental short stories, and both are almost redolent of
a Sunday-school magazine. Two more of his few lapses into senti-
mentality in "Prattle" occurred in 1891 in connection with the knife
slaying in San Francisco of a young man named Samuels by another
named McGregor. When McGregor was first apprehended by the
police, Samuels's mother told reporters that she forgave him for his
murder. Bierce's comment on that action was rhapsodic.

> [I]n souls like hers shines inextinguishable a light that is not of
> earth. Good Heavens! Was ever such an act as this? It is worth

all the prayers of all the preachers. It distinguishes the doer like the jewel of an Order of Merit. It parts her from her sex a long remove; it thrones her a measureless height above the race, yet lifts us all a little too. Between the ordinary woman bereft of her whelp and this incomparable mother what an unthinkable distance!—not to be overpassed but in eons and eons of spiritual development. (E, 18 January 1891, 6)

Several months later, McGregor was acquitted by a jury. Again Bierce lauded the mother's character, and in noting that the mother had asked his cooperation, concluded:

I did not feel that it would be proper—even if it were practicable—for me to assist in what her saintly heart, having justification of its great mercy, might rightly undertake. Yet to that superior spirit I did not dare to signify my refusal, for I could not hope intelligibly to explain a baser nature's checks upon its will. In the added sorrow that has recently fallen upon this sister to the angels I hope she may be sustained by some consciousness of her own worth and a faith that somewhere and somehow in the scheme of existence a Christlike spirit is commuted into peace. (E, 17 May 1891, 6)

Both of these passages reveal an interesting and not sufficiently studied impulse toward sentimentalism in Bierce and point up a weakness in Bierce's style about which little is known because it is so seldom seen. Neither one of these passages nor the stories mentioned above are far removed from the maudlin. These passages especially are too extreme in their claims, trite in their metaphors, and commonplace in their concluding sentiments. The simple truth of the matter is that Bierce could not handle sentiment. Whenever he wore his heart on his sleeve, he almost invariably lapsed into stilted or ornate language and became sermonical. Perhaps his awareness that he departed from art when he tried to express feelings was one of the reasons behind his later injunctions against mixing reform and literature. Whatever the cause, Bierce rarely indulged any stray whim to overwhelm his readers by the purity of his ideals and force of his emotion. In his stories, Bierce did try to convince his readers to reassess their values and their outlook on life, but he did not entreat their hearts; he aimed at, and attacked, their heads.

One evidence of this characteristic may be seen in his craftsman-like attitude toward writing. From his first acquaintance with James Watkins, Bierce was concerned with style: he deliberately strove for precise diction, correct grammar, and close logic. With Bierce, however, style was more than ornamental; it was functional. That it meant to him an organic relationship of reason, language, and morality is apparent from a "Prattle" of 1889, in which appears an unusual and interesting crusade metaphor:

> Professor Max Muller has recently distilled the results of a lifetime of study into two lines:
>
> "No Language without Reason;
> No Reason without Language."
>
> How can you know that a man who cannot express his thought has the thought? Are you a mind-reader? The individual with a copious and obedient vocabulary and the will and power to apply it with precision thinks great thoughts. The mere "glib-talker"—who may have a meager vocabulary, and no sense of discrimination in the use of words—is another kind of creature. A nation whose language is strong and rich and flexible and sweet—such as English was before the devil invented dictionaries—has a noble literature and, compared with contemporary nations barren in speech, a superior morality. A word is a crystallized thought; good words are precious possessions, which nevertheless, like gold, may be mischievously used. The introduction of a bad word, its preservation, the customary misuse of a good one—these are sins affecting the public welfare. The fight against faulty diction is a fight against insurgent barbarism—a fight for high thinking and right living—for art, science, power—in a word,

civilization. A motor without mechanism; an impulse without
a medium of transmission; a vitalizing thought with no means
to impart it; a fertile mind with a barren vocabulary—than
these nothing could be more impotent. Happily they are impossible. They are not even conceivable. (E, 21 April 1889, 4)

That his opinion in this article is not an isolated opinion is made
clear by his use of the same idea in other "Prattle" columns. The
most important adumbration of this position occurred two weeks
earlier:

It is not permitted to you to think, good reader, that because I
sometimes write without seriousness that these hateful perver-
sions have a hateful intent—that they are set down in a spirit
of irreverence. You will not think so unless you are a fool, and
then nobody will care what you think. My design is to show in
the lucidest conceivable way the supreme importance of
words; their domination of thought, their mastery of character. Had the Scriptures been translated, as literally as now,
into the colloquial speech of the unlearned, and had neither
the original nor any other version been thereafter accessible,
only a direct interposition of the Divine Power could have
saved the whole magnificent edifice of Christianity from tumbling to ruin.

Conduct is of character, character is of thought, and
thought is unspoken speech. We think in words; we cannot
think without them. Shallowness or obscurity of speech
means shallowness or obscurity of thought. Barring a physical infirmity, an erring tongue denotes an erring brain.
When I stumble in my speech I stumble in my thought. The
poets, who have the richest and most obedient vocabulary,
are also the wisest thinkers; there is little worth knowing but
they have thought. The most brutish savage is he who is
most meagerly equipped with words; fill him with words to
the top of his gift and you would make him as wise as he is
able to become. The man who can neither write well nor

talk well would have us believe that, like the taciturn parrot of the anecdote, he is "a devil to think." It is not so.

Though such a man had read the Alexandrian library he would remain ignorant; though he had sat at the feet of Plato he would be still unwise. The gift of language—by tongue or the sign-language—it is the measure of mental capacity; its degree of cultivation is the exponent of intellectual power. One may not choose to utter his mind—that is another matter; but if he choose he can. He can utter it all. His mind not his "heart"; his thought, not his emotion. And if he do not sometimes choose to utter he will eventually cease to think. (E, 7 April 1889, 4)

One month later, with extraordinary frankness, Bierce vividly expanded his concept of language as a weapon of morality and culture in another "Prattle" column. Although the article is devoted to an explanation of his ideas of strategy and tactics in newspaper controversies, it is of obviously wider significance, especially since it was written at the height of Bierce's career as a short story writer. In this article, it is noteworthy that Bierce lapses into war imagery: the "controversy" becomes a "fray," then a gladiatorial combat; the other controversialist is variously described as an "adversary," an "antagonist," and, finally, a "gladiator"; the outcome is conceived of in terms of victory and defeat, victor and vanquished. Typically, Bierce expresses unconcern for the reading public: his concern is only with the man who thinks. "The public, in most cases, neither cares for the outcome of the fray, nor will remember its incidents." The writer, therefore, is advised to accomplish "two main purposes: 1—entertainment of the reader; 2—a personal gratification." In achieving the second purpose, the writer is advised to (1) guard his self-respect, (2) destroy the self-respect of his adversary, (3) force the adversary to respect him against his will, and (4) betray the adversary "into the blunder of permitting you to despise him." Every dodge, lie, and evasion offered by one adversary is a score for the other. It is not important that the public understand; the combatants will. Loss of honor, dishonesty, and the use of falsehoods are all tantamount to defeat:

Remember that what you want is not so much to disclose his meanness to the reader (who cares nothing about it) as to make him disclose it to your private discernment. That . . . is the whole gospel of controversial strategy.

You are one of two gladiators in the arena: Your first duty is to amuse the multitude. But as the multitude is not going to remember, after leaving the show, who was victorious, it is not worth while to take any hurts for a merely visible advantage. So fight as to prove to yourself that you are the abler swordsman—that is, the more honorable man. Victory in that is important, for it is lasting . . . and is enjoyed ever afterward whenever you see or think of the vanquished. (E, 26 May 1889, 4)

Thus, Bierce considers words as weapons, symbols, and military agents of reason and truth. In controversies, language is used with special strategy, but it must be used circumspectly at all times, for whoever understands the words he uses, fights for civilization if not for personal gratification. No intelligent man is exempt from strife; language, by definition, is a weapon in use, and discourse, a form of combat. It follows from this that a man may be his own enemy. Just as failure to act rationally on the battlefield may cost a soldier his life, so a failure to think carefully and to use language with precision may deprive a man of his honor and self-respect. To Bierce, seeking truth and speaking it were not just good deeds; they were moral imperatives. He considered them binding upon himself because he considered himself reasonable. And that he expected all other reasonable and thinking humans to accept the same obligations is evident in his constant challenging of his readers and in his continual assaults upon their minds and sensibilities. In more ways than one, Bierce's manner of involving himself in challenges that turned a reader into either an opponent or a victim is strikingly pedagogical. He believed the function of literature is to please and instruct. As he took care that almost every piece of writing he composed for publication should please, so also did he take care that it could instruct, when reflected on.

In his poetry and nonfictional prose, Bierce teased his readers into controversy—and thought—by the time-honored pedagogical tactic of provoking them from his previously prepared strong positions. In his short fiction, however, while he continued to aim at the minds of his readers, he used radically different and much more subtle strategies. One such strategy is briefly but unmistakably[1] described in a "Prattle" written in 1892, just as his major period of activity as a short-story writer was ending. It was his wont, from time to time, to reply in "Prattle" to various letters received from readers. From his answer, other readers could deduce the question. In such a reply to "F. H. L." Bierce said: "May not art follow nature? May not fiction resemble fact in leaving something to conjecture? In life do events always wholly disclose the purpose and meaning of the Master of the Show? From your neighbor's words and acts can you always infer his character, his motives; from your glimpses of his character and motives always forecast his deeds? Are there no broken lights, no parted clews, no paths leading nowhither?—no caves and abysses of eternal shadow? The story-teller is not bound to address those only who do not wish to think" (E, 29 May 1892, 6). In the last two lines, Bierce clearly indicates that he has not been working in the trick-ending tradition of O. Henry. There are clues in his stories, but they are "parted." Thinking readers, however, can put them together, and Bierce intends that they should.

The reply furthermore strongly implies a profound seriousness in Bierce's stories. In the first three lines, Bierce not only suggests that his stories may be "true-to-life" but indeed, also opens the door of possibility to allegorical truth. The sarcastic phrase "the Master of the Show" at once reflects Bierce's resentful accession to "the Scheme of the Universe" and also implies that a thinking reader may, by reflection, find an author's hidden purpose in his stories.

Another strategy Bierce employed to capture the attention of his readers' minds—*and hold it*—was his technique of shock, of etching on the minds of his readers some unforgettably awful scene or action described in brutal detail. This technique has been generally misunderstood, especially by the large group of casual critics of Bierce who consider him simply imitative of Poe. One of the best of such critics is Fred Lewis Pattee, who asserted that Bierce "lacked Poe's imaginative sweep and his romanticism and his lyric soul," and complained that Bierce's use of shock was not very artistic, that it physically harrowed the reader. A little further on in the same discussion, however, Pattee was moved to concede grudgingly to Bierce a genuine ability to create "hauntingly suggestive stories," many of which begin for the reader where the last sentence ends. "It is the last touch of art: it is the art that compels the reader to search his own soul."[2] Pattee's criticism of Bierce thus alternates between reluctant admiration of Bierce's power and censure of that same power for being too intellectual and too horrible.

Pattee was not the first to note a similarity between Bierce and Poe, and the comparison has been made many times since then. Bierce was a strong admirer of Poe at a time when it was not fashionable to be one. He long shared the fate of Poe, to be considered all manner but no content, to be read for shudders, and to be wondered at as a technically talented but psychologically disturbed personality. Bierce, however, might have been one of the earliest acute students of Poe, for insofar as an influence of Poe might be verified in Bierce, it is likely to show that the same depth of theme and penetration into character that are now recognized in the earlier writer are also present in the later.

Pattee's very censure of Bierce's use of shock is in itself a form of tribute to its effectiveness. A more direct tribute, however, was tendered by Frederic Taber Cooper, who praised it as "a pitiless realism unequalled by Stendahl . . . and at least unsurpassed by Tolstoy or Zola."[3] But Bierce's use of shock must be judged on more substantial grounds than individual reactions to horror and brutality. To this end, Grenander advanced the discussion when she contended that Bierce made a unique contribution to the short story in the particular way in which he combined irony with terror. "He added an ironic twist, which rests primarily on a certain kind of relationship between plot and character, so that we feel an intense fear coupled with a bitter realization that the emotion is cruelly inappropriate. What emerges is really a new form. Poe's tales of terror are nearly all simple in plot and cumulative in their emotional impact; Bierce's best ones are complex in plot and involve an element of irony in their emotional effect."[4] Her application of this theory to two classes of Bierce's stories—those in which the actual situation is harmful, but in which the protagonist conceives it to be harmless and acts accordingly; and another class in which the reverse holds true—is convincing. If she underestimates the subtleties and ironies of Poe, she at least points up a major difference between Bierce and O. Henry, whose effect, as she subsequently notes, is derived from the narrator's having concealed or held back vital bits of information.[5] Bierce's technique, at least in his serious stories, is to conceal nothing from the protagonist's *perception,* but then to enable readers to see that the protagonist has misinterpreted his perception. The first awareness of readers of this "gruesome inappropriateness" of perception to the facts of the real situation comes with a sudden shock when they discover that the protagonist has blundered into a possibly fatal trap of his own making. Grenander has chosen to call stories in which this sequence of thought occurs "not ironical tales of terror, but tales of ironical terror," because the irony lies "in a certain relationship between a given character and the incidents of the plot" rather than in a "self-conscious coyness on the part of the narrator."[6]

If it is true, as John Mason Brown once said, that irony is concerned only with the trip and not the fall, then the pattern of irony that Grenander has discovered in Bierce's tales of terror is not an end in itself but rather a means to subserve Bierce's primary goal of involving his readers in the moral issues of his stories. Like his respected model Swift, Bierce uses shock for moral purposes, and behind both the story plots and mechanics that are productive of ironical terror, and the sudden glimpses of unexpected horror that appear in his stories, is a calculated plan to force the reader into intellectual activity. Whoever has read *Gulliver's Travels,* for example, will remember having experienced physical disgust at the well-known passages on the skins and persons of the Brobdingnagians and the Yahoos; yet those passages, precisely because of their shocking vividness, stick in readers' minds like barbed arrows, pricking truths about themselves that they might have preferred to ignore, and rankling in their memories, ever recalling them to painful reflections. It is not hard to see in Bierce, who admitted to imitating Swift,[7] the use of this same Swiftian skill of harrowing readers with a memorably detailed glimpse of something disagreeable to them. Bierce's use of shock, in other words, is not a self-indulgent assault on readers' minds and sensibilities; it is a tactical maneuver to drive them into defensive intellectual and moral combat on issues carefully chosen by Bierce. To see how Bierce militantly advances a definite philosophy of life in the most of the stories in *Tales of Soldiers and Civilians* and the best ones in *Can Such Things Be?*, it is only necessary to look into the history and function of several examples of his use of shock.

Certainly one of the most famous instances of shock in his stories occurs in "The Coup de Grâce" (1889), in which Captain Downing Madwell, searching a battlefield for a missing friend, finds him mortally "hurt" and his clothing strangely disarranged. The wound is like none other Madwell has ever seen, and he is baffled by it until he notices something nearby:

> Fifty yards away, on the crest of a low, thinly wooded hill, he saw several dark objects moving about among the fallen men—a herd of swine. One stood with its back to him, it shoulders sharply elevated. Its forefeet were upon a human body, its head was depressed and invisible. The bristly ridge of its chine showed black against the red west. Captain Madwell drew away his eyes and fixed them again upon the thing which had been his friend.
>
> The man who had suffered these monstrous mutilations was alive. . . . (CW, II, 128)

It is impossible to read this passage without some feeling of revulsion. This specific passage, in fact, was one of those Pattee had in mind when he censured Bierce's use of shock as being too horrible.[8] The subjective merits or drawbacks of the passage need not be argued here, but it can be demonstrated that it was used deliberately and that it was also an expression of Bierce's hatred of war and his consequent view of life as hostile and implacable.

The origin of this incident in "The Coup de Grâce" was in

Bierce's own experience as a soldier in western Virginia twenty-eight years before. In his autobiographical prose piece "On a Mountain," he recalls retreating past a spot where, the day before, he had seen for the first time some fatalities of the war, corpses with repulsive "yellow-clay faces." With details used again in "The Coup de Grâce," Bierce describes the same scene on the next day:

> Repassing the spot the next day . . . some of us had life enough left, such as it was, to observe that these bodies had altered their positions. They appeared also to have thrown off some of their clothing, which lay near by, in disorder. Their expression, too, had an added blankness—they had no faces.
>
> As soon as the head of our struggling column had reached the spot a desultory firing had begun. One might have thought the living paid honors to the dead. No; the firing was a military execution; the condemned, a herd of galloping swine. They had eaten our fallen, but—touching magnanimity!—we did not eat theirs. (CW, I, 233)

The tone of grim humor in this passage should not be misconstrued as facetiousness or callousness. On the contrary, it is an indication of seriousness and sensitivity. Bierce used several literary devices, among them an ironic mask, and the appearance of inappropriate humor or sarcastic tone, to create artistic distance between himself and a subject about which he had strong feelings. We already have the testimony of his daughter on the continuous impact the recollections of the dead and wounded had upon him in later life,[9] and the prose piece itself, published years after the war, argues by its very vividness that the original scene shocked Bierce into permanent memory of it.

The picture of animals ravening human corpses was not solely a war scene to Bierce, though he clearly used it to shock his readers out of stereotyped romantic responses to war. That he believed civilian life had such horrors, too, is evidenced by his repeated and broadened uses of the theme of animals gorging on human carrion. In an 1888 "Prattle," for instance, Bierce sarcastically enlarges upon a farmer's claim that hogs foretell "cyclones" by boring into a hill. "After the elemental warfare is accomplished," Bierce comments, "it [a hog] emerges from its pit, and with a tranquil mind goes about its business—which consists, generally speaking, in eating its former master and his family" (E, 11 March 1888, 4). One year later, in the *same month* that saw the publication of "The Coup de Grâce," Bierce pursued the theme again in "Prattle": "A man in New Jersey recently had the misfortune to die. His body was prepared for burial, when his favorite dog, being admitted into the death chamber, manifested so sharp a reluctance to leave that it was decided to let it remain. Unfortunately the watchers fell asleep that night, and the dog took a reprehensible advantage of their weakness: it bit off one of the dead man's ears and ate it" (E, 30 June 1889, 4).

Finally, in 1906, Bierce published a story called "John Mortonson's Funeral," in which the pet cat of the deceased is accidentally enclosed in the coffin with the body. The mistake is discovered in the funeral parlor when the widow takes one last look through the glass at the face of her beloved and faints in horror. One of the mourners who comes to her aid also looks at the face and, sickened by what he sees, stumbles against the coffin and accidentally knocks it to the floor, breaking its glass. "From the opening crawled John Mortonson's cat, which lazily leapt to the floor, sat up, tranquilly wiped its crimson muzzle with a forepaw, then walked with dignity from the room."[10] With this conclusion, what had begun as an experience in Bierce's life, and had been subsequently utilized as arresting incidents in memoirs and journalism and as a poignant episode in a war story, is finally put in the center of the stage in a short story. Biographical criticism might brush off this story—admittedly one of his lesser ones—with the explanation that here Bierce was indulging his well-known hatred of pets. But seen in the larger context that has been outlined, the story may be understood as a bitter reminder of the ignoble end to which all humans are subject. Constantly imperiled by a hostile Nature and their "fellow man," Bierce reiterates, human beings cannot even look forward confidently to the sufficiently degrading end to which they have by custom reconciled themselves, mold and worms; even in death their remains may be mutilated or dishonored. Neither the beast of the field nor the "domesticated" and beloved pets of home have either fear of or lingering devotion for their human masters when their life or force go out of them.

An ironic twist to this idea is given in "One Summer Night" (1906), which appeared in the same issue of the *Cosmopolitan* as "John Mortonson's Funeral." In this story, Henry Armstrong regains consciousness in his coffin and discovers that he has been buried alive. (Poe gave literary prominence to this situation in his 1844 tale "A Premature Burial," but stories about being buried alive were not uncommon items in newspapers of the late nineteenth century, including the *Examiner.*) Just as Armstrong accepts his fate, he hears a noise overhead. It is three grave-robbers at work, one mercenary laborer and two young medical students in need of a fresh cadaver. When the coffin lid is removed, and the "cadaver" sits up, the two "scientists" flee. The laborer does not. Later, back at the medical college, the two students meet the laborer, who asks for his pay. In the dissecting room he has deposited Armstrong, this time a real cadaver, his head split open by a blow from the laborer's spade (CW, III, 58–61). Bierce effectively sinks human beings below the pets of the household and the swine of the field as he returns in this tale to a variation of his theme of war, human beings killing each other for pay.

We flatter ourselves with our conception of man as a special, higher form of life; we fondly foster a sentimental ideal of the sacred inviolability of the human cadaver; and we find it a humiliating affront to our collective ego to admit that a human being when dead is merely carrion to Nature, to be disposed of indifferently by any one of several purely natural methods. But Bierce uses shock to shatter these cherished illusions and compel us, by means of this disturbing new vision of life, to use our reason to begin drawing new conclusions. The real shock, after all, is not so much in the brutality of the deeds represented in the stories as it is in the outrage done to our idealized conceptions of the nature and significance of man. But lest these macabre episodes be passed over too lightly as sensational stoicism, it must be kept in mind that their genesis was in a shock to Bierce's sensibilities, and that with the sincerity and purposefulness of writing that we have seen to be a peculiar trademark of his, his use of them in his tales, such as "The Coup de Grâce," evidences a sensibility still lacerated by their recollection. Bierce shocks his readers with what was shocking to him, and arraigns the veracity and compassion of the rationales of human beings that are founded upon wishful thinking instead of close and honest observation. By so doing, he challenges readers to replace a discredited generalization with a more accurate view of life that, by not raising unrealistic expectations, might result in less suffering for humans instead of more.

Another example of purposeful, but compassionate, use of shock occurs in the story "Chickamauga" (1889). On all sides it is acclaimed as a great work of realism and as a compelling denunciation of war. The story certainly qualifies for both of these commendations, but it is quite possible that these points are ancillary to a still larger purpose, one suggested to us through Bierce's use of shock. The one incident in this story of unrelieved horror that no reader of it ever forgets is the "hideous pantomime" of a deaf-mute child mounting one of a line of maimed and bleeding soldiers crawling away on all fours from the ruddy conflagration of a forest fire lit by the battle of Chickamauga (CW, II, 52). Here is the allegorical picture of hell Bierce remembered in his account of Shiloh, but instead of the demons, it is peopled with the damned. The allegory in "Chickamauga" is almost transparently clear. There are no "normal" people in the entire story, just the newly dead, the dying, the maimed, and the "naturally" abnormal. What were "normal" people were destroyed, and are being destroyed, by the twin cataclysms of military warfare and the elemental warfare of fire. All are crushed in spirit as well as body by the horrors, except the child, who is both too young and too deficient in perceptive capacity to understand quickly. But when he finally does understand, he, too, is crushed. "Then he stood motionless, with quivering lips, looking down upon the wreck." But who could say more? What was there to say? It is apparent that in this allegorical picture of hell, it is life that is hell, and the living who are the damned.

Here again Bierce has used shock to attack the reader's mind. By shifting the story's point of view back and forth between the intellects of an omniscient narrator and the deaf-mute child, he forces the reader to see contrasts where comparisons are alleged, and comparisons where contrasts are pretended. A violent contrast occurs in the parallel of the child at play and soldiers at war. The child is first described as "the son of an heroic race"—significantly, he is playing soldier. Bierce effects a sudden transition to the next scene, where the child sees lines of wounded dragging themselves away from the nearby battle, which the child's deafness prevents him from apprehending. He misinterprets the soldiers to be adults playing a "merry" game ("these were men, yet crept like babes"); in fact, he is reminded of having "seen his father's Negroes creep upon their hands and knees for his amusement—had ridden them so, fancying them his horses." In the final scene, the deaf-mute loses his childishness when he finally understands the tragedy before him. The story's conclusion shows the handicapped child and the maimed soldiers to be equals in their common victimhood; the child a victim first of Nature and then war, and the soldiers victims first of war, then Nature.

Another strategy Bierce employs to engage the mind of his reader in controversy arises out of his own ambivalent attitude toward reason. Like his eighteenth-century predecessors, Bierce was intensely interested in the capabilities and limitations of reason, and explored the subject in stories that are at once ironic and serious, pleasing and instructive. Without exaggeration, it may be said that one of the most distinctive (and perhaps unique) characteristics of Bierce's style of fiction is his conscious use of reason and his treatment of reason to arrive at conclusions in his stories that call into doubt the value of reason.

Most critics of Bierce who have been aware of a deliberate use of reason in his stories have tended to take too simple a view of it. Thus, even Carey McWilliams, for example, once charged that Bierce regarded the world as a hard and fast equation, and existence a pattern that could be unerringly traced, and that he warped his stories to fit into the mold he had devised.[11] Robert Littell, a critic who objected to what he considered to be stories cut to a predetermined pattern, felt that Bierce's tales were deliberately constructed from beginning to end for the sake of an "unnatural and artificial end," and that

Bierce was so eager to shock the reader that the outcomes of the stories were predictable.[12] Even so appreciative an advocate of Bierce's art as Vincent Starrett yielded ground on this issue, although he tried to turn his concession to advantage. "It has been said that Bierce's stories are 'formula,'" Starrett wrote, "and in a measure it is true; but the formula is that of a master chemist, and it is inimitable."[13] Paul Fatout is content to note thoughtfully that the sequence of mystery and murder, and a supernatural atmosphere cleared by a rational denouement, was a "frequent technique" in Bierce's tales.[14]

The objections, direct or indirect, well-intentioned or adverse, of these and other critics to what has seemed to them to be formularized stories rigged at the end to conform to reason are in almost every case founded upon the assumption that Bierce had assigned a simple, traditional value to reason in his personal philosophy and in his stories, and upon a consequent failure to recognize the stories as the serious explorations of reason they really are. In this case, interpretations founded on inadequate biography have rather muddied the waters of Bierce criticism. They accurately reported that Bierce valued reason above almost every other tool of knowledge,[15] but it failed to discern that Bierce still did not wholly trust it, that he regarded it as being far from dependable. A more penetrating observation on the matter comes from Percy Boynton: "In the way of thoughtful doubters Bierce was out of tune with any set of extremists."[16] The accuracy of this position can be substantiated by an examination of the fates of Bierce's rationalistic protagonists.[17]

With few exceptions, Bierce's stories center on protagonists who are eminently rational. Accordingly, either out of habitual confidence in reason or out of pride, readers are encouraged to identify themselves with these protagonists. When readers do this, however, they deliver themselves into the hands of Bierce, whose intention it is to make them reassess their estimation of reason. He accomplishes this by letting readers see their intellectual alter ego betrayed by a dependence on reason. Readers feel themselves threatened by any disaster occurring to their favorite, especially a disaster that they themselves could not have avoided. As almost every rationalistic protagonist in Bierce's stories is ultimately brought to grief, we may see in this pattern a reflection of Bierce's complex and ambivalent attitude toward reason: it is necessary to human existence, but it is of limited use. Far from formularizing his stories and short-circuiting thought, the use of the rationalistic protagonist device induces thought in the reader and makes tragedy possible in the tales.

When disaster occurs to the rationalistic protagonist, the reader may, of course, unquestionably accept the disaster as either pathos or irony. But to do this is to ignore Bierce's deliberate use of a *rationalistic* protagonist. If Bierce had had no other purpose than that of evoking empathy, a less complex protagonist—a moral hero, for example—would have served his purposes better. Irony, also, might have been achieved more easily, such as through the manipulation of plot. But more important than plot or even character in Bierce's stories is his study of mind. His protagonists are distinguished by intelligence precisely because he wants to call our attention to their rationalism. He has purposely endowed them with reason, the finest human defense against disaster, and has given them a measure of control over their own futures by according them a choice in which they can exercise their reason. Therefore, when one of them is undone, readers who have identified themselves with the protagonist are provoked to reexamine the details of the story and their own reactions to them. When they do this, they find that the cause of disaster was not the circumstances of plot or some carelessness in the protagonist who made maximum use of his reason; the cause was the human mind. Thus, readers, far from being deceived by Bierce, are rather included in an exploration of reason that points out its limitations and the consequent tragedy of human existence. That Bierce does not detach himself, Olympian fashion, from the implications of his tales, but freely acknowledges himself a potential victim of his own mind, is a point made first by Carey McWilliams: "I have often thought that the satirical motivation of the horror stories was two-fold: in part aimed at the timorous reader and in no small measure directed at Bierce himself, as though he recoiled from his own frightful fantasies. . . . At times Bierce seems to have satirized his own, as well as the reader's fright."[18] It is also a point that is likely to occur to close readers of Bierce's stories of the supernatural and of extreme fear, and to those who have access to his stories in their original context of the *San Francisco Examiner.*

The stories that originally appeared in the *Examiner* were published in a context of fiction and articles noticeably keyed to the macabre, the exotic, and the apparently inexplicable. Science-fiction and stranger-than-fiction news articles were regular fare in the daily editions; in the Sunday feature section there was a feast of them. In addition, the Sunday feature section typically included a number of mystery stories and tales of the supernatural, and lurid narrations of murders, executions, burials alive, strange disappearances, and uncanny occurrences. Bierce's tales, in fact, competed for readers' attention against usually more lengthy Sherlock Holmes mysteries by Arthur Conan Doyle, Guy de Maupassant's shockers, Frank Stockton's offbeat narratives, and W. C. Morrow's supernatural thrillers (sometimes subtitled as "blendings of fact and fiction").[19] It would have been strange if Bierce gave no attention to his literary environment and the sort of subjects then in vogue. As it was, however, not only did he give attention to these matters but he even acquired a reputation for being a connoisseur of the supernatural. More than once, subtitles of feature articles he wrote about reported instances of supernatural occurrences described him as being an expert on the subject, and on at least one occasion he himself referred to "rather voluminous memoranda" he kept on the subject (E, 29 April 1888, 9).[20]

Seen against this literary background, Bierce's employment of the supernatural and the terrifying in his stories is rendered more understandable. He obviously found the Sunday *Examiner* feature stories convenient models of what was marketable, but, in addition, he saw in the very themes of the supernatural and the terrifying a splendid opportunity to demonstrate and test his developing convictions about reason. The connection between the two themes is made explicit in his definition of a ghost, "The outward and visible sign of an inward fear" (1885). An implicit connection is that both terror and the perception of the supernatural either paralyze the human mind and bring its reasoning function to a halt, or else leave the reasoning function intact but pervert its end by feeding it false premises or by encouraging inappropriate methods of reasoning.

Thus, in the story "A Tough Tussle," originally entitled "The Facts about Byring's Encounter with an Unknown,"[21] the protagonist, Lieutenant Byring, recognizing his own intense fear of a nearby Confederate corpse and his irrational suspicion that it is somehow stealthily drawing closer to him, in fact brings his doom upon himself by attempting to rationalize his fears away. First, he accepts the false, but plausible, premise that his fear is an inherited legacy handed down to him over the centuries from primitive and superstitious ancestors who lived in "the cradle of the human race—Central Asia" (CW, III, 113). Next, proceeding a priori from this premise, he not only fails to dispel his fear but actually intensifies it by justifying and tolerating it. Eventually, Byring's fear grows into a chimera that turns his own reasoning against him and paralyzes him with terror. When he is subsequently triggered into action by a sudden Confederate attack, he instinctively leaps upon the corpse with his sword but somehow plunges it accidentally into his own heart. At this point, the ironic ambiguity of the work "unknown" in the original subtitle is made apparent—the unknown is not so much any supernatural being as it is Byring's own mind. This point is stated sympathetically in the story by the narrator in an editorial comment: "I repeat that Lieutenant Byring was a brave and intelligent man. But what would you have? Shall a man cope, single-handed, with so monstrous an alliance as that of night and solitude and silence of the dead—while an incalculable host of his own ancestors shriek into the ear of his spirit their coward counsel, sing their doleful death-songs in his heart, and disarm his very blood of all its iron? The odds are too great—courage was not made for so rough use as that" (117). Significantly, Byring is defended in this comment against any lack of reason or unwillingness to use his reason. His death is ascribed to the inherent limitation of his rational nature rather than to some flaw in it. A protagonist with less sensitivity, intelligence, and reason either would have been too dull to symbolize man as a rational creature or would have fled the scene. But given such a man as Byring, Bierce implies, such a person as we probably flatter ourselves to be, what other conclusion, under the circumstances, would have been more likely?

Three traps are laid in this story for credulous readers—that is, readers who are proud of their ability to reason and who do not think that it would deceive them. The first trap is inherent in the very nature of the story. It is a ghost story—and there are no such things as ghosts. The assumption that ghosts do not exist cannot be proven rationally, however; it is a point of faith. Merely to entertain the thought that spirits may operate among us, therefore, as Byring did briefly, is to permit rationalization to carry one into superstition. In other words, it is basically faith and not rationality that separates credibility from credulity. Reason indifferently serves any premise; logic leads to validity, not truth. Or, to put it differently, faith in something beyond reason is a natural and necessary part of the mental process. A wholesome faith imparts some protection against credulity; in its absence a vacuum will be created that an inferior faith may fill. The first trap is sprung when readers proudly believe that reason by itself is self-sufficient, and put their entire faith in it.

The second trap is sprung when the readers' alter ego, Byring, reasoning a priori from a plausible premise, in fact creates a fatal chimera that provokes him into accidental suicide. At this point, Bierce's ambivalent attitude toward reason can be recognized. In the sense that the story can be read as a tale of ironical terror, Bierce can be understood to be discounting reason as an infallible defense against the perils of life.[22] While it is true that the reader has been trapped through overconfidence in reason, Bierce softens the blow, in the passage quoted above, by suggesting a tragic dimension in the significance of Byring's doom for all humans. Even granting that pure reason might have saved Byring, the story demonstrates that he is psychologically unable to use it.

The trace of compassion for man implicit in the narrator's sympathy for Lieutenant Byring is likely to be forgotten by readers who spring the third trap, because its function is to drive home forcefully the lesson of the second trap by repeating it on *them*. The third trap is set up in the understatement of the few, short paragraphs of the conclusion. In them is described the site of Byring's "encounter" as seen, on the following morning, by a Federal captain and a surgeon. The reader is briefly informed that the Confederate corpse, gashed several times by Byring's sword, not only was bloodless and stiff, but was also decayed and maggoty—indications that it had lain there a long time. The reader is also notified that the sword in Byring's breast was his own (120).[23] The trap is baited by the last two sentences, short and deliberately noncommittal: "The surgeon looked at the captain. The captain looked at the surgeon" (120). As these two sentences are somewhat ambiguous, readers are moved to interpret them. If readers did not participate in Byring's reasoning or if they read the conclusion carefully, the last two lines are anticlimactic and superfluous, adding nothing of importance to the story. If, however, they did identify with Byring, then it seems that Bierce expects them to remain so thoroughly caught up in Byring's reasoning as to be carried by the momentum of his logic over the inconspicuous details of the matter-of-fact conclusion, and to interpret the last two sentences to mean that the two officers suspect the corpse of having killed Byring. Readers who reach this opinion have sprung the third trap, for the interpretation is untenable for two reasons. In the first place, it puts a reader in the absurd position of defending the proposition that there are ghosts; and in the second, it ignores the contradicting factual explanation of the conclusion. By virtue of the fact that any reader who springs the third trap does so despite two major advantages—the factual explanation of the conclusion, and the absence of the "monstrous alliance" of night, solitude, and the presence and silence of the dead—Bierce continues to point up the dangers of inappropriate mental responses and to develop the tragic dimension of the rationalistic protagonist, for when Byring dies, readers who identified with him take his place as rationalistic protagonist. Partly by their own repetition of Byring's mistakes, but mostly by a dramatic revelation of the subtle but powerful opposition of psychological forces in the mind to the correct use of reason, such readers are led to the brink of an inevitable conclusion: reason is not an unqualified good, and humans are not naturally constituted to make full use of even such benefits as reason seems to offer them.

A similar conclusion can be derived from a close reading of "The Suitable Surroundings" (1889), another story from *Tales of Soldiers and Civilians* that seems to make use of the supernatural. As its title suggests, this story is founded upon the notion that no one who thinks about the supernatural under "suitable circumstances" is immune from irrational fear, not even a rationalistic individual who is fully aware that he is the subject of an experiment in reason. The proposition is put to the test in the story by the rationalistic protagonist Willard Marsh, who, stung by the imputation of a writer of ghost stories that he was too cowardly to risk feeling "fear—at least a strong sense of the supernatural" by reading "in solitude—at night—by the light of a candle" (CW, II, 357) a manuscript the author had written, accepts the dare. That night, alone in a deserted house in a forest, Marsh reads the document. He learns from it that the writer plans to commit suicide at midnight and will appear to him, in spirit form, with the intention of frightening him to death. As he finishes, Marsh looks up, and in the feeble rays of the candlelight unexpectedly sees a face. Simultaneously, a shriek rends the air. Marsh springs to his feet—and dies.

This is the bare plot of the story, told in chronological sequence. Bierce, however, begins in medias res, with a boy lost in the woods who sees a light in an old house, goes over to the window, and sees a man staring apprehensively into the darkness. Just as the boy's face is illuminated by the candlelight, an owl shrieks, the man jumps up, and the candle is dashed to the floor. The boy flees. This sequence of events is essential to Bierce's purpose, for by means of it the reader is told all the details *of* Marsh's death.

The next development of the story is a flashback to the events of the previous day. In this section, the reader learns all the details *leading up to* Marsh's death. The next development is a narration of events occurring on the day after Marsh's death. The boy returns to the house on the next morning, bringing some men with him. They find Marsh's body, and the fatal manuscript alongside it.

At this point, Bierce tests his readers. Although the first section of the story—the section about the fatal night—has given readers all the details of Marsh's death, the readers do not know this. Consequently, they have not been prevented from ascribing Marsh's death to the malignant spirit of the suicidal writer. The details of the boy at the window and the owl shriek could be interpreted as attendant circumstances; they might have caused Marsh to faint, but it is hard to believe that they are meant to suffice as the cause of his death. Moreover, inasmuch as this is a ghost story, it would seem that the spirit of the writer must have killed Marsh. But if Bierce had meant this tale to be nothing more than a ghost story, he could have ended it here and satisfied the credulous—probably the average—reader. It is traditional in ghost stories, after all, for the writer to discount the evidences of the senses and to leave readers enough clues to reason their way to the conclusion that their secret, inner fears have some basis in fact.

But Bierce adds one last paragraph, a newspaper article reporting the commitment to an insane asylum of the writer who convinced Marsh to dare death by fright. According to the article, the writer was observed in his preparations for suicide and captured in time. Of course, readers who never wavered for an instant from their firm disbelief in ghosts—if such readers exist—are not abashed by misinterpreting the ending. The rest of us are.

In retrospect, this story can be seen to be a very considerable work of the storyteller's art. First of all, Bierce set up *two* protagonists who prided themselves on their rationalism—Marsh and the reader. Then, Bierce broadens the scope of action by inducing the reader to participate in the story. Next, Bierce accomplishes the difficult feat of arming the reader against deception yet inducing the reader to deceive himself. Finally, as in "A Tough Tussle," Bierce advances his ambivalent evaluation of reason: it has inherent limitations, and it has further limitations consequent upon the circumstances of its use.

The utilization of the motif of a rationalistic protagonist's fatal hubris can be seen at work in a number of other stories, among them "The Man and the Snake" (1890), which Grenander uses to good effect to illustrate Bierce's use of ironical terror,[24] and "One of the Missing" (1888). It is true that Bierce wrote a number of purely formularized stories of terror and the supernatural, but as I have tried to indicate, those stories that touch on the supernatural or the terrifying but that are also carefully crafted to stay within the bounds of possibility are neither frivolous nor formularized. On the contrary, they are speculative and serious, and occasionally develop tragic dimensions. As in the case of his stories of shock, they disturb the thoughtful reader with the same problems that had disturbed Bierce for years. The stories represent articulations of the problems, but not solutions.

We have seen in Bierce's various strategies, and even in his very insistence on craftsmanship in writing, evidences of a pattern of thought or values; and at least in the years leading up to the publication of *Tales of Soldiers and Civilians* and *Can Such Things Be?*, some of Bierce's most important values were contrary to reason. In these years, Bierce struggled to find meaning in life; to discover some satisfactory explanation for the existence of evil, torment, and death; to learn some way of coping with life. The stories of which we speak are the terrifying battlefields of the most intense phase of that struggle, when the combatants were Bierce's mind and heart, pitted against each other as reason and humanitarianism. The ferocity and desperation of this struggle can only be comprehended when it is understood that the stories are channels to thinking readers, and that the struggle that rages in Bierce rages also in the stories and, through them, finally rages in the readers, too. By having been induced to participate in the stories, readers have a personal stake in the outcomes of the struggles the stories represent. Readers' perceptions, their reasoning, their self-knowledge, and ultimately, their values are tested; all come under fire. For a little while, at least, they share with Bierce a concern for mind and collaborate with him in their dual roles of experimental volunteers and researchers. How much stress can the mind take? How reliable is it? What values does it lead to? Precisely because Bierce is so painfully thorough and so scrupulously honest in his examination of the mind, his stories cannot all be dismissed with the disparaging generalization "formularized." On the contrary, each story represents a unique problem and is so far from being rigged as to depend for its success upon an engaged and thinking reader.

Because Bierce insisted upon scrutinizing the mind *reasonably*, he is a long remove from those sentimentalists of reason who idolize it indiscriminately. It is not an accurate summary of Bierce's philosophy that broadly claims that reason is, or should be, the greatest good in life, for such a conclusion could only be reached in contradiction to the implication of his stories. Furthermore, Bierce's stories are central to his philosophy rather than adventitious; his reaching out from journalism to fiction in the important years from 1887 to 1893 is indicative of this fact.

From our knowledge of Bierce's standards of writing, we can be sure that he opposed obscurantist writing—i.e., writing that was not founded on precise thinking and was not precisely expressed—and lying. It may seem odd, then, that Bierce, who placed a heavy responsibility for truth upon a writer, would deliberately advocate values in fiction he knew to be false, a medium prone to warp truth by slighting syllogistic reasoning, to say nothing of religious reasoning, for such imponderables as tone, mood, and feeling. It may also seem odd that Bierce not only resorted to fiction but opposed William Dean Howells and his school of realism because they stressed probability, and, in Bierce's previously stated opinion, "Fiction has nothing to say to probability."

Resolutions of these seeming paradoxes can be deduced from several of Bierce's remarks on writing. In a "Prattle" note to "Mr. H. L.," Bierce says sarcastically, "You were not born to write stories. Stories are not true and you are too conscientious to make them seem true, and so mislead your fellow creatures. Try writing sermons, which are all true."[25] Here we have a strong suggestion that Bierce realized that fiction, though in itself not true, nevertheless opens on to a higher level of truth than can be reached by purely rational and strictly literal discourse, especially the sermonizing kind of discourse.

This is borne out by a study of his "Prattle" columns from 1887 to 1893, for as we have seen, many of the philosophical ideas present in his stories are stated less ambiguously in the journalism of the same period. Interestingly enough, however, while the significant years for the publication of short stories in the *Examiner* are 1888 to 1892, the significant years for the publication of "Prattle" commentaries that speculate on the nature of reason and man are 1887 to 1890. One conclusion that can be derived from this discrepancy is that Bierce gradually abandoned "sermonizing" to his "Prattle" readers as he became increasingly aware of the limitations, for him, of logical exposition, and of the wider capabilities for precision in fiction. This may have led him to transfer his energies from the less to the more efficient genre.

This conclusion is reinforced and enlarged by another of Bierce's remarks, in an introduction he wrote in 1913 to an anthology of short stories by his friend Josephine McCrackin: "A great writer has said that life is a farce to him who thinks, a tragedy to him who feels. But he who most deeply thinks most keenly feels; so his are the high lights and the black shadows; and however he move among them—with passive acceptance or dissenting activity—his life is more than a life: it is a career! Its every feature is 'out of the common,' and all its mutations are memorable."[26] The devotion to literature obvious in this passage is significant, for literature was a cause as well as an effect of Bierce's refusal to accede willingly to reason. He had examined the life of the mind carefully, and had found it deep but narrow. Reason and philosophy prescribed theoretically adequate ways of coping with life and understanding it, but in practice, reason and philosophy could not always be used. Love, hate, fear, cowardice, bravery, and loyalty were qualities only partly explicable, to Bierce, by the mind; happiness, not at all. Furthermore, Bierce also sensed that reason was not a pure good in that it would, of necessity, "level" humanity too much. In other words, the same moderating force that reason could exert to prevent people from acting foolishly could also prevent them from acting nobly. And, in his stories, when the noble deed is also unwise, the question of which set of values to follow is left unanswered. So in literature Bierce found an opportunity to examine the life of the spirit as well as that of the mind, to explore and ponder the memorable "high lights and black shadows" that are present in life, common or not, probable or not. In his devotion to literature, in his linking of deep thinking and deep feeling, Bierce expresses a concern for the mind of man and, through that, a concern for the whole man.

~ 5 ~

POIGNANT CLARITY
The Achievement of Tragedy

F OR AN INTRODUCTION to Bierce's concern for humanity, no better story exists than his first, "The Haunted Valley." Originally published in July 1871 in the *Overland Monthly*, whose editorship Bret Harte had recently relinquished, the story shows us Bierce at the most transparent stage of his literary evolution—the stage at which he still stated his aims explicitly. No other story he wrote reveals so simply his basic compassion for his fellow human beings and demonstrates more clearly the relationship between that compassion and the technique that he was even then developing to express it.

To anyone who has read many of Bierce's stories, "The Haunted Valley," at first glance, will appear to be atypical of him. In a formal sense, it is. It is a local-color story with all the familiar outward trappings: gruff but heart-of-gold characters, an extensive use of dialect, an educated narrator, a quick sympathy for regional types, and a sentimental moral. On closer scrutiny, however, its points of resemblance to the more familiar Bierce story will become apparent. There are not as many differences between this story and the best ones in *Tales of Soldiers and Civilians* and *Can Such Things Be?* as one might expect from first impressions.

Except for the use of dialect, which Bierce very seldom used again,[1] almost every other important feature of the story, thematic as well as stylistic, can be found in the best of later tales, although in a deepened and much more subtle form. The polished and educated narrator, for example, the "Easterner" of this story, is to undergo an artistic sea change and reemerge as the rationalistic protagonist, the character in the story with whom the reader is most likely to identify. A definite prototype of the parted clue occurs in "Ah Wee's Epitaph":

AH WEE—CHINAMAN.
Age Unknown. Worked for Jo. Dunfer.
This monument is erected by him to keep the Chink's
memory green. Likewise as a warning to Celestials
not to take on airs. Devil take 'em!
She Was a Good Egg.

This can be seen in the epitaph's "meager but sufficient identification of the deceased; the impudent candor of confession; the brutal anathema; the ludicrous change of sex and sentiment" (CW, III, 144)—this last referring to the "She" on the tombstone, which is the only digression from Whisky Jo.'s otherwise uniform habit of referring to a female Chinese ("Chinaman") as "him." The themes of fear and the supernatural are present in the apparent transformation of a knothole in a wall into a human eye, and in the effect of this apparition in precipitating Whisky Jo.'s death. The subsequent logical explanation of the apparition implies a typical Biercian commentary on the tendency of the human mind to err through a priori reasoning. This is demonstrated in both Whisky Jo. and the educated narrator. Gopher's sudden and passionate confession of lunacy or, more accurately, the unexpected confrontation of the reader with the spectacle of a man driven mad by grief, is perhaps too pathetic an incident to be called "shock," but it may be said to foreshadow Bierce's strategy of shock in its violent nature and its abruptness. It may further be said to foreshadow Bierce's use of shock insofar as Bierce at least partially induced shock by an intensification of pathos. Remarkably adumbrative of Byring's rationalizations in "A Tough Tussle" is the failure of reason as it is unmistakably depicted in a passage of self-analysis by the narrator:

I began by analyzing my pet superstition about the place. Having resolved it into its constituent elements I arranged them in convenient troops and squadrons, and collecting all the forces of my logic bore down upon them from impregnable premises with the thunder of irresistible conclusions and a great noise of chariots and general intellectual shouting. Then, when my big mental guns had overturned all opposition and were growling almost inaudibly away on the horizon of pure speculation, the routed enemy straggled in upon their rear, massed silently into a solid phalanx, and captured me, bag and baggage. An indefinable dread came upon me. (CW, III, 141–42)

Finally, in the story's sudden shift of focus from Whisky Jo. to Gopher, Bierce makes a last minute, and not wholly unsuccessful, attempt to rise above the sentimental pathos of the local-color story and achieve tragedy with a grander theme, the failure of a man's mind and heart to cope with the vicissitudes of life.

By way of amplifying this latter point, let us take a close look at Whisky Jo. and Gopher. The most obvious comparison lies in the fact that both men loved Ah Wee. An extension of the girl's very name, "ah, we," binds the two together through her, and the similarity of the names of the two men also infers a parallel relationship. Beyond the obvious suitability of their respective nicknames is a more subtle appropriateness, as suggested by Whisky Jo.'s epitaph—"JO. DUNFER, DONE FOR." Gopher's name also lends itself to this grim kind of punning—GOPHER, GONE FOR—and the pun is relevant to him, for he is experiencing a sort of death-in-life. The contrasts between the two men are even more significant. Whisky Jo. represents Bierce's adherence to the local-color tradition. In accordance with it, the love affair between Whisky Jo. and Ah Wee has overtones of social criticism—the prejudice of the white Westerner against the Chinese[2]—and leads straight to a melodrama complete with poetic justice. Gopher represents Bierce's attempt to transmute the local-color tradition into a vehicle suitable for studying a man destroyed in mind as well as in spirit. The most significant feature of Gopher's characterization is not his pertinence to social problems of the day, or even his tender devotion to Ah Wee, but his terrible mental collapse under the shock of seeing her killed. His own words, "it was Gopher to the dark" (153), have an extended meaning, tragedy as well as madness. In portraying Gopher, Bierce rises above the particularities of regionalism and the limitations of social criticism and creates, simply, a tragic human being.

In the shift of focus from Whisky Jo. to Gopher, then, we catch Bierce's art at the exact instant when it began to respond to the influences of the ancient and modern classical literature and philosophy that Bierce, under the tutelage of Watkins, had been studying for the past three or four years. Just as the sentimentalism and generous feeling for humanity, which was the stock in trade of the local-color story appealed to the sensitive and idealistic side of Bierce's nature, so did the pessimism and sense of limitation of the Stoics and the Enlightenment writers appeal to Bierce's intellectual honesty and his memories of the war. The reconciling of these radically different values was never perfectly accomplished by Bierce, but "The Haunted Valley" at least shows him taking his first decisive step in the direction he would thenceforth follow toward that end. That step was a compounding of the essence of local color—compassion—with that of classicism—skepticism. In keeping with the humanistic tradition he subsequently followed, not any particular notion of God, nor any particular notion of society, nor any particular doctrine of philosophy, but the most universal subject of all[3]—Man, "the glory, jest, and riddle of the world"—was to be his theme.[4] From 1871 to 1891, Bierce's art of the short story was to develop immensely, but even at its peak of excellence it retained essential similarities to the local-color tradition from which it began; even at its most indirect and "cynical," it was inspirited by the same generous feeling for victims of life that is explicitly manifested by the first-person narrator of "The Haunted Valley" in his simple but eloquent gesture of compassion for the grief-maddened Gopher: "I followed the little wretch back to his wagon and wrung his hand at parting" (154).

Once he began to write more stories, however, Bierce worked toward greater subtlety and understatement. Although some stories of

his mature period still have vestiges of the sort of explicit interpretation present in the last paragraph of "The Haunted Valley," in
which the first-person narrator relieved readers of the necessity of
coming to their own conclusions, most of the tales reflect Bierce's
characteristic determination to make his readers grapple with the issues that motivated him to write the stories in the first place. This
trend toward subtlety and understatement is evident not only in the
progressively better stories that came from his pen but also in his editing of them, and in his deliberate efforts to rise above pathos.
These two points are related. Insofar as a story is obvious in its intention of evoking a particular emotion in the reader, it obviates
thought. In fact, it may do more than that; it may discourage
thought. With the goal of provoking thought in his readers a primary consideration, Bierce made use of his distinction between perception and discernment. To him, pathos, or an emotional
evocation of sympathy and pity, involved only perception and feeling. If we may narrowly define tragedy as pity or sympathy evoked
by discernment rather than perception, we may say that Bierce
aimed at tragedy because he wanted his readers first to perceive,
then to discern, and only finally to feel compassion. Each step is important by itself, and the sequence of all three is important. The
third step cannot be achieved until the first and second are executed
properly, but the third must be achieved if the story is to be properly
understood. In his stories, therefore, Bierce increasingly omitted
from the start, or cut out in the editing process, details that were not
absolutely necessary to an understanding of them. To a great extent,
the versions of *Tales of Soldiers and Civilians* and *Can Such Things Be?* to
be found in the *Collected Works* are models of economy. The stories
will "please" the average reader, but only the thoughtful reader who
is able to put together their parted clues will derive instruction as
well as pleasure from them. In Bierce's omission or excision of
pathos from his stories, he rejected the temptation of popularity to
make instead a daring bid for artistic precision of a high order. He
assumed that the man who thinks deeply also feels deeply, and we
can see in his stories the pattern of his standard of success—
poignant clarity. By furnishing only just enough clues to the reader

and no more, Bierce exalts the action from the page to the reader's mind, there to be catalyzed by discernment and self-knowledge into tragedy.

Three of Bierce's most famous stories from *Tales of Soldiers and Civilians* illustrate both the way in which Bierce's literary style matured and became increasingly sophisticated and the way in which he informs his reader's mind with a sense of tragedy. The three stories, written about a year apart in the period 1888–90, are "A Son of the Gods," "A Horseman in the Sky," and "An Occurrence at Owl Creek Bridge." They will be discussed chronologically.

Of the three, "A Son of the Gods" (1888), is the least sophisticated. For one thing, Bierce continues in it to divide the reader's attention and identification between an educated narrator and a sympathetic protagonist, as he did in "The Haunted Valley." Bierce also continues to make use of a first-person narrator, although in "A Son of the Gods" it is a first-person *plural* "we." The plural pronoun is a decided improvement over the singular because readers are led to feel that they are being given a consensus of opinion rather than a single point of view, and because they are encouraged to include themselves in the reactions of "we" and become more involved in the tale. Consequent to the use of a first-person narrator, however, Bierce still feels it necessary to guide his readers' reactions. He does this through overt manifestations of sympathy—"A tremendous cheer bursts from our ranks, relieving the insupportable tension of our feelings" (CW, II, 67)—and through an explicit interpretation at the end: "Ah, those many, many needless dead! That great soul whose beautiful body is lying over yonder, so conspicuous against the sere hillside—could it not have been spared the bitter consciousness of a vain devotion? Would one exception have marred too much, the pitiless perfection of the divine, eternal plan?" (70).[5]

The incident in Bierce's life upon which the story is probably based is quoted by McWilliams from an 1883 *Wasp*, in which Bierce tells how he once recklessly exposed himself on horseback to draw Confederate fire. "I never felt so brave in all my life," he remembered. Fortunately for Bierce, McWilliams says, his heroism was superfluous, for it was found that the Confederates had already retreated.[6] On an obvious level, therefore, the story can be seen to be a "study" of bravery. The seminal escapade, though well-meant and undoubtedly gallant, was nevertheless foolhardy, for Bierce put his life in jeopardy. By chance, his life was not forfeited; there was no enemy to take it. He knew his experience was atypical, however; his survival, a freak long shot that proved nothing. It raised problems, in fact, for it implied a lawless universe in which nothing could be predicted. In "A Son of the Gods," Bierce took the dice back into his hands and cast them once again. This time, the protagonist did not beat the odds. No exception was allowed.

The story itself is about a heroic young Federal officer who futilely sacrifices his life for his comrades. Volunteering to take the place of a skirmish line usually sent ahead by the Union army to detect suspected ambushes, the officer suicidally rides alone up an ominously quiet hill and gives the signal that the Confederates are hiding on the opposite slope. The Confederates open fire on the man who has discovered their trap and, though he almost escapes back to the anxious Union lines, eventually shoot him down. Ironically, the Union troops for whom the officer gave his life charge from their shelters seeking revenge, and many are killed needlessly.

McWilliams complains of this story that it "is romanticized to an unbelievable degree. . . . The gallant fellow . . . dies and our hearts are broken. It is a good illustration of how Bierce invariably chose the wrong incident for his stories. To see his great energy and vitality being cramped and beaten into the obsolete riggings of the story form is a pitiful sight. After Poe the story must be 'unusual'; it must be weird."[7] This complaint, reflecting an early negative attitude toward the stories that McWilliams later reversed, is still worth considering for the important part preconceptions play in it. Almost as often as Bierce has been compared to Poe (usually unfavorably), Poe has also been underestimated. Certainly few literary scholars would argue today that Poe's stories are merely weird or unusual, that stories after Poe had to imitate his lead, or that "A Son of the Gods" is even weird. More important, behind the claim that Bierce "invariably" chose the "wrong" incident for his stories is the underlying assumption (still current) that Bierce was more substantial as a biographical entity than as an author. Rather than further dispute these doubtful assumptions, let us examine this story for evidence of artistic quality.

A clue to the significant area of action in the story can be found in its original subtitle in the *San Francisco Examiner,* "A Study in the Historical Present Tense."[8] Through his use of this tense, Bierce creates an atmosphere of immediacy, strengthens the illusion of actuality, and encourages readers to become involved in the story. As mentioned previously, he heightens the illusion of actuality even more through his use of the inclusive "we," but beyond including readers in the observation of the officer's ride, Bierce also includes them in the illusion of action—and in the fatal consequence of the action. "Ten thousand pairs of eyes are fixed upon him with an intensity that he can hardly fail to feel; ten thousand hearts keep quick time to the inaudible hoof-beats of his snowy steed. *He is not alone—he draws all souls after him: we are but 'dead men all'*" (emphasis mine). In the *Collected Works* version, the clause after the colon in the last sentence has been deleted. It was too obvious.

The story has a double significance. The more obvious level is summarized in one of Bierce's later epigrams: "Courage is the acceptance of the gambler's chance: a brave man bets against the game of the gods" (1909). Bravery, in one sense, is not reasonable; the man who exposes himself unnecessarily in war or life simply multiplies the odds against his survival. A question of values beyond reason is also involved, however. If by "reason" we are to understand only those actions that are conducive to the preservation of one's life, does not reason cancel out bravery? If so, should reason be a higher good than bravery? Also, which course of action is more reasonable: keeping oneself as protected as possible, or altruistically risking one's life to save others or to accomplish a larger goal? This point is explicit in the text's statement of the issue: "Ah, what a price to pay for gratified curiosity! At what a dear rate an army must sometimes purchase knowledge. 'Let me pay all,' says this gallant man—this military Christ!" The comparison to Christ raises the stakes to the limit, especially since Bierce earlier characterized Christ as a perfect moral calculator.

The questions posed here are raised in the story by the tension that is developed between our having joined the "we" narrator in admiring the officer, and our simultaneous fear that the officer—and our hopes—are ill fated, a fear that is too obviously justified in the clause Bierce later dropped. That Bierce insists that these questions not be quickly answered and lightly dismissed is evident from the ironic conclusion, which in effect keeps them before us by having them lead to another, deeper question. If the officer's action is judged unreasonable, Bierce asks, is it unreasonable in itself, or is it our learning at the end that the bravery was for naught that makes it seem unreasonable? Bierce's possible answer to this last question is given in the previously cited "Prattle" item, which followed this story by less than three months, about judging the wisdom of an act by the light the actor had at the moment of decision. But that is only a partial answer, and it is not in the text of the story. "A Son of the Gods" articulates the issue of whether reasonableness or bravery is a higher value, but it does not solve it.

The less obvious level of significance in the story inheres in readers identifying with "we." To the extent readers are so inspired by the bravery of the officer and so overcome by his pathetic death that when "the spell is broken," they, too, would have disobeyed orders and joined in the charge, to that same extent they would have jeopardized their lives had they been there. In the penultimate paragraph, Bierce calls impetuous readers back to sanity and to an understanding of their own nature with a sudden shift of focus to the "Commander": "The Commander has not moved. . . . He sees the human current flowing on either side of him and his huddled escort, like a river parted by a rock. Not a sign of *feeling* in his face; he is *thinking*. . . . He addresses a calm word to his bugler. . . . The colors move slowly back" (emphases mine). A judgment of the spontaneous charge—it was an example of mass psychology rather than bravery—can easily be inferred from the description of the calm Commander as thinking instead of feeling, and in the contrast of his image as a rock to the derogatory connotation of the flowing-river imagery applied to his men, unthinking units swept along by a current.[9] In this last vignette, Bierce clearly depicts cold reason as a quality to be followed. From the post mortem standpoint, which sees the vain sacrifice of lives that resulted from the mass charge, the superior worth of reason is even more patent; but in an evaluation of the young officer's intent, it is not. In fact, the story's main issue is very similar to the one Dostoevsky raised in "The Grand Inquisitor" chapter of *The Brothers Karamazov:* Is Christ, who revealed to humans the moral sublimities they may choose, the ultimate benefactor of humanity, or is it the functionaries who cannot work miracles but who have to lead mankind on a reduced and mundane scale by dealing with humanity and the world as they are? The Commander and those like him are obliged to be aware of and work within "the pitiless perfection of the divine, eternal plan," "the Scheme of the Universe," the immutable laws of strategy. In the final analysis, "A Son of the Gods" is a tragic allegory of mankind's dilemma—we cannot always know what reason teaches, and even when we can know, we can still be seduced by our feelings, to our destruction.

"A Horseman in the Sky" (1889) represents a considerable advance in literary style,[10] for by 1889, Bierce had largely withdrawn himself from his stories. This story is told by an omniscient narrator, and Bierce avoids having to commit himself either as "I" or "we" to any statement that could be tied back to him as an explicit interpretation. Another improvement in the story is its focusing of attention upon a single main character; readers are not distracted by the unnecessary intrusion of a narrator into the action. A third improvement is the use of the omniscient narrator's point of view to make known the protagonist's thoughts and impressions. A fourth is an advance in literary economy: the language is very spare; virtually every detail is functional. Finally, Carter Druse, the main character, is a fully developed rationalistic protagonist. An intelligent, sensitive, and well-bred Virginia aristocrat, he seems an attractive individual with whom the reader can identify.

Bierce did not make the transition from semi-autobiographical fiction to pure fiction without some difficulty, however. The edition of "A Horseman in the Sky" that appears in the *Collected Works* differs in some important respects from the *Examiner* version. Interestingly enough, the problem that seemed to cause Bierce the greatest difficulty was how to express his compassion for Carter Druse. The additions and deletions in the later edition make that compassion less obvious, but they do not eradicate it.

Briefly summarized, "A Horseman in the Sky"[11] is about a young Virginia aristocrat who decides to fight for the Union side in the Civil War. This decision involves more than fighting against just his native state, for his father is to fight on the side of the Confederacy. In the course of the war, Carter Druse returns to Virginia with the Union army. While on sentry duty in the mountains one day, he sees a mounted Confederate officer ride to the brink of a cliff and reconnoiter the Union army in the valley below. He takes aim, looks closely again at the figure, hesitates briefly, then pulls the trigger. Horse and rider arch into the air and plummet to the valley floor. Shortly after, when Druse is reached by his sergeant, he reveals his knowledge that the rider of the horse was his father.

Even in summary, the plot is shocking, and if Bierce had done no more than flesh out the bare plot with a few scraps of dialogue and some detailed description, he would have merited the label of "Bitter Bierce." As it is, however, almost every additional detail of theme and action is marshaled to soften the harshness of the plot. This is done partly through the sympathetic characterization of Carter Druse, which is accomplished in four stages. First, a landscape setting is described in which Druse, a sentinel, lies sleeping in a clump of laurel. Second, Druse is described as a civilian. Third, he is represented as a soldier. In this stage, the issues of the story are brought to a head. Finally, he is shown again simply as a man, a tragic victim of an impossible choice.

A great deal of significance is compressed into the four paragraphs of the first section, much of it the result of internal contradictions. The scene is set in "western Virginia," a section in which young Bierce fought his first battles of the Civil War, but also a section in which Union sentiment was sufficiently strong for it to break away from the rest of secessionist Virginia to remain in the Union. Thus, Virginia itself had its own microcosmic civil war, and this was paralleled on an even smaller scale by that of the Druse family within it. These interlocking conflicts establish the story's putative theme of civil war.

Related to this theme is the contrast between the initially Edenic setting of the story—a sunny afternoon in a picturesquely wooded country of cliffs surrounding a deep valley with a meadow and small stream—and the hellish "rat-trap" into which it is swiftly transformed. "No country is so wild and difficult but men will make it a theatre of war; concealed in the forest at the bottom of that military rat-trap . . . lay five regiments of Federal infantry" that were vulnerable to destruction by as few as "half a hundred men in possession of the exits" (CW, II, 17). This perilously beautiful country, again like Eden, is the stage for the fall of man, a grim pun for the descent of the aerial horseman.

Finally, the picturesque first two sentences of the story that describe Carter Druse asleep contrast ironically with the next four in the paragraph. Although mountain laurel is a native plant in West Virginia, laurel also has classical overtones of honor and award. Immediately contrasted with the peaceful pose of the first two sentences are the jolting details of the next two—that he was grasping a rifle and wearing a cartridge belt. The next line informs us that "He was asleep at his post of duty," and the last line of the first paragraph explains that the award for this "crime," if discovered, would be death. Within six lines, a peacefully sleeping soldier becomes a criminal, and within four paragraphs an Edenic scene becomes the stage for the fall of man and hellish war, and the combatants diminished from humans into rats.[12]

Central to the second stage is the scene in which Carter announces to his father his intention of joining the Union army. The father does not remonstrate with him. He remains silent for a moment, then says: "Well, go, sir, and whatever may occur do what you conceive to be your duty. Virginia, sir, to which you are a traitor, must get on without you. Should we both live to the end of the war, we will speak further of the matter" (18). The father requests only that the son not disturb his dying mother with the news. The son "bowed reverently to his father, who returned the salute with a stately courtesy that masked a breaking heart." This is not a story about a dysfunctional family in which hatreds boil beneath the surface and either father or son is villainous. Both father and son are decent and principled individuals who care deeply for each other.

"Virginia . . . to which you are a traitor, must get on without you." The phrase "to which you are a traitor" does not occur in the *Examiner* version but was added later. The addition sharpens the issue dividing father and son: both possess the virtue of loyalty, but their allegiances are contradictory—the father is loyal to Virginia and the son to the Union. The other side of that coin is that the father regards the son as a traitor to Virginia and, although it is not stated, the son must regard the father as a traitor to the Union. Long before Bierce wrote this story, many true stories had circulated about loving families that were divided by the war, and fathers and sons, or brothers, eventually found themselves shooting each other.[13] This situation, then, has the makings both of a civil war and of inevitable tragedy.

"Go, Carter, and whatever may happen, I hope that you will do what you conceive to be your duty." In this line from the *Examiner* version, the father addresses his son more intimately and paternally, by his first name, instead of the formal "sir" in the familiar *Collected Works* version. In either version, these are the most important words of the story. They are more than a condensed codification of the high-minded principles to which father and son both subscribe; they are also a product of a gracious culture whose courtliness and aversion to inflicting pain stem from a cultivated compassion. They are a product of the home life of the Druses, a life that places a high value on familial devotion and filial obedience. But, inadvertently and with tragic irony, they lend themselves to war.

The third stage of the story begins when Carter, having been awakened by a "good or bad angel," gets the enemy horseman in his sights and prepares to fire.

> At that instant the horseman turned his head and looked in the direction of his concealed foeman—seemed to look into his very face, into his eyes, into his brave, compassionate heart.
>
> Is it then so terrible to kill an enemy in war—an enemy who has surprised a secret vital to the safety of one's self and com-

rades—an enemy more formidable for his knowledge than all his army for its numbers? (21)

The sudden recognition of his father and his immediately resulting crisis of being torn between the conflicting emotions of bravery and compassion temporarily disables Carter. He is reduced from a cool and capable soldier to an inept civilian who takes his finger from the trigger and nearly swoons "from intensity of emotion." He returns to his senses, however, and "conscience and reason sound," he fingers the trigger again.

In the *Examiner* version, when Carter prepares to fire again, he seems to have settled the issue completely in his mind: the horseman is an enemy. Just before he fires, he is described as being calm—his nerves were as tranquil as a sleeping babe's—and the reader is told that "Duty had silenced conscience; the spirit had said to the body: 'Peace, be still.'[14] He fired." In the *Collected Works* version, the text reads "Duty had conquered" (23). But the implication of "pacified" in the replaced word "silenced" is made more explicit in two crucial sentences added to the first part of the paragraph that follow his re-aiming his rifle and that explain Carter's disciplined calm. "But this time his aim was at the horse. In his memory, as if they were a divine mandate, rang the words of his father at their parting: 'whatever may occur, do what you conceive to be your duty'" (23). The added two sentences eloquently supply a clue whose significance is central to the story. A whole volume is spoken in the first sentence. Before, Carter had aimed at the *horseman*. The tiny gesture of slightly lowering his rifle to aim at the horse is the only concession he can make to compassion. In the second sentence, Carter is seen to be doing more than his soldierly duty, he is obeying his father first.

The choice is inhumanly terrible. The seconds of agony and horror that the horseman must have felt as he and his mount plunged to the ground in a shocking "flight" that is incongruously described with beautiful vividness can only be imagined. Bierce wisely does not attempt to record the father's feelings. But a Federal officer in the valley is "filled with amazement and terror" and "overcome by the intensity of his emotions" at the awesome sight he sees in the air above him. There is "a crashing sound in the trees—a sound that died without an echo—and all was still" (24–25). The sergeant who crawls up to Carter's post is also stunned when he learns who it was that Carter shot. In the *Collected Works* version, of the story's three observers of the death of Carter's father, only Carter seems to remain steady. "The man's face was white, but he showed no other sign of emotion. Having answered, he turned away his eyes and said no more. The sergeant did not understand" (26). The statement is spare, but there are parted clues in it that, when matched up with other parted clues, lead to a shocking conclusion.

In the *Examiner* version, however, Bierce was not yet willing to leave so much up to the reader. The ending is much fuller in detail than the later version, and its significance is such that it deserves substantial quotation.

"Did you fire?" the Sergeant whispered.

"Yes."

"At what?"

"A horse. It was standing on yonder rock—pretty far out. You see it is no longer there. I am a great marksman. You know I once shot a match with the Devil in hell and beat him."

The Sergeant was shocked and startled. He looked searchingly at Druse. The man's face was white; his eyes were restless and glittered with a strange, uncanny light. The Sergeant, still on hands and knees, involuntarily looked a little away from him.

"See here, Druse," he said, after a moment's silence, "it's no use making a mystery. I order you to report. Was there anybody—anybody at all—except the horse?"

"Do you mean the horse which had wings?"

"Well, yes, if that's the kind of horse you shot. Was there anybody else?"

"Yes."

"Who?"

"My father."

The Sergeant rose to his feet and walked rapidly down the road toward the valley.

Here, in the *Examiner* version, the blending of Bierce's art and philosophy in this story is more easily discerned. Carter Druse is mad! His personal and private civil war between mind and heart, between reason and compassion, is no less devastating for its silence and restrained display. "Duty had conquered," and Carter Druse had lost. The penalty for a sentinel sleeping at his post was death, and Druse does pay for this crime with more than his father's death. Reason prevails long enough for Druse to pull the trigger. After that, he is as destroyed in mind as his father was in body. The *Collected Works* text is not as explicit but the result is the same. Given the situation and relationship between father and son, what other possibility is more likely?

It is worthwhile, at this point, to note the similarities and differences of "A Horseman in the Sky" and "The Haunted Valley." The techniques introduced in the earlier story have almost reached ultimate development in the later. In addition, there is a striking parallel between the madness of Gopher and that of Carter Druse. The minds of both men have their breaking points. Druse's superior reason, far from staving off doom, actually precipitates it. Profound compassion for both protagonists is also evinced in both stories. The obvious way in which these points are expressed in "The Haunted Valley" are replaced in the later story by fine and subtle strokes, such as Druse's eloquent gesture of lowering the sights of his rifle to the horse, a parted clue in the understatement "Duty had conquered," and in the shocks of the sight of the horseman in the sky and the description of Druse at the end of the story, particularly in the more restrained *Collected Works* version. Bierce has increasingly elevated the story by engaging the readers' minds, has involved them in a desperate struggle, and has forced them into looking at life from a new perspective. Also, by way of difference, it can be seen that Bierce's themes have grown grander. From his early attempt to extol the simple folk of California, he has risen to contemplating the lot of humanity at a universal level. Carter Druse epitomizes the tragedy of man. Following his best lights, reason and compassion, he eventually reaches a point where they split away from each other. The soldier and civilian must go separate ways. When that happens, one or the other—mind or heart—must die within the man. Unless that happens, the man himself must die.

⇥ 6 ⇤

"AN OCCURRENCE AT
OWL CREEK BRIDGE"
Nothing Better Exists

To BIERCE, reason, although imperfect, remains humanity's best hope for preventing a needless death or at least for delaying death's inevitability. Conversely, the failure to use reason, or the misuse of it, will hasten death or bring it on needlessly. This is the theme of Bierce's most famous story, "An Occurrence at Owl Creek Bridge" (CW, II, 27–45). "Nothing better exists," said Stephen Crane. "That story contains everything."[1] Crane was right. Certainly it is the finest story that Bierce wrote, and it has deservedly achieved the status of a classic. In it Bierce finally mastered his medium. Compared to "A Horseman in the Sky," even after that story's subsequent revisions, "An Occurrence at Owl Creek Bridge" is the work of a much surer pen. Just four changes from the *Examiner* version, only one of which is longer than a phrase, are significant. And although the plot of "Owl Creek" is about war, the Civil War per se is not the story's main subject. By the time Bierce wrote it, he had assimilated his past and was able to create something entirely new from his experiences. The Civil War armies and campaigns are of auxiliary use rather than central importance in the story; the tale could be equally compelling told in the settings of the Revolutionary War or the Spanish Civil War. Less about armies than about man, the story's specific military situation is used as a symbolic vehicle for a philosophical message. "Owl Creek" is about war, but it is a war that involves all readers, for the war is life.

It took twenty-five years of reflection and meditation on Shiloh before Bierce could achieve the artistic distance necessary to use it in one of his stories. Much of what he learned permeates "An Occurrence at Owl Creek Bridge." The story is an allegorical reflection of his conclusions. It is not directly autobiographical, although the setting of the main action appears to be Shiloh. The battlefield is in southern Tennessee, approximately twenty miles from the Alabama line. In the story, Peyton Farquhar's northern Alabama plantation is located "about thirty miles" from the Owl Creek bridge (CW II, 33). That Bierce moved a railroad so that it had a bridge across the creek is an indication that he had some use for the name, probably the owl's symbolic connotation of wisdom.[2] If so, wisdom is a darkly brooding concern in the story, an ironic element against which Farquhar's impulsive, arrogant, and foolish rationalizations, and his and the readers' fantasies, are measured and found fatally flawed.

The story obviously foregrounds the mind-contrived but unconscious fantasy that deludes Peyton Farquhar in his last moments of life. Farquhar, the protagonist of the story, is a Southern planter who is being hanged by Federal troops for, among other reasons, having attempted to burn down a bridge. Less obviously and more deeply, the story describes various delusions that lead Farquhar to his death. Least obviously and most deeply, however, the story is not about Farquhar at all, but about the reader's mind. What Bierce attempts to disclose at this deeper level is that the reader's mind is inclined to make the same fatal mistakes that Farquhar's does. Herein lie the story's tragic implications.

Although Bierce constantly mused about the Civil War, the genesis of "Owl Creek" was probably not so much any specific reminiscence of the war but rather, as in the case of "Coulter's Notch," printed sources, including *civilian* material, that came to his attention from his reading over the years. In the absence of evidence leading to definitive connections, we can only speculate on which printed items might be considered sources, but some likely candidates are worth consideration. In addition to those previously mentioned, another one is "The Reporter's Revenge," a story by his Nevada friend Sam Davis, included in an 1886 collection of his works that Davis family tradition claims Bierce encouraged him to publish. In the course of that story, one of its characters walks out upon a platform where some prisoners will soon be hanged and begins to play with a noose as he talks to the narrator, an associate:

> "Did you ever think how it must feel to be hanged?" he asked me, with a smile, as he worked the soaped rope through the hangman's knot. "It seems to me that however dreadful the preliminaries may look to others, nature kindly sends a paralysis upon the brain long before the black cap shuts out the sunshine forever. The most hideous moment of all must be just when the trap caves from under your feet and you shoot down to oblivion. There is an appreciable interval of time between the beginning and the end of that awful fall—and in that last instant of life how the mind must blaze and the heart pump!"[3]

Because it is virtually certain that Bierce read this story, it is not hard to imagine the seed that these lines might have planted in his reflective mind.

In any case, inasmuch as Bierce read the *San Francisco Examiner* as well as wrote for it, he undoubtedly noted at least some of its many articles about hangings, and some of those might also have fed into his meditations.[4] Three years into Hearst's ownership of the paper, the *Examiner* was already featuring the yellow journalism that was directed to the masses' appetite for sensationalism and scandal, and which Hearst correctly guessed would boost his paper's circulation. Executions were considerably more frequent in the late nineteenth century than they are today, and *Examiner* reporters fully satisfied the public's morbid curiosity about the details of hangings: how the gallows were constructed, how the condemned prisoner was reacting to his imminent death, how the execution itself was carried out, etc. At least ten hangings were reported in the *Examiner* in 1889 alone, sometimes with several columns and large artists' illustrations being luridly devoted for days on end to individual executions. One report in particular, appearing on 10 December and headlined "Man Almost Hung," was an interview with a man named McCarthy who survived a hanging:

> Well, it don't hurt so much after it's done. Jest a little pain at de furst. When dey kicked de box an' I fell four feet, dere was a sort of prick and den I saw stars and rockets and b'imeby de whole Fourth of July bizness was a boomin' fur all it was worth.

> Den I didn't know nuffin till I was dead fur 'bout an hour, and den I wus getting alive agin. Dat hurt mor'n de hul bizness, sure. . . . Me neck feels as if it was stretched over de bay and forty Goat islands was layin' in de middle of it, wid a million tons of iron piled on de bloody top.

Because Bierce was clearly interested in what happened in a mind at a hanging, his imagination must have been spurred by at least some of these accounts. This article in particular might have been of special interest to him because it supplied a survivor's testimony about the sensations of being hanged and what it felt like going from life to death. But Bierce would have realized that, for an interesting story, he needed a deeper theme than that of a mere hanging, and a protagonist more appealing and with a better mind than McCarthy. Peyton Farquhar would have filled the bill.

"Owl Creek" is a hoax as well as a tragedy, an intentional misrepresentation by the use of details that make plausible something at odds with fact, impossible, or highly improbable. Normally, to thus categorize it would imply that it was a work of inferior literary quality, but as I indicated earlier, the writers of the Sagebrush School raised the literary hoax to the status of a high art form.[5] Although elsewhere in his canon Bierce demonstrates his mastery of the literary hoax, "Owl Creek" is so superior to any other he wrote as to be in a category of its own, and it must rank as one of the most accomplished literary hoaxes ever written. In the first part, we learn that a man is about to be hanged by some Federal soldiers. All readers of the story are aware, at the end, that they misinterpreted the story and are mistaken in their belief that Peyton Farquhar escaped. The ending, however, is not the only hoax, nor even the most important. It is only the most obvious, a string that, if pulled, can unravel the rest of the hoaxes. Since all readers are misled, it is natural that they should want to know who misled them, and how. A short answer is that Bierce gives them the chance to mislead themselves, and they do it by projecting their expectations into the story and letting those expectations blind them into not reading carefully and thoughtfully enough.

I.

THE FIRST of the story's three sections establishes its ironic tone and lays the foundations of the issues on which readers are hoaxed in the narrative. As in the case of "The Suitable Surroundings," Bierce supplies readers with all the necessary details, although the readers do not yet know this, but he withholds the principle by which the details are sorted out into a practicable pattern. The operant principle that Bierce uses here as well as elsewhere is the one previously discussed, and implied in his *Devil's Dictionary* definition of "pray," i.e., "To ask that the laws of the universe be annulled in behalf of a single petitioner confessedly unworthy." Peyton Farquhar is, in the story, that unworthy petitioner, and neither his nor the reader's wishful thinking will keep events from running their natural course. The hanging will be successful.

This section begins unfolding the first hoax, the character of the omniscient narrator. Most readers trust a story's omniscient narrator unless it becomes apparent that the narrator is channeling the thoughts of another character. But the narrator of "Owl Creek" moves seamlessly and without warning into and out of Farquhar's mind; therefore, it is not always readily obvious if the narrator is speaking from a neutrally factual point of view or if he is being ironic. He is *very* ironic, but his irony is often very subtle. Hence, he is an unreliable narrator, unless one is able to accurately recognize when he is ironic. Even in the less polished *Examiner* version (13 July

1890, 12), his irony is never fully obvious, and in the *Collected Works* version, it is extremely subtle and complex. We would expect such a narrator to be ironic *about* something—a statement, a situation, a character. And this narrator does satisfy that expectation, for there are a number of recognizable targets of his irony. In addition, however, this narrator is ironic *toward* his audience. He is constantly playing mind games with unwary readers and setting traps for them. Many of the traps have to do with whether his language is to be read literally or figuratively. In reading the story, we can take nothing for granted. Every sentence is functional, and all possible meanings have to be considered and weighed if the reader is to escape being caught in the hoax or, having been caught, to understand it.

The story's third paragraph provides a good example of how this ironic narrator works. Its first sentence is a bit unusual. It begins: "The man who was engaged in being hanged. . . ." Grammatically speaking, the phrase "engaged in" is superfluous, and because it sounds quaint and overly formal, it adds an ironically jocular tone to the sentence. We might say that a man is engaged in eating—that is, he is busily absorbed in the process of eating—but it is uncommon usage to say that he is engaged in dying. In this case, however, that is exactly what is being said because, given the circumstances of Farquhar's total focus on his imminent hanging, the phrase is peculiarly exact. Next we are told, "He was a civilian, if one might judge from his habit, which was that of a planter" (29). This statement includes a pun on "habit" (in the *Examiner*, the line itself is humorless—"if one might judge from his dress"), but its intended grimness cannot be fully appreciated unless one is familiar with the lines deleted from the conclusion of the *Examiner* text. The line conveys additional ironies that are likely to become evident only upon rereading. Insofar as much of the story's philosophical punch depends upon whether Farquhar is a civilian or soldier, it is significant that this sentence opens by affirming that he is a civilian, then backs slightly away with the impartial qualification "if one might judge from his habit" (or dress). At first glance, the issue seems to be whether or not one's identity depends on the clothing he wears. (That is the only meaning of the *Ex-*

aminer sentence.) This is, of course, a superficial standard of judgment, and that is exactly the point, for it is the working theory of Farquhar, who is not a careful thinker—and as we shall soon see, Bierce is sharply critical of him. When the ambiguous word "habit" is used in the *Collected Works* version, the standard may deepen, for "habit" can refer to a person's customary actions as well as clothing. In either case, however, the matter is settled by the line's last clause. Farquhar looks like a planter, and he also acts like a planter. In other words, he is no soldier.

Then follow several sentences of seemingly favorable description emphasizing that he had "good" features and a "kindly" expression. Such explicitly favorable comments are easy to comprehend, whereas most of the negative descriptions of Farquhar, far greater in number, require more thought to recognize because they are either muted or stated ironically. For this reason, most probably, these sentences and a few other similar ones taken out of context have led many readers to consider Farquhar a hero and to identify with him. It is naïve, however, to believe that the face is an accurate indicator of character. The next line, in fact, undercuts this belief: "Evidently this was no vulgar assassin." The irony of this sentence rides on the fact that it affirms what it appears to deny. The issue of whether or not Farquhar was vulgar is quite separate from that of whether or not he was an assassin. Read carefully, while the line denies he was vulgar, it does concede that he was an assassin, no doubt for using stealth in attempting to kill one or more Union soldiers while posing as a civilian. Farquhar is being hanged not only for attempted sabotage but also for attempted assassination.

Finally, the last sentence ironically addresses the question of why Farquhar is being hanged: "The liberal military code makes provision for hanging many kinds of persons, and gentlemen are not excluded" (29). (The words "if patriotic and daring" follow in the *Examiner* version.) The irony consists in calling Farquhar a "gentleman." From the perspective of his high status in Southern society, the title could be appropriate. But would a real gentleman be an assassin? That question is not so easily answered. And would Southern society still consider Farquhar a gentleman if it were known that he avoided military service and sat back in safety while others fought and died in a war that he had helped cause? These questions cloud his right to the title. Again, however, the ironic narrator treats questions like these as academic quibbles. The military code is liberal and doesn't care what title a person has or wants to assume; it will hang him, gentleman or not.

Apart from the hoax that results from our being misled, unless one can determine when the narrator is or is not being ironic, another hoax results from Bierce's progressive undercutting of readers' sense of familiar reality by his manipulation of perspective. He does this in four subtly graduated and overlapping stages: a change of perspective from telescopic to microscopic; a shift from objective reality to fantasy; mental movement from the present to the future; and the sectional shift from the present to the past. This fourth stage is obvious as a step, but its relationship to the previous three is a subtle continuation of the process they set into motion. The story begins with a telescopic view of the scene that zooms in more and more narrowly on the civilian, but which in its descriptions of the physical situation remains only factual. We learn that Farquhar is about to be hanged by some Federal soldiers from the middle of a railroad bridge over a stream. He is standing, a noose around his neck, on the loose end of a plank that almost spans four railroad ties. A sergeant is standing on the other end. When the sergeant steps off his end, Farquhar's end will tip down and Farquhar will be hanged.

The next sentence makes an adroit escalation from the domain of the objective to the subjective when the zooming process suddenly but inconspicuously advances into Farquhar's mind and microscopically reveals his thoughts. "The arrangement commended itself to his judgment as simple and effective" (30). From this point on until the last short paragraph of the first section, it is clear that the omniscient narrator is channeling Farquhar's thoughts and impressions. We learn that his senses have become preternaturally acute but are distorting reality. First, it seems that the external world is slowing down; the stream beneath him and a piece of driftwood in it appear to be moving sluggishly. Then, he comes to recognize that what seemed to be the sound of hammer strokes upon an anvil is actually the ticking of his watch. Farquhar has now begun the process of fantasizing.

Understandably, Farquhar's drift to fantasy is the result of his mind's instinctual and unconscious wish to escape from the dreadful situation that is imminent. It has begun to race; hence, it makes maximum use of the few moments left to it by concentrating on smaller and smaller units of time, first seconds and then milliseconds, and by appreciating mundane details normally passed over. That *seems* to make time run slower by making fuller sensory use of it, but because Farquhar's present is too limited, under the best of circumstances, his mind shifts to the future.

Naturally, it contemplates escape. Farquhar wishes to return to his family, so his mind accommodates him with a wish-fulfillment scenario. It is worth noting that the fantasy of escape in the third section follows *exactly* the sequence of the events Farquhar wishes for in section one's penultimate paragraph: "'If I could free my hands,' he thought, 'I might throw off the noose and spring into the stream. By diving I could evade the bullets and, swimming vigorously, reach the bank, take to the woods, and get away home. My home, thank God, is as yet outside their lines; my wife and little ones are still beyond the invader's farthest advance' (31–32). Therefore, when the trap is sprung, and as Farquhar's consciousness is being ended, his unconscious mind continues to play out this "hopeful" scenario.

The short final paragraph of the first section assumes that readers have sympathetically "bought into" Farquhar's fantasy, and Bierce briefly and daringly offers them two chances to return to the world of reality. What he does with the paragraph is similar to what a hypnotist does after putting a subject into a suggested trance: check to see if the subject is under his influence or is still awake. The first chance occurs with this curious phrase: "As these thoughts . . . were flashed into the doomed man's brain rather than evolved from it. . . ." Readers are given the opportunity to pause and ponder this statement and realize that Farquhar is not reasoning with his head but with his heart. The far-fetched "thoughts" originate in his heart and are transferred—"flashed into"—his brain, which then willingly elaborates them. But almost all readers are too much caught up in the action to want to slow down and reflect on the unusual wording. The second chance occurs when the narrator informs us that Farquhar is "doomed." He is, as the plot will demonstrate, but most readers who have identified with him hope that some miracle will occur and save him. Readers are thus given a chance to take this last warning literally and seriously and to recover from infatuated involvement with him. As Bierce expects, almost no one does.

Coleridge famously described the desired psychological response of readers to literature as "that willing suspension of disbelief for the moment, which constitutes poetic faith." He embraced this state of mind as being a concomitant of artistic success because it awakens to "the loveliness and wonders of the world before us." Bierce, on the other hand, skeptical of abandoning reason in a moment of decision or crisis in a world that he saw as seldom benign, addresses the mental peril of *willing surrender to belief* in real life. In this state of mind, individuals will subordinate cold reason and a grasp of empirical reality to theory, desire, or impractical hope. Such individuals abandon their best weapons of defense against the dangers of existence and become susceptible to being rendered vulnerable by a hoax.

In "Owl Creek," Farquhar is self-deluded from the start and underestimates the difficulty of achieving his desire. He concocts a game plan that is to his liking but that has no other merit. Bierce is not seriously concerned about Farquhar, who is only a "shadow of imagination,"[6] but about readers, who are real. Bierce targets readers in order to teach them something of vital importance about their mental dispositions. In his experience, readers who let their wish for a desirable conclusion govern their critical reactions to a fictitious character are also prone to being willingly governed by nonsensical expectations in real life. The text of "Owl Creek" abounds in warnings about Farquhar. Only readers who disregard all Bierce's warnings and allow themselves to be manipulated by his mind games, including the fantasies of his protagonists, can become victims of his hoaxes. But Bierce writes so that readers who do succumb to the hoaxes of literature can still learn something about their minds that might save them from tragedy in real life.

II.

T HE SECOND SECTION, a flashback to the events that led up to the hanging, is an interruption of the narrative flow at its precisely climactic moment—"The sergeant stepped aside"—and distracts readers by introducing them to a whole new set of events in a seemingly disjunctive new section. Instead of allowing readers to be carried by the momentum of events to the logical and natural culmination, Bierce maneuvers the readers into accommodating a common literary convention that involves an unnatural suspension of action. Accepting this disruption of natural order and sequence helps prepare readers for the apparent suspension of normality in the last section. It accustoms them to disruption just enough that they remain unaware they have been led into an ambush.

The second section is the most brilliant and underestimated part of the story. It shows Bierce at the peak of his artistry, and his daring skill is awesome. Generations of readers have misinterpreted it not because of any deception that Bierce practiced on them but because, as Bierce correctly gauged, they produce their own deception by allowing themselves to be governed by emotion instead of reason. Instead of following the text carefully and thoughtfully, they "read into" the story; they project their own insufficiently considered values into the plot and wish, futilely in the final episode, for an unreasonable ending. In short, most readers miss the subtle but scornful ironies in which this section is drenched, and are unaware of the fact that an omniscient narrator is taking them by degrees into the mind of Farquhar, who is an unreliable source of information. It will be necessary to proceed slowly through this part, sometimes phrase by phrase, because it is so intricately put together yet so dense in meaning.

The great majority of readers initially regard Peyton Farquhar as the hero of the story. This is exactly wrong. He is not a hero in any way; he is an arrogant, self-serving, and self-important rationalistic protagonist. "Peyton Farquhar was a well-to-do planter, of an old and highly respected Alabama family." This does sound like someone readers can favor, someone with standing and breeding. "Being a slave owner and like other slave owners a politician, he was naturally an original secessionist and ardently devoted to the Southern cause" (32). If we make allowances for the fact that Farquhar is a Southern gentleman, it is to be expected that his politics and loyalties support the South and that he resemble other Southerners of his class in his possessions, a plantation and slaves. But why should we make allowances? Strongly implied by its first phrase is the clarification in the sentence of that otherwise unexplained phrase "the Southern cause." For Farquhar, it seems not to have been state's rights, sectional loyalty, attachment to friends and kin, but slavery. Slavery was a main cause of the Civil War, and the essence of slavery is the belief that it is right and natural for certain creatures who look, think, feel, and act like human beings not to have human status at all, but to be treated as property, like livestock; and for other creatures who basically resemble slaves in physical, mental, and spiritual endowments to be their lords and owners. Slave owning is the faith issue that determines the direction reason will take. Properly understood, therefore, this second line damns Farquhar and his kind.

Farquhar's contagion even spreads to his wife. When the dusty rider stops at their plantation, "Mrs. Farquhar was only too happy to serve him with her own white hands" (33). This line by itself is a study in ironic tone. The phrase "only too happy" is a meaningless cliché that normally projects a false sincerity. Mrs. Farquhar's complicity in her husband's values is indicated by her readiness to personally "serve" the horseman when she might have called a slave. And she will serve the rider with "her own white hands." "White" is the word, that extra touch, that oh-so-daintily reminds us of the dehumanizing racism that underlay the institution of slavery. Secessionists precipitated the tragic war that wrecked the South and killed millions of men, including many of themselves, for false ideals. What they got they deserved, and they brought it on their own heads.

"Circumstances of an imperious nature, which it is not necessary to relate here, had prevented him from taking service with that gallant army." What imperious circumstances could be referred to? As the war dragged on, the South put almost every able-bodied man, and even many teenaged boys, into service. What was Farquhar doing that was so important, or what "imperious" events were occurring in his life, that he was "prevented" from joining the army? The first sentence of the second paragraph finds "Farquhar and his wife . . . sitting on a rustic bench near the entrance to his grounds." Nothing imperious about that. As long as he is prevented from joining the army, he seems to be doing a good job of making lemonade from life's lemons, and resting on a rustic bench while he does it.[7]

"[H]e chafed under the inglorious restraint, longing for the release of his energies, the larger life of a soldier, the opportunity for distinction. That opportunity, he felt, would come, as it comes to all in war time" (32). The ironies of these lines are grim but brilliant, and each separate phrase forecasts Farquhar's end. They all seem to be written in romantically lofty abstract language, but their literal meanings are exact and brutal. We might guess what inglorious restraints could be chafing Farquhar's romantic mind, but shortly his neck will be chafed by a hangman's noose, and that will certainly be an inglorious restraint. The longing for the release of his energies will be satisfied when his neck is stretched (i.e., made longer) and he dies (which will definitely release his energies). He also longs for "the larger life of a soldier." This is romantic claptrap, reflecting an ideal notion of heroism and fame.[8] The hard truth is that soldiers commonly die in war in ways that are rarely ideal, and the only "larger life" that is likely to happen to a soldier would have to be an afterlife. He longs for "the opportunity for distinction." One sure venue for distinction is the gallows. Someone hanging at the end of a gallows rope is certain to be noticed. Farquhar is confident that the opportunity for distinction "would come, as it comes to all in war time." Yes, sooner or later all die, and in war time it is usually sooner. For Farquhar the opportunity will come sooner than he expects.

"Meanwhile, he did what he could. No service was too humble for him to perform in aid of the South, no adventure too perilous for him to undertake if consistent with the character of a civilian who was at heart a soldier, and who in good faith and without too much qualification assented to at least part of the frankly villainous dictum that all is fair in love and war" (32–33). This entire passage is utter nonsense. It is not the report of a neutral narrator, but the mental rationalization of Farquhar, and it shows either how confused or how completely self-deluded he is. Farquhar was doing nothing for the South, and "he did what he could" is a polite way of covering up that bald truth. He was certainly not performing any humble service, but the word "adventure," with its romantic connotation of derring-do, suggests that he thinks a person of his class and station (and with his special virtues!) is suited for only some task of high emprise. The rest of the sentence makes no sense at all. The grand, sweeping volunteerism of the first part—"no service was too humble . . . no adventure too perilous"—suddenly runs up against a qualification, "if." If what? "[I]f consistent with. . . ." But who determines the measure of consistency? Farquhar. This goes some way toward explaining the "imperious" circumstances that "prevented" him taking service thus far.

He thinks of himself as "a civilian who was at heart a soldier." To Bierce, these were two very different and mutually exclusive kinds of people. An individual may be one or the other, but cannot be both simultaneously. A soldier is someone who is trained for war, is disciplined to be a professional warrior, and knows he is in a war. A civilian is someone who is not trained or disciplined for war, and who cannot function as a soldier. There was a vast difference, in Bierce's mind, between these two types, and the distinction is at the heart of the title of his collection *Tales of Soldiers and Civilians*. That Farquhar thinks he can be both, slip back and forth from one role to the other, again shows that he either does not know what he is talking about or that he is self-deluded.

The second half of the sentence, after the word "if," breaks into three qualifications. The "if consistent with" one has already been dealt with. The second one, "in good faith and without too much qualification," is, again, internally contradictory. "[I]n good faith" sounds good but is brought up short with the admission that there will be a qualification. That means that we cannot be sure of what *he* means about undertaking something "in good faith." How much qualification will there be? "[N]ot too much." Is this clear? Who will do the qualifying? Farquhar. Again he is really offering far less than he seems to be at first.

The third qualification sounds suave and sophisticated but is actually foolish. Farquhar assents "to at least part of the frankly villainous dictum that all is fair in love and war." "Dictum," as opposed to "dicta," means that the statement is singular, unified, and indivisible. One can agree with a dictum or disagree with it, but how can one assent to part of it? "Fools rush in where angels fear to tread" is a dictum. What part of it can be assented to? Farquhar even qualifies his qualification. He will assent to "at least" part of the dictum. In other words, he may give more or less of an already impossibly divided assent to the dictum. Even assuming that this can be done, who will decide how much "at least part of" will be? Farquhar. Farquhar may think himself clever as well as noble to have described himself so well, but that is because he may not realize how meaningless the description is. Readers who swallow this gibberish have fallen into Bierce's trap. Finally, the dictum is "frankly villainous." To assent to a frankly villainous proposition makes one a villain. But Farquhar assents only to "at least part of" it. All right, if at least part of Farquhar is a villain, that part is going to be hanged.

As Farquhar and his wife sit on their rustic bench, a "grey-clad soldier" rides up. Most readers figure out that "grey-clad" doesn't necessarily mean Confederate. The soldier, we learn at the end of the section, is a Federal scout in disguise. Whether one is a soldier or a civilian is a matter somewhat deeper than whether or not one is wearing a uniform, or the color of that "habit." This event is a test of what Farquhar means by his partial assent to the frankly villainous dictum. Would Farquhar object to being deceived by someone posing as a Confederate? He seems not to object to disguise, a few minutes later, when he plans to wear civilian clothes in order to deceive Federal soldiers on his proposed military mission of destroying the Owl Creek bridge. Does this mean that he will assent to his being frankly villainous, but will not assent to someone else being so? That hardly seems fair. In fact, that double standard would be wholly villainous.

The majority of readers consider the incident that ensues from this encounter the part of the story where Farquhar is tricked into volunteering for his doomed "adventure." Farquhar is tricked, all right, but he is the only one who does the tricking. To read the dialogue between Farquhar and the scout carefully is to see without doubt that all the scout does is answer questions *that Farquhar puts to him.* Moreover, he answers those questions directly and honestly. He does not lead Farquhar; he makes no suggestions whatsoever. The crucial question comes from Farquhar. "Suppose a man—a civilian and a student of hanging—should elude the picket post and perhaps get the better of the sentinel . . . what could he accomplish?" (34). Here again, Farquhar reveals both his inflated sense of himself and his fundamental confusion. He obviously thinks he is describing himself when he says "a civilian and a student of hanging." Apart from the already discussed distinction between a soldier and a civilian implied by this question is a new term, "a student of hanging." What does this mean? What course of study does it entail? A hangman, perhaps, might be called a student of hanging, but it is secondhand study. The only real student of hanging that is possible is someone who is being hanged. Only he can study it firsthand, and only he knows *exactly* what it is. Farquhar, of course, does not intend to be that devoted a student of hanging, but he will be; and the phrase, like those earlier in the section about his chafing under an inglorious restraint and longing for the release of his energies, ironically forecasts his doom. Also, like the earlier nonsensical passage at the beginning of the section, this phrase sounds impressive but is really foolish. Readers who identify with Farquhar, therefore, are allowed to share with him some of the things he "learns" about hanging. For most, even the secondhand experience is unsettling.

One more aspect of Farquhar that is almost always overlooked can be inferred from yet another phrase from his smiling question, "Suppose a man . . . should elude the picket post and perhaps get the better of the sentinel. . . ?" A picket post was usually a small group of soldiers in an outlying location, placed as part of the outermost ring of defense for the main camp. It makes sense for Farquhar to elude the post because he would almost certainly be outnumbered in a showdown. But when he proposes to "get the better of the sentinel," he is using a euphemism for violence. It is almost certain that he intends to kill the sentinel by making use of his civilian habit to get close to the deceived soldier. If not, why does the text describe him as an assassin? If Farquhar ever took his chances in battle with other uniformed Confederates, disguising himself for a special mission could be seen as clever. But inasmuch as Farquhar seems to think himself "prevented" from army service and conventional warfare, and available only for "adventures" where he can play civilian but be a soldier in disguise (or vice versa) and inflict injuries in safety, there is a hint that his kind of subterfuge warfare has an element of cowardice in it. Farquhar does not want to be a soldier except on his own terms, which means, practically speaking, that he is willing to fight only when he judges it unlikely that he will get hurt.

Bierce despises Farquhar. Never before or afterward did Bierce create a character upon whom he lavished such utter scorn. In his journalism, Bierce often excoriated some real-life fool, scoundrel, or knave with insult that was both elegant and corrosive. With serious offenders, he let his hatred shine through his words; it was a personal matter as he lashed them with invective and held them up to ridicule for what they did or said, and it earned him the sobriquet of "the man with the burning pen." But Bierce has contempt for Farquhar not just for what he does or says but for what he is. He represents everything that Bierce loathed: pompous arrogance; muddled thinking; self-delusion or intellectual dishonesty; hollow rhetoric or, even worse, nonsense; deception; personal cowardice; influence unmatched by ability; unmerited respectability; and cruelty and immorality (he was a slave owner). And, to top it all, he thought war was a game! Bierce achieved the very peak of his control in his brilliantly restrained portrayal of a character who was his very antithesis. Bierce's irony was never before or afterward deeper and more caustic yet more subtle. The outstanding mastery of language displayed in this second section is a major reason why "An Occurrence at Owl Creek" is a world classic, and Bierce the only American author who can justly be compared to Swift.

III.

THE MOST FAMOUS part of "Owl Creek" is its striking third section. Every reader of the story comes to realize that it is an elaborate fantasy that is played out in the mind of a dying man, and that the reader is stunningly deceived by it just as Farquhar was. Most

diligent readers are able to review this section and retrospectively recognize in it both signs of his delusion and evidences of his approaching death. His supposed (because impossible) ability, for instance, to
see from a considerable distance the forest "leaves and the veining of
each leaf . . . the very insects upon them: the locusts, the brilliant-
bodied flies, the gray spiders stretching their webs from twig to twig
. . . the prismatic colors in all the dewdrops upon a million blades of
grass," and to hear "the humming of the gnats that danced above the
eddies of the stream, the beatings of the dragon-flies' wings, the
strokes of the water-spiders' legs," and "the rush of [a fish's] body
parting the water" (37–38), are reluctantly conceded to have been
imaginary impressions of the moribund Farquhar. I say "reluctantly"
because this passage is poetry approaching that of Whitman's magnificent catalogues, in which a finite list somehow suggests the infinite
variety and beauty of creation, and not many readers are keen about
relegating such sublime sensitivity and praise of life to the hallucinations of a hanging culprit. In this passage of incredible beauty but
poignant irony, however, is evidence of a tragic but conscious tension
in Bierce's mind between the consequences of a Coleridgean willing
suspension of disbelief and that of his own tendency to be skeptical
of a willing surrender to belief.

The third section opens with a brilliantly ambiguous sentence: "As
Peyton Farquhar fell straight downward through the bridge he lost
consciousness and was as one already dead" (34). Not until the very
end can any reader be sure what it means.[9] But Bierce forces a choice
upon his readers based on the standard he had earlier enunciated:
"[A]n act is wise or unwise the moment it is decided on and according to the light which the person making the decision then had." In
this case, the observation applies to the readers. Most ignore the literal import of this sentence and interpret it only in a figurative sense
to mean that the knot of the hangman's noose stunned Farquhar but
did not kill him. In this they are abetted by the next sentence, especially if they overlook the sign of ambiguity in its word "seemed" and
its possible broad application: "From this state he was awakened—
ages later, it seemed to him—by the pain. . . ."

The back-and-forth movement of the narrator between Far-

quhar's unconscious mind and his own ironic commentary is so deli-
cate as to be almost undetectable through most of the third section.
Only a few passages indicate it. For instance, still in the first paragraph we are told, "The intellectual part of his nature was already ef-
faced" (35). The second paragraph of the section begins: "He was
not conscious of an effort." This clause, in contrast to passages that
give a direct expression to his reactions, continues the original implication of fatality in "he lost consciousness and was as one already
dead." Farther along in the fantasy, the *Examiner* text reads, "The
hunted man . . . was now swimming, *consciously and* vigorously, with
the current" (emphasis mine). The *Collected Works* text drops the em-
phasized words and the commas separating the adverbial phrase in
this sentence. This removes a misleading clue and heightens the sense
of continuing action. And as Farquhar, in his fantasy, walks the road
"in what he knew to be the right direction" (43), with exquisite irony
the narrator remarks that he is on an "untraveled avenue" (44).
These fine touches, individually and collectively, may warn an attentive reader, but few readers are that attentive. Why? Because readers
get caught up in the action, are fascinated by Farquhar's engrossing
adventures, and hope for his escape from the deceptive Federal soldiers who tricked and trapped him.

As Farquhar approaches the end of his mental journey, he senses
marvel and mystery. But the association of fantasy and death in this
story is consistent. Farquhar believes he sees "great golden stars . . .
in strange constellations" and hears "whispers in an unknown
tongue. His neck pains him, his eyes feel congested and cannot be
closed, his tongue feels relief in thrusting itself into the cold air, and
he no longer feels the roadway beneath his feet." Again, diligent
readers are retrospectively able to recognize these unusual reactions
as attempts by his unconscious to reinterpret the grim physical symptoms of hanging for adaptation to his ongoing fantasy.

At the very end, an important verbal change occurs. The entire
story up to this point is written in the past tense, but Bierce in the
penultimate paragraph subtly and deftly shifts to the historical present tense.[10] It is a subtle change, but even though it speeds up the action and the sense of immediacy, it also functions as one last

indication that Farquhar's brain is speeding up its fantasy as it senses its own end. "Doubtless, despite his suffering, he had fallen asleep while walking, for now he sees another scene—perhaps he has merely recovered from a delirium. He stands at the gate of his own home. All is as he left it, and all bright and beautiful in the morning sunshine. He must have traveled the entire night. As he pushes open the gate and passes up the wide white walk, he sees . . ." (44). In the original *Examiner* version, Bierce wrote "he fell asleep" instead of the past perfect "had fallen asleep," but probably replaced it because of its clash with the next verb, "sees," and the one after that, the present perfect "has merely recovered." "Fell" is also too hard and definite for the suppositional context, and it is too distant from the historical present tense that immediately follows: "pushes," "passes," "sees," "steps," "stands," etc. Through this shift of tense, Bierce is, of course, delicately but precisely representing Farquhar's imaginary perceptions that are disguised to him—and to readers—as realities, and he is also laying out one more trap for unwary readers who, racing to find out what happens next in the plot, slight the text.

The story's last trap is Farquhar's perception that his wife, "looking fresh and cool and sweet, steps down from the veranda to meet him" (44). This romantic vision of home and wife, with its strongly positive connotations, refreshes for the reader the favorable impression of Farquhar that derived from such earlier and explicitly positive descriptions of him as having good features and a kindly expression, and coming from an old and highly respected family. This final perception permits readers to revert to the sentimental image of Farquhar as a devoted family man—and allows it to be their last impression of him alive.

By now it should be apparent that most readers of this story feel that they have a great deal in common with Farquhar. We view him as a hero because of his good looks, good background, devotion to family, and patriotism, and his audacious cleverness in an adventure of perilous service to his native land. We see him as a victim of provocation and deceit. We are thrilled when the rope breaks and we are with him as he makes a heroic dash for freedom. We are anxious for him to reach home and safety, and are shocked when we learn that he has been deluded all along—and that so have we. Ultimately, the true shock of this story is ours, for by identifying with him, we, by implication, prove that we would have done the same things he did and our lives would have ended like his, with the noose around our neck. *Where did we go wrong?*

Bierce helped us go astray but did not cause it. He placed before us two sets of signals, the dominant one leading to the conclusion of the hanging, and another leading to a more soul-satisfying and heroic ending wherein the underdog, with a little help from chance, overcomes the enormous odds against him. To miss the realistic set and choose the sentimental, we had to read superficially and uncritically, pay little attention to the abundant presence of irony, and ignore a number of textual warnings and parted clues, including forecasts of death and even the sequence of events in the final fantasy. We had to allow theoretical shifts in perspective to numb our reliance upon familiar empirical reality. We had to be eager to swallow a lot of errant nonsense without ever once putting it to the test of intelligibility. We had to forget what the war was about and cheer for the slacker and self-important slave owner. We had to believe that such a civilian could outwit seasoned, professional soldiers at their job. We had to believe that hangmen do not check their ropes and knots, that sharpshooters miss a plain target, and that there is nothing fantastic about a series of coordinated miracles that add up to a man successfully dodging cannon and gunfire and surviving hanging, drowning, and capture all in one day. We had to encounter peculiar physical symptoms without ever pausing to ponder their strangeness. And after all of these, we have to resent what is after all a literary hoax meant to teach us something for our own good, blame its author for our failures and shortcomings, accuse him of a trick ending, and impute to him feelings of misanthropic bitterness.

The conclusion of the story is fittingly brief: "[H]e feels a stunning blow upon the back of the neck; a blinding white light blazes all about him with a sound like the shock of a cannon—then all is darkness and silence."[11] Readers are caught almost as unawares by this as Farquhar, and need the final sentence to explain to them what happened. Although the fact of what happened is indisputable, the significance of what happened has occasioned a variety of interpretations, many ranging from the ingenious to the strained. F. J. Logan, however, to cite one of the better interpretations, is almost certainly correct in linking a paradox of Zeno to the story.[12] According to the paradox, Achilles running after a tortoise will never overtake it if at any instant he reaches only the place where the tortoise was the moment before, because at any given instant, even infinitely far into the future, the tortoise would have left that place and moved ahead to a new one. If we apply Zeno's infinitely divisible space and time to the story, we can see that Bierce believes in neither. In real life Achilles would overtake the tortoise, and in the story Farquhar's neck breaks. The application of this paradox to the story has a direct relationship to Bierce's attitude toward reason. Zeno's paradox shows us what reason can do, but reason-generated theory and empirical reality are at odds. As Logan puts it, "Bierce pairs unanswerable philosophical logic [i.e., that the man's death will never occur] with the implacable logic of natural law" (110). How beautiful it would be if infinitely divisible time could be lived. But it can't. The story's mind games are all theoretical constructs, but life is not theoretical. Farquhar—and we—must live in the real world, where "the immemorial and immutable principles of strategy cannot be violated with impunity." Those principles are empirical, and so is Bierce.

The original ending of the story, in the *Examiner* version, made very clear Bierce's scorn for the baseless theorizing he associates with Farquhar. The last line in it reads: "Peyton Farquhar was dead; his body, with a broken neck *and suspended by as stout a rope as ever rewarded the zeal of a civilian patriot in war-time,* swung gently from side to side beneath the timbers of the 'Owl Creek Bridge'" (emphasis mine, indicating the passage that was deleted). As with many of his deletions from *Examiner* versions of other stories, this passage was too pointed in its moral; the ironic *Examiner* text unmistakably establishes Bierce's criticism of Farquhar. The leaner *Collected Works* version was improved by Bierce's editing, but his position is the same. Precisely because life is precious, the world of reality must be looked at clearly and assessed coldly with the aid of reason. It will not do to paint the world of reality in rosy hues after our desires, because it is deadly.

Thomas Beer, himself a fraud whose ingenious fabrications have deceived generations of literary scholars, may nevertheless have conceived an appropriate response to all those many critics who have misinterpreted this story and blamed Bierce for their discomfort. In a perhaps imaginary exchange, he has Bierce reply to an amateur critic, "If it scares you to read that one imaginary person killed another, why not take up knitting instead of reading?"[13] Bierce wrote fiction not to entertain all readers but to spur thoughtful readers into reflection. "An Occurrence at Owl Creek Bridge" is Bierce's crowning achievement, a masterpiece of subtle and controlled irony. Even though nothing else that Bierce wrote reached its level of artistry and power, with it he touched the level of Swift and Mark Twain, and it justifies the recognition accorded to genius.

⊰ 7 ⊱

"SUCCESS IN LITERATURE"

BIERCE BEGAN his literary career with short and pithy comments about people and events, a pattern he followed in his journalism for the rest of his life, with occasional variations for short essays, verse, and ironic sketches. Some of these sketches evolved into narratives, and this led him into the domain of fiction. Typically, irony, satire, and sarcasm dominated the narratives, but writing them extended his range and afforded him an outlet for his rapidly growing creative talents. While many of these early fictional ventures seem contrarian, in that they put an ironic spin on fables and myths, they remain moral exempla. Underlying their reversals of plot and characterization is a coherently skeptical view, grounded in experience, of human nature, but coupled with that is a humanitarian intention to teach humans how to at least recognize their plight and perhaps minimize their suffering.

It is more obvious in the less-complex short pieces of his early period, but it is true of his entire oeuvre, that Bierce adhered to the traditional principle that literature had dual purposes: to please and to instruct. This principle is a key to his fiction, and it is most evident in his early and short works. The pleasure comes from his wit and skill and sense of fun; the instruction, as previously shown, derives from his reflections on the ideas and experiences he writes about. He admitted this latter purpose in a "Prattle" reply to a correspondent: "F. McA.—No doubt 'the people' would 'prefer a different mental diet.' I can only say to them, as Euripides answered the Athenians: 'I do not compose my works in order to be corrected by you, but to instruct you'" (E, 19 May 1895).

Bierce objected strenuously to any fiction or poetry that was patently didactic or homiletic, but he also understood that literature worthy of the name engages life, and that lessons therefrom might be drawn inferentially. Although he tended to disparage much of his fiction, it is now possible to see that while striving to write literature that both pleased and instructed, he experimented with form and technique in his early, middle, and late periods, and had a high degree of success from an aesthetic point of view. The unconventionality of his ideas and style, his concision, and the depth of his irony, combined with the preference of many critics for less-demanding literature, have worked against him, but literary history records other cases of ultimately established authors suffering the same experience, a delay in being understood and appreciated.[1] Once Bierce's experiments are understood and recognized as having a common root, it becomes obvious that he was a serious and a sometimes brilliant literary artist. All throughout his fiction are signs of a serious and thoughtful commitment to literary artistry that leads to rewarding intellectual and moral depth. One group of his stories appears humorous and even playful, another romantic, and yet another reveals him as being a serious social critic. Because these separate manifestations of his character are all related to each other, and to his more than forty years of nonfiction journalism, it is a mistake to consider only a handful of stories from his two major anthologies as the sum total of his successful writing.

Signs of his literary genius are apparent very early in his career. One example, from the many fables and myths Bierce revised and collected in the books he published in England, is "The Grateful Bear" (1873). In it, Bierce reworked the familiar story of Androcles and the Lion to show how a malefactor and a victim are attracted to each other. A bear with a thorn in its paw is aided by a widow with two daughters. After the good-hearted widow extracts the thorn, she gives the bear something to eat. Unstated but implicit to this story is the moral that humans and bears, even talking ones, are natural enemies of each other, and that the widow put herself in danger by attempting to do a good deed for a creature incapable of appreciating the gesture. The bear immediately learns that it will be fed at the widow's if it comes with a thorn in its paw, so it begins to stick thorns into its paws. Soon the widow runs low on food, and when she shows hesitancy about doling out more food, the bear licks the hand of one of her daughters, a sign the widow correctly interprets as a threat to the girl. So the widow offers the bear a heifer. And each day afterward, the widow surrenders another animal from her stock until she has nothing more to give. At this point, driven by desperation, she decides to close her door. She is never again bothered by the bear. It now becomes clear that the title is ironic; the bear was not so much grateful for the widow's good deeds as for her susceptibility to intimidation and her slowness in realizing that she could end her victimhood simply by shutting the door on it.

Bierce astutely recognized in the original Androcles fable a romantic fairy tale, contrary to nature. His version lacks high moral idealism but is eminently more sensible. It is easy to see in it that the widow, because of her good heart, made an erroneous assumption of how a bear would behave, and built an erroneous expectation on top of that. This situation is a precursor of what Bierce was later to do in his more advanced stories, which are much more subtle, sophisticated, and complex, but which have similar basic lessons at their hearts.

Although Bierce's skill is most impressive in his great stories of 1887–93, there is striking literary quality in other lesser-known short works that he wrote before 1887, and others he wrote after 1893. They demonstrate that he was multitalented in the field of fiction. Indeed, it may come as a surprise to those who have read only a few of his war tales or have imbibed the simplistic myth of his bitterness that neither his personality nor his range of fiction was narrowly limited or fundamentally negative.

As testimony that there was a congenial side to Bierce, McWilliams quotes Hugh Hume, the editor of *The Wave,* a literary journal to which Bierce sometimes contributed: "Bierce was the mildest and gentlest gentleman I have ever met. . . . In his conversational discussions of people and events, he was kind, considerate, and friendly."[2] A similar perspective is advanced by William Chambers Morrow, a younger writer whom Bierce befriended and encouraged, in a humorous sketch that I discovered. The sketch, entitled "A Strange Adventure" (1891), in which Bierce plays a prominent part, attests to Bierce's friendliness and sense of humor and also explains "A Lady from Redhorse" (1891) as his playful response to the sketch's friendly ribbing.[3] Included in *Tales of Soldiers and Civilians,* it may even be described as a lighthearted romance.

Bierce's range is also considerably wider than has been generally recognized, for he wrote in a surprising variety of subgenres of the short story, in each of which he demonstrated literary craftsmanship. Among his light humorous stories are "The Race at Left Bower" (1874) and "The Failure of Hope & Wandel" (1874). But as previously noted, a story like "Jupiter Doke, Brigadier-General" shows that Bierce can combine humor with sophisticated depth. He even composed sentimental stories, such as "A Baby Tramp" (1891),[4] "An Inhabitant of Carcosa" (1891), "A Resumed Identity" (1908), and "The Stranger" (1909), the last three of which have autobiographical elements. "Beyond the Wall" (1907), also of possible autobiographical value, may be the closest Bierce ever came to writing a love story. All of these stories, and others like them, are examples of Bierce's mastery of familiar categories of the short story.

As for his experiments, an example of how original and successful Bierce could be is the rediscovered powerful story "Hades in Trouble" (1888). Wittily entertaining, and more than a little sardonic, this parody of *Paradise Lost* ingeniously suggests that the human race was created for the vindictive purpose of punishing the fallen angels and turning their Pandemonium into Hades. Yet it is not a facetious tale. Its bold conception is one of Bierce's bleakest assessments of mankind as well as of Milton's theodicy.[5] If the story were intended to be only cynical, this assessment and the superficially humorous plot would have sufficed to achieve that end. Instead, the story anticipates Mark Twain's *Letters from the Earth* (1909; 1962) in that it opens up to a deeper level of theologically serious reflections about God, man, Satan, and existence. "Hades in Trouble" inverts the relationship between humans and devils and ironically supports the description of man as "little lower than the angels" by comparing humans negatively to the fallen angels. It even develops some relative sympathy for Satan and the fallen angels by making them appear naïfs at immorality, compared to Eve. Further, insofar as the story's character Time seems to entertain, but actually oppresses, both devils and humans, Bierce allows Time to be understood as a means by which a vindictive Deity has made earth and Hades a punishment for their two categories of inhabitants.

The story's deeper level derives from its deviation from Milton's conception of a struggle between those who are absolutely evil and those who are relatively good, to a contest between those who are evil and those who are even more evil. With this touch (paralleled in the Parenticide Club tales, written at about the same time), Bierce pressures his readers to think in unconventional ways by presenting a narrative without heroes. This upsets readers who are looking for someone in the story with whom to identify, for the only alternatives are between evil characters who differ only in degree. The choice is not even the lesser of two evils, for that distinction is not always clear, and Bierce does not spare his readers' feelings by allowing them the small comfort of at least being able to think of their own kind as the victims, or of God as benevolent. As in his Civil War tales, the only option before the reader is a lose-lose one. Again, this story parallels, if not anticipates, the position of Mark Twain, who simultaneously disparaged "the damned human race" and also the God who created the race as it is.

Bierce's contemporaneous *Examiner* contributions are of little help in ascertaining the mood in which he wrote this piece, for he rarely allowed whatever was going on in his personal life to be reflected in print. His pursuit of a philosophy of life overrode the ups and downs of his life, and almost constitutes a constant element in his works. Although "Hades in Trouble" appeared on the same page as his political allegory "The Fall of the Republic," it also followed by one week the publication of "For the Ahkoond," one of his more humorous satires. "Hades in Trouble" is rich in erudite wit and offers further evidence of Bierce's complexity and wide range of talents, and the seriousness of his thought.

While "Hades in Trouble" is somewhat unusual for Bierce—a satire with theological implications—Bierce's political and social satires constitute a large and impressive area of his writing.[6] A great deal of his ironic and satiric work was written either anonymously or pseudonymously, including, during his English years, the books he published as "Dod Grile" and what he wrote as editor of *The Lantern*. On the light side are works such as "How Not to Eat," a two-part un-collected double-spoof that ridicules the extremes both of "vulgar-ian" habits of eating and of the excessively fastidious views on etiquette espoused by its fictitious author, "Jamrach Holobom," a class-conscious snob (E, 6 and 13 May 1888, 10). On the serious side, Bierce expressed his trenchant and thought-provoking criticisms of society and culture abundantly in both nonfiction and fiction. It is practically impossible to read more than two consecutive "Prattle" columns without realizing that "Prattle" itself was mainly a vehicle for Bierce's commentaries on his milieu. A survey of several years of those columns not only would put his troubling stories into the larger perspective of the full spectrum of his interests but would addition-ally demonstrate, beyond the shadow of a doubt, that Bierce was an "old Roman" when it came to social ethics.[7] Like Edgar Lee Master's character "English Thornton,"[8] Bierce was devoted to the moral and intellectual standards of the Founding Fathers, and the columns help illuminate his stands on social issues.

The rich vein of pointed social criticism in Bierce's fictional canon has barely been touched by scholarship and has hitherto been invisible to those who miss his irony or who expect him to be merely grimly facetious or psychologically disordered. The four tales com-prising the set known as "The Parenticide Club,"[9] for example, are frequently read and often alluded to, but are generally misunder-stood as evidence of his warped personality. Among the most fa-mous—or, rather, notorious— sentences Bierce ever wrote is the one that begins "An Imperfect Conflagration" (1886), the first of the four tales: "Early one June morning in 1872 I murdered my father—an act which made a deep impression on me at the time." Critics eager to support the alliterative epithet "Bitter Bierce," and the notion that he was more important as a personality than an author, have seized upon these four tales as all-too-obvious proof that he hated his parents (and, presumably, additional relatives, for an aunt, uncles, and cousins are featured in the other stories).

To arrive at this misguided position, it is necessary, to begin with, to believe that Bierce usually wrote directly out of his own experience; that these stories can be relied upon to constitute valid autobiographical evidence; that Bierce was either unaware that they resemble morbid, self-indulgent, adolescent, and possibly psychopathic fantasies, or was such a misanthrope that he didn't care; and that beyond their obvious and shameless cleverness they have no other literary merit. It is further necessary either to be ignorant of, or to disregard, the previously mentioned letters (see chapter 1) that Bierce wrote to his mother in 1876, and the abundant additional evidence from biography and correspondence that contradicts the "Bitter Bierce" myth. Finally, if the best of Bierce's stories are granted talent but still regarded as bitter at their core, little more than heartless and shallow gloatings over human misery, then it follows that the Parenticide Club tales are simply the most transparently bitter of Bierce's stories.

Sadly, the majority of critics, shocked by the outrageous plots of the tales, have tended to believe the worst of Bierce, and their comments on the Parenticide Club tales have usually been negative. Stuart Woodruff considers the Parenticide Club tales the worst that Bierce ever wrote, and Roy Morris Jr. disagrees only because he believes that Bierce "wrote several that are worse." He considers them "invaluable," however, from a biographical point of view because "[t]hey contradict the popular assumption that Bierce was somehow warped by the Civil War. A man driven to kill his parents over and over again in his stories . . . is a man who was a casualty long before the first cannon fire at Fort Sumter." Jay Martin sees in these tales exposés of the irrational hatreds that underlie family life and reflections of the psychic tensions Bierce "suffered deeply both as a child and as a parent." Cathy N. Davidson saw in one of them a "Kafkaesque quality of Oedipal tragedy reduced to transient comedy of manners." Even M. E. Grenander dismisses them briefly as absurd "mimetic tales of action."[10]

Those who mine these stories for autobiographical revelations ignore Bierce's criticism of domestic murders in the *Examiner* of 24 February 1889. Although his article begins by reporting on fathers who murdered their families, it goes on to note that only 10 percent of murderers are executed, partly because the murderers are tried "in courts of acquittal instead of making them answer for their deeds before tribunals of larger powers and more austere character," and partly because the law surrounds "the accused with an almost impregnable wall of technicalities and presumptions of innocence." The piece concludes on a more general view of domestic murders: "What we need are energetic and repeated affirmations of the crimes of braining, disemboweling, throat-cutting and shooting—especially in families." It is obvious that Bierce is responding with sincere moral indignation to problems of domestic violence and failures of the legal system to correct them. Modern scholarship has thus far overlooked this social background. "The Parenticide Club" and related stories are most satisfactorily understood as fictional counterparts to his attacks on social ills in his "Prattle" columns.

Far from being embarrassingly inferior or sickly or blackly humorous expressions of Bierce's wounded psyche, the Parenticide Club tales, though shocking and exaggerated, are undeniably skillful and morally vigorous. Basic to any competent reading of them must be the recognition that they are satires, one of his favorite forms of literary expression. All four stories in the set share a pattern of ironic features: they pretend to be defenses of parenticide; the "autobiographical" accounts are humorously euphemistic and unremorseful; the forms of legalism and custom so prominent in them are extravagantly treated as ends in themselves, and morality as an irrelevant nonissue; the victims are no better than the murderers; and the first-person narrators are urbane, sanctimonious, and unreliable. Goodness is reduced to the technical excellence of a deed—any deed, even a crime—well done (e.g., an "artistic atrocity" [CW VIII, 162]), sin is reduced to alleged crime, and crime is itself reduced by considerations of moral and even technical relativism. The society portrayed in these stories is one that has kept the words "right" and "wrong" but, in practice, has emasculated them by altering their definitions.

A good case in point is the story "My Favorite Murder," originally published in the *Examiner* of 16 September 1888. Somewhat typical of the group in its use of technique, it begins with a shocking and attention-catching paragraph: "Having murdered my mother under circumstances of singular atrocity, I was arrested and put upon my trial, which lasted seven years. In charging the jury, the judge of the Court of Acquittal remarked that it was one of the most ghastly crimes that he had ever been called upon to explain away" (CW, VIII, 147). Irony is (or should be) immediately apparent in the story's title and in the paragraph's reference to a Court of Acquittal, in which crimes are to be dismissed by rationalization. The irony spreads as the narrator's attorney promptly supplies the assistance the judge needs by allowing his client, the defendant, to relate the details of another, much ghastlier crime he committed, by comparison to which the matricide should seem tame and uninspired. This earlier crime involved catching his uncle unawares, mutilating him by severing his Achilles tendons, and then hanging him in a bag from the limb of a tree where a notoriously vicious ram butted him to death in a series of concussions of seismic force. As a consequence of this testimony, the confessed matricide is acquitted of the less ghastly crime before the bench.

Bierce averts legitimate moral outrage in his readers by his use of gross exaggeration and by skillfully maintaining a humorous tone. This prevents them from feeling much sympathy with the victim, who is a highway robber. We learn that, in one way or another, the entire family made its living by robbing the public. The narrator's father had established a "road agency" (i.e., gang of highway robbers) in California, but when the family had been nominally converted to religion, the father invited his brother, "the *Hon.* William Ridley of Stockton" (emphasis mine), to accept as a gift "the franchise," which consisted of a Winchester rifle, a sawed-off shotgun, and some masks (149–50). While the uncle and his two sons crudely held up stagecoaches, the narrator's immediate family rose to a "higher" status in

the world by running a tasteless dance hall. Bierce deliberately op-
poses his readers' inclination to favor some character in the story by
carefully making them all morally unsavory. Readers, therefore, who
attempt to fall back upon some familiar moral precept, e.g., the commandment to honor one's father and mother, are bound to be frustrated in discovering any virtue worth honoring in any of the family
members. As always, Bierce is endeavoring to break his readers away
from platitudes and automatic responses and make them think. Because there is no morality worthy of the name in the story, a moral
basis for evaluating actions must come from the healthier source that
generates the irony. This has to be Bierce, for the story's ironies target
the actions and values of the main characters, and the author is the
source of the ironies.

The family relationships in the tale are so ridiculously formal as to
preclude feeling. When the narrator sets out to kill his uncle, he first
gives notice of his intention to his parents. His father expresses his
pride in his son, and his mother sanctimoniously "promised that although her religion forbade her to assist in taking human life I should
have the advantage of her prayers for my success" (151). He then tells
his uncle's wife, Aunt Mary, "one of the most fair-minded women
that I have ever met," who smiles, expresses a courteous doubt about
his chance of success, and wishes that the best man would win.
When Uncle William is hamstrung, he does not express either pain
or emotion but accepts the situation matter-of-factly, without surprise
or rancor. Earlier, the narrator tells us that when his uncle denied
having been responsible for the robbery of a stagecoach in which he
had been riding, he and his sons "affected a belief that my father and
I had done the job ourselves in dishonest violation of commercial
good faith" (151). When the narrator is turned down in his subsequent request of his uncle and cousins to be accepted as a partner in
the gang, the matter to be kept secret from his father, the narrator's
commercial conclusion is cold-bloodedly rational: "This fair offer he
rejected, and I then perceived that it would be better and more satisfactory if he were dead" (151).

From the first, the narrator is made to appear cultured, well
spoken, and, if conventional poses and pious platitudes count for

anything, refined. Although his refinement is superficial, that is enough for him, for appearance is everything in his world. Freely admitting to ghastly murders, he is concerned only with social standing, and is gratified by an acquittal on a technicality: "I left the court, without a stain upon my reputation" (149). The statement he gives describing his murder of his uncle shows him to be fastidious, but only about appearances: "I was born," he says, "of honest and reputable parents, one of whom Heaven has mercifully spared to comfort me in my later years" (149), and he subsequently alludes delicately to the parent he murdered as "my now sainted mother" (150). He praises himself for having acted "a most honorable part" in permitting himself to be robbed by what he mistakenly thought were his kinsmen. He greets his uncle "pleasantly" before suddenly knocking him out by a blow to the head with a rifle butt; he plumes himself for being "reasonable" in granting his uncle's request to be finished "in the bosom of [his] family"; and he sorrowfully refers to his "poor uncle" as he describes in elegant language the effects of the ram's batterings.

With these obvious and audacious ironies—of Bierce's, but not the narrator's—coloring the narrative, readers are unlikely to identify emotionally with victims who themselves are so flat and stiff that they are not believable. The story may be perceived, therefore, as being as absurd and ridiculous as the legal hair-splitting that has a place in a world of Courts of Acquittal, Courts of Exception, and Courts of Objections and Technicalities. Compared to such well-known stories as "An Occurrence at Owl Creek Bridge" or "Chickamauga," a tale like "My Favorite Murder" may even seem trivial. Nevertheless, the same passionate commitment to truth, justice, and compassion that drives the other stories drives the Parenticide Club tales also.

These tales are social criticisms in the manner of the satire of Swift's "A Modest Proposal." Bierce's target is a world of hypocrisy and self-deceit where hard words are replaced by soft ones or, if retained, are fitted with soft meanings. This world resembles ours. The appearance of respectability, e.g., being a deacon in a church or not being idle (although one's work consists of disposing of murdered bodies), is equated with virtue. Religion has almost no impact on character and actions, for any course of action can be justified by excuses. It has the familiar fundamental injunctions: "Honor thy father and mother" and "Thou shalt not murder"; but in practice, its society, through its legal system and mores, construes these commandments so loosely as to negate them. By implication, if absolute and fundamental laws are rendered relative or circumventable by subversive technicalities, both the legal and the moral codes become nothing more than matter for logic chopping, which becomes in effect the new absolute. The narrators are morally shallow, but they are no worse (or better) than any of the other characters. The world described in these tales is what society has chosen to make it. The only thing more absurd than the stories themselves is the belief that Bierce could be in some way identifying with characters he is patently satirizing with such elaborate scorn.

The earliest Parenticide Club story, "An Imperfect Conflagration" (1886), similarly excuses parenticide, ironically, for reasons of financial expediency. "It was that music-box which brought disaster and disgrace upon our family. If we had left it my poor father might now be alive" (CW, VIII, 171). The narrator and his father were in the robbery "business" and squabbled over how to divide a music box that the father stole for himself. "I could not help admiring his spirit and sensitiveness; for a moment I was proud of him and disposed to overlook his fault, but a glance at the richly jeweled music-box decided me, and, as I said, I removed the old man from this vale of tears." To conceal the murder of his father, the son murders his mother also. Then he goes to the chief of police, "told him what I had done and asked his advice. It would be very painful to me if the facts became publicly known. My conduct would be generally condemned; the newspapers would bring it up against me if ever I should run for office. The chief saw the force of these considerations; he was himself an assassin of wide experience. After consulting with the judge of the Court of Variable Jurisdiction he advised me to conceal the bodies in one of the bookcases, get a heavy insurance on the house and burn it down. This I proceeded to do" (174).

The evidence of the murders is not destroyed, however, because the bookcase he uses unexpectedly turns out to be fireproof. "Not a hair of them was singed, their clothing was intact. On their heads and throats the injuries which in the accomplishment of my designs *I had been compelled to inflict* were conspicuous [emphasis mine]. As in the presence of a miracle, the people were silent; awe and terror had stilled every tongue. I was myself greatly affected" (175–76).

Of course, the son is not jailed, but is set free to enjoy life, liberty, and the pursuit of happiness, which in this case consists of passing counterfeit United States bonds. Again we deal with a world in which appearances are more important than realities, where awful deeds that are both immoral and criminal receive the connivance of the police and judiciary and go unpunished, where blame is displaced, and where the narrator is allowed to get away even with parenticide while yet indulging in sentimental platitudes. This world is not wholly imaginary, except, perhaps, in the transparency of its hypocrisy.

The same world appears in "Oil of Dog" (1890). "I was born of honest parents in one of the humbler walks of life, my father being a manufacturer of dog-oil and my mother having a small studio in the shadow of the village church, where she disposed of unwelcome babes" (CW, VIII, 163). Everything about this sentence is ironic, especially its euphemism about disposing of "unwelcome babes"—for that function involves the narrator's "dear mother" murdering cherubic babes (165)—and its location of the "studio" in the "shadow" of a nearby church. This last detail is especially rich, implying as it does that both church and society have willingly turned a blind eye to murder, and downgraded from immoral and illegal to "disreputable" an activity that is permitted because it apparently has some social utility. These stories were almost certainly occasioned by specific social problems that disgusted Bierce; he was not given to attacking abstract or theoretical vice.[11] Although American fiction in his time seldom openly addressed such social issues as abortion, child abuse, and murder of children, those practices existed then as well as now, and there must have been some connivances of political authorities, clergy, and even society to hush up but not halt these activities that angered Bierce into satirizing the sanctimoniousness of those involved in coverups.[12]

Eventually, in "Oil of Dog," the occupations of the parents merge once they learn by a "happy" accident that superior dog oil results when the bodies of the "unwelcome babes" are added to the vats of dead dogs, and the parents graduate from being passively dependent on orders to remove the "small superfluous" to actively scouring the region for raw material, and extending their scope from newborn infants to older children, and even to such adults as could be enticed to the "oilery." Ultimately, the activities become publicly known. The neighbors then hold a meeting at which "resolutions passed severely censuring them. It was intimated by the chairman that any further raids upon the population would be met in a spirit of hostility" (167).

Again Bierce has created a world not all that far removed from the one we know, which countenances abortions and mercy killings and then "harvests" cells and organs from the "unwelcome babes" and terminated patients—thus creating an interdependent connection between abortion and euthanasia and "social utility"—and where spineless authorities chastise evil with temporizing, ambivalent, and morally mushy resolutions. When greed and zeal lead the husband and wife to kill each other and both fall into their boiling vat, Bierce's narrator sorrowfully sums up these events as a "commercial disaster" that, additionally, has closed off for him all avenues to an "honorable career" in that town (169–70). Even this phony rationalization has been realized in our world, where individuals arrested by the police for pursuing illegal but unofficially tolerated activities complain that they are being "forced" into more extreme criminal activities. It is incredible that such a powerful story of social criticism has been read purblindly as mainly an example of a misanthropic personality resentful of his parents.

"The Hypnotist" (1893), the last of the ironic four stories, features a narrator who is an amoral individual with hypnotic powers that he uses to indulge his whims. He is sentenced to prison when he is caught taking advantage of a small girl but, upon his release, avenges himself on the warden by making a fatal hypnotic suggestion. He decides to punish his parents also. He blames them because, in his eyes, "all my misfortunes had flowed like a stream from the niggard economy of my parents" (CW, VIII, 181). He hypnotizes them to believe themselves broncos, and they kick each other to death, leaving him "an orphan." Fifteen years later, his trial in the Court of Technicalities and Continuances is still in process, and his lawyer is "moving heaven and earth to get the case taken to the Court of Remandment for New Trials." (The "heaven" part of the cliché provides additional irony.) At the time of writing, the narrator thinks of himself as somewhat of an experimental scientist. As for his power of hypnotic suggestion, he spins it with a lofty, butter-wouldn't-melt-in-my-mouth rationalization: "Whether or not it could be employed by a bad man for an unworthy purpose I am unable to say" (184). Again, what is revealed in this tale is not Bierce's resentment of his parents, but rather his ridicule of individuals who refuse to acknowledge guilt and blame others instead of themselves for their actions, and his disgust at a legal system that bends over backward to avoid punishing criminals.

Bierce's scorn for a society that failed so ingeniously to live up to its professed principles was by no means restricted to the Parenticide Club stories. "The City of the Gone Away" (1888), for example, originally subtitled in the *Examiner* "A Tale of Medical Science and Commercial Thrift," begins: "I was born of poor because honest parents, and until I was twenty-three years old never knew the possibilities of happiness latent in another person's coin. At that time Providence threw me into a deep sleep and revealed to me in a dream the folly of labor" (CW, VIII, 52). Here, "poor because honest" makes explicit the irony underlying the recitation of the formula by the narrators of the Parenticide Club stories. Led by his revelation that he had "broken the First Commandment of the Natural Decalogue: you have labored!" (53), the narrator sets himself up as a physician who practices euthanasia, and appends to his "dispensary" a cemetery flanked by "some very profitable marble works" and an extensive flower garden as well as a "Mourner's Emporium" that "was patronized by the beauty, fashion and sorrow of the city" (54–55). The story connects the charlatan narrator with corrupt city officials and priests who manipulate, respectively, government and religion for their mutual benefit. The alliance continues profitably until the narrator is accidentally discovered to have been taking an unfair bonus from the operations by not burying his "patients" at all but instead converting them into fancy soap. Practically every sentence of this story is steeped in irony.

"A Bottomless Grave" (1888) and "The Widower Turmore" (1891) are additional stories written in the same vein of social satire.[13]

Bierce was serious about life, and stories like these, only slightly offset from the real world, depict it with thought, passion, honesty, and skill. Duplicating "Swift's method of inflaming rather than convincing," Bierce attacked his targets with a combination of "savagery and mirth,"[14] seeking not to reconcile with those he considered morally or intellectually bankrupt but to reduce them to ashes. In these tales no one stands up to expose false values, hypocrisy, amorality, or even immorality. The stories' pervasive irony, however, is dependent upon a norm, and Bierce's values constitute that norm. Upholding a moral norm was the role he fulfilled in real life. For close to forty years, he fiercely castigated society for being "frothing mad" because of its sicknesses of materialism, moral cowardice, deceit, false reasoning, and hypocrisy. Bierce's intense dedication to moral values was behind his lashings of rogues and rascals in his weekly "Prattle" columns in the *Argonaut*, *Wasp*, and *San Francisco Examiner*, his exposure of Collis Huntington and the Central Pacific Railroad scandal of 1896, and his attack on American militarism and imperialism in the Spanish-American War period and its aftermath, 1897–1901. He outspokenly held individuals and society to account. Of course they resented it, and not being able to substantively criticize his arguments, they retaliated with slurs and ad hominem depreciations of his style and personality, responses that have infected Bierce criticism ever since. The shallow and fallacious charges that he was a misanthrope and an irascible cynic have always been the easiest ones to infer shallowly from the sensationalism of his plots and the vigor of his indignation. It is ironic that, again like Swift— also a writer to whom integrity and strong moral convictions were central—Bierce the messenger has been denigrated by those for whom his message might do the most good, either because it was too disturbing or because they did not take the trouble to comprehend it.

The traps that Bierce lays in his satires for unwary readers are closely related to those he employs in his hoaxes, another category of writing in which he excelled. As Carey McWilliams observed, it is impossible to discuss Bierce apart from the hoax tradition.[15] Early and late, Bierce fully participated in both the playful and serious aspects of the Sagebrush tradition of the hoax. Bierce's lifelong fondness for the ghost story genre, for example, is closely related to his propensity for hoaxes, as is his solemn use of the first-person narrator in other stories that prey upon readers' credulity. His central technique, the use of shock, is also connected to the tradition of the hoax when it depends upon the tricks the minds of his protagonists—or Bierce's readers—play on them. McWilliams, therefore, even underestimates the importance of the hoax tradition to an appreciation of Bierce's literature. "An Occurrence at Owl Creek Bridge" stands head and shoulders above all of Bierce's other hoaxes, but it is still related to them in its basic lineaments and must be understood as arising out of a context.

Among the early hoaxes in the playful line is "Mr. Swiddler's Flip-Flap" (1874), a lightly ironic and humorous tale with grisly overtones about a protagonist named Swiddler who was frustrated by the collusion of his unsympathetic townsmen against his last-minute attempt to save a murderer friend from the gallows. One of these townsmen hoaxes Swiddler into doing a somersault while he is racing on foot to beat the clock. As a result, Swiddler gets turned around and runs instead in the opposite direction from where the hanging is to take place, thus losing his chance to save the criminal. Readers, typically, are trapped in a no-win situation. Swiddler was clearly deceived; on the other hand, he was trying to restore a sentenced murderer to society.

A more elaborate but still playful hoax is *The Dance of Death* (1877), which Bierce coauthored with William Rulofson and T. A. Harcourt. Using the pen name of William Herman, these three conspirators concocted the book as a seeming attack on the popularity of the waltz from the right-wing religious position that it was conducive to immorality. Once the book was published, Bierce boosted its commercial success by fiercely attacking its supposed author for having a prurient mind, but his "attack" was written in language that could not fail to arouse interest in the book: e.g., "From cover to cover it is one sustained orgasm of a fevered imagination—a long revel of intoxicated propensities."[16]

Bierce collaborated in another literary hoax in 1899, when he, another friend, and the young poet Herman Scheffauer attempted to pass off Scheffauer's Poesque poem, "The Sea of Serenity," as a rediscovered work written by Poe. As before, Bierce distanced himself from the joke by judiciously worded comments in "Prattle" about the potential importance of the poem. The three had expected that it would occasion much discussion but were disappointed in the public's response. Little interest was expressed in the "discovery," and the friend eventually revealed that Scheffauer wrote it.[17] Bierce's participation in the hoax, apart from the fact itself, is of chief interest for the praise he lavishes on Poe—a consistent position in his oeuvre.

Two of Bierce's later and better-known stories are still not widely recognized as hoaxes, but they are. The first of them is "The Death of Halpin Frayser" (1891), an intricate and fascinating tale with too many red herrings, which has generated some ingeniously overread interpretations. Cathy N. Davidson's treatment of the story, however, presents a convincing case for identifying the story as a hoax. Her analysis identifies and persuasively explains a number of its false leads and concludes that it is a "comic detective yarn."[18] Once the story is approached as a hoax, it is possible to see how skillfully Bierce laid his traps, perhaps tailor-making them for the critical approaches most likely to be used on the tale.

"Moxon's Master" (1899) appears to be the same sort of insoluble story, a trap for the critic who gets carried away by theory and leaps of logic. Bierce had a wholesome respect for formal logic and a good deal of ability in its use.[19] As a consequence, what can only be deliberate misuses or errors of logic add to the abundant evidence of irony in the story's composition. Moxon is an inventor heavily dependent on theories so abstruse as to be mystical. His central argument—to persuade the story's first-person narrator that a machine can think—is ingenious and developed in subtle stages, but it is demonstrably false in its parts as well as its whole. He begins by quoting a definition of "machine" from a popular dictionary—"Any instrument or organization by which power is applied and made effective, or a desired effect is produced"—and then applying it to man. An argument based on definition can only be as valid as the definition, and in this case the definition is obviously faulty by being too broad. Moxon then claims that man "thinks—or thinks he thinks" (CW, III, 88), a statement intended to blur the distinction between man and machine and thus help prove Moxon's point. It is clever word play but nothing more, for if man doesn't really think then he cannot think he thinks, either.

Next Moxon argues that plants can think, using as an example a vine that keeps creeping toward a stake, even changing its direction several times when the stake is moved, but again he uses faulty logic. That plants move toward things they need—water, light (or shadow), support, or some other element—can be satisfactorily explained in biological terms, but this kind of movement does not make them thinking beings, although Moxon on this account extravagantly places plants in the "philosopher class" (90). Further, in describing roots of a eucalyptus that seek water, he uses personifying verbs and then claims that this search "proves that [plants] can think" (91). Building on these deficient analogies, he moves to a more clever but also false analogy when he similarly implies evidence of intelligence and volition in patterning phenomena as far apart as soldiers forming in lines or squares, geese flying in a "V" formation, and atoms being arranged ("arrange themselves," he says) into mathematically perfect shapes (92).

Then follows a series of linked ingenious theories, eloquently described, each an example of pure rationalism unsupported by empirical fact. Moxon first claims that all matter is sentient, disarming the narrator (and credulous readers) with flattery that releases Moxon from the obligation of identifying the authors he professes are his authorities ("I need not name them to a man of your reading" [93]). From there he denies death ("There is no such thing as dead, inert matter; it is all alive; all instinct with force, actual and potential" [93–94]), and moves on to praising, as being beyond his power to "profitably" change, add to, or remove a single word from, Herbert Spencer's definition of Life: "a definite combination of heterogeneous changes, both simultaneous and successive, in correspondence with external co-existences and sequences" (94). Bierce himself, however, had years earlier quoted that same definition in *Fun* (27 July

1872, 37) and the *Argonaut* (15 December 1877, 5) and ridiculed it for its obscurity. When the narrator both concedes and objects that the definition "defines the phenomenon . . . but gives no hint of its cause," Moxon cites John Stuart Mill to establish that all causes are effects of previous causes, but that the final cause is one that we do not know. We are close to being back with Zeno's arrow in this case of an infinitely regressing cause. Nevertheless, in the empirical world, effects do have definite, provable causes.

Moxon is an extreme—*excessive* might be a more accurate term—rationalist who persuades the narrator (and readers) with word play and logic chopping. By his chain of increasingly theoretical and unprovable assertions, Moxon brings the narrator to the point where Spencer's definition of life seems plausible. When the narrator looks toward Moxon's workshop and asks, "Moxon, *whom* have you in there?" (my emphasis), readers are moved one step closer to expecting someone (or something) sentient in the room. Then Moxon asks, irrelevantly, "Do you happen to know that Consciousness is the creature of Rhythm?" (96), and the narrator—and the credulous reader—are hooked, en passant, by this erudite-sounding but nonsensical theory. The idea is repeated rhythmically in the story, as if to establish it by incantation, and Bierce "mocks on" as impressed but mystified readers (and, judging from several ingenious interpretations of this story, also some critics[20]) hunt in vain for a plausible solution to an impossible situation. It is a test of readers. Those who overlook or misinterpret the clues will remain caught in the story's dead-end mazes of absurd propositions and fallacious reasoning. It is as close in its character to *Alice in Wonderland* with its plays on logic as it is to Poe's essay "Maelzel's Chess Player," which is sometimes considered its inspiration and which also involves the exposure of a robot hoax. The main inferable lesson of "Moxon's Master" is that only cold reason can recognize the story for what it is, and only reason can save one from needlessly wasting time and effort in a futile attempt to make sense of it.

Bierce's entire literary career was devoted to exploring the advantages and the limitations of reason. It is not, he believed, a gift of nature, but an achievement that requires constant effort and strict discipline. Even though, as we have seen, it had tragic limitations and its use might even incur tragedy, he early on concluded that it was humanity's best weapon and most useful tool, and that those who do not use it or use it improperly—most of us all of the time and all of us some of the time—forgo its invaluable potential for saving human beings from folly and unnecessary grief or tragedy. How few are those who achieve it, and how influential in human affairs those who do not, is implicit in his *Devil's Dictionary* definition (1884) of a "fool":

> n. A person who pervades the domain of intellectual specula-
> tion and diffuses himself through the channels of moral activ-
> ity. He is omnific, omniform, omnipercipient, omniscient, and
> omnipotent. He it was who invented letters, printing, the rail-
> road, the steamboat, the telegraph, the platitude and the circle
> of the sciences. He created patriotism and taught the nations
> war—founded theology, philosophy, law, medicine and
> Chicago. He established monarchical and republican govern-
> ment. He is from everlasting to everlasting—such as creation's
> dawn beheld he fooleth now. In the morning of time he sang
> upon primitive hills, and in the noonday of existence headed
> the procession of being. His grandmotherly hand has warmly
> tucked-in the set sun of civilization, and in the twilight he pre-
> pares Man's evening meal of milk-and-morality and turns
> down the covers of the universal grave. And after the rest of us
> shall have retired for the night of eternal oblivion he will sit up
> to write a history of human civilization.

A man who considered the great majority of his fellow human beings fools was not on the track to popularity, and Bierce, obviously, did not seek that. Respect, including self-respect, was more important to him. He told hard truths, as he saw them, not out of a cheap misanthropy but out of a sense of duty. He believed it was everyone's obligation to tell the truth, but everywhere he looked he saw that most people preferred some soft substitution for the real thing, or some comfortable view conducive to their own interests. The Civil War had opened his eyes to the dangers and horrors of life that lurked behind its attractive exterior and, shocked and wounded, he could not thereafter bring himself to conform to the polite fibs sanctioned by society. To do so, in his mind, would have been a betrayal of humanity and made him an accomplice of suffering and death, a goat leading his fellow humans to their doom. So Bierce devoted his entire career to stripping away deceit and calling things by their true names. This made him an eccentric to most readers, and an unpleasant eccentric to readers who are upset by the surfaces of his stories.

Bierce joined Herman Melville, Emily Dickinson, and Mark Twain, and was later joined by Stephen Crane, Frank Norris, and Jack London, in recognizing that life is not benign. The Civil War proved to him that human society is capable of unthinkable viciousness and cruelty, and his years of observing human nature as a journalist disabused him of any illusions about its innate goodness. These were not new discoveries in Bierce's age, and his reading of classical literature and philosophy convinced him that truth does not alter with time. He devoted his art to developing techniques to tell these old truths in a new way. Bierce's way, previously pioneered by Swift and Poe, was to analyze violence and deception, including self-deception, under a microscope and reveal them and their processes, mental as well as physical, in detail. He despaired of a cure, but aimed at prevention. The task he set himself was to get the attention of his readers by shocking them out of their familiar grooves, to make them see how undependable were the assumptions and habits of mind they had naively trusted, and where they were unthinkingly heading. Even their goals, Bierce believed, were often misplaced.

Civilization and progress, Bierce was convinced, have made mankind more active and powerful but not any better or any happier.[21] If Bierce had been a cheap cynic, he would have railed at everything, mocked humanity, and been done with it. Instead, as we have seen, he was passionately engaged with humanity. His animus, his scorching satire, was directed toward the fools and scoundrels who made its lot worse, but his sympathies were with those who did the best they could but who were overwhelmed by forces too strong for them to cope with, or who were betrayed by the inadequacies of their best weapon, Reason. Regarding life itself as a state of war, and a war that all would sooner or later lose, Bierce accepted his place in the ranks and conducted himself with honesty and dignity. His stories, properly understood, never glorify the war—that would have been dishonest and cruel—but rather counsel his readers to be humane toward each other, rational, and moral, and to follow these standards with soldierly discipline. Bierce promises no reward for being virtuous except that of not being a fool or a scoundrel. The fictional record of his struggles with this severe creed has made him deserving of the status of a classic writer. Even in his own time, readers regarded him as an outstanding literary figure. What it cost him can be deduced from his reply to a reader: "J. S. If success in literature were so simple a thing that I could tell you how to win it, it would not be worth winning. I cannot write a prescription for adversity."[22]

≼ APPENDIX A ≽

A YOUNG WOMAN stood before the mirror with a razor. Pensively she twirled the unaccustomed instrument in her jeweled fingers, fancying her smooth cheek clothed with a manly beard. In imagination she saw her pouting lips shaded by the curl of a dark moustache, and her eyes grew dim with tears that it was not, never could be, so. And the mirrored image wept back at her a silent sob, the echo of her grief.

"Ah," she sighed, "why did not God make me a man? Must I still drag out this hateful, whiskerless existence?"

The girlish tears welled up again and overran her eyes. Thoughtfully she crossed her right hand over to her left ear; carefully but timidly she placed the keen, cold edge of the steel against the smooth alabaster neck, twisted the fingers of her other hand into her long black hair, drew back her head and ripped away. There was an apparition in that mirror as of a ripe watermelon opening its mouth to address a public meeting; there were the thud and jar of a sudden sitting down; and when the old lady came in from frying doughnuts in the adjoining room she found something that seemed to interest her—something still and warm and wet—something kind of doubled up.

159

Ah! poor old wretch! your doughnuts shall sizzle and sputter and swim unheeded in their grease; but the beardless jaw that should have wagged filially to chew them is dropped in death; the stomach which they should have distended is crinkled and dry for ever!

✦ APPENDIX B ✦

THE BAPTISM OF FIRE
How It Feels When a Soldier Goes Into His First Battle.

COURAGE AND PRIDE.
Lapses of Bravery in Men Distinguished for Good Conduct.

AN INTERESTING short story, translated from the French or German, was published a few weeks ago in a leading weekly journal of this city. It bore the title, "Was He a Coward?" leaving the reader to answer the question in his own mind. Briefly outlined, a scene in a restaurant is described wherein a stranger stares so steadfastly at a young lady seated with some friends at another table that she became annoyed. A high-spirited young nobleman of her party goes to the stranger and commands him to desist. Angry words lead to a challenge, and arrangements for a hostile encounter are made. The story is perused with interest, the reader hoping all the time that friends will intervene and explain that the staring stranger has a glass eye or some hereditary weakness that accounts for his conduct and thus avert the duel; but nothing of this kind occurs. In brief, the young nobleman insists on a sanguinary affair, naming pistols at short range.

As the time approached for the fight, he began to think of dying, and also the apprehension comes that he might falter on the field and forever be disgraced in the eyes of the world. The mental strain is intense, but he professes to his seconds that he is ready to fight, and docs not want to recede from his choice of pistols. The wear on his system—loss of sleep and failing appetite for food—begin to tell, and he fears that his friends will perceive his weakness. He finds that his hand trembles when he holds his weapon. To quiet his nerves he drinks brandy freely but the liquor fails to strengthen him. The last night before the appointed time for meeting is one of agony. He cannot expel from his mind the fear which has now reached a conviction that he will falter, drop his pistol and fall a nerveless, abject figure in the presence of his adversary, exposing his friends to chagrin and himself to shame. To live and be called a coward is more than he can endure. In the agony of despair he takes the pistol and sends a bullet through his own brain.

EXCHANGE OF STORIES.

Speaking of this story, an *Examiner* man brought out in exchange from several veterans of the late war, some observations be[ar]ing upon the subject of personal bravery and moral courage, and also personal recollections of the baptism of fire. In relating these reminiscences it is not the purpose to invade the field of the *Century Magazine* by mapping out blind roads, bald mountains or country taverns in the region of battle-plain, but merely to note what happened in a small individual way, without regard to the enemy who felt our left in the morning or the friendly corps who supported our right in the evening.

UNDER FIRE FIRST.

General Coey was asked how he felt when under fire for the first time, and replied that the feeling was difficult to describe. "The first impulse in all men in self-preservation, and it requires a general bracing-up to stand the ordeal. It is self-pride that makes the soldier stand firm."

"Did you make a study individually of the men who went out from your town in your regiment?"

"I was Second Lieutenant when my company went to the front. Several well-known citizens of the town enlisted and served in the ranks. Two I remember particularly well on account of their prominence. I studied the men closely at Chancellorsville. One who was a large, fine looking man, well known in the regiment because of his prominence at home, acted in a very singular manner. He had never been under fire before, and as we were taking position under a brisk fire, he seemed to lose his self-possession, and laughed and talked in a peculiar manner, almost hysterical. He would say: 'I know I will fall down, but I am going on—going through it.' He did go in and fought well, but did not seem to be a rational person during the battle. In the same regiment was an officer whose position in the community at home was very high. His family connections were of the best, and his own ability as an editor contributed to his prominence. It was expected that he would make a model soldier, but in this regard his friends were disappointed. At the first day's fight at Gettysburg he was missed early in the action and no one saw him for several days. I was wounded there and taken to the field hospital, where I saw this officer and asked him where he had been and what was the matter. He gave an incoherent story about a shell dazing him by concussion. In fact, he said he could remember nothing more, as he became unconscious and either wandered off the field or was carried off. I knew that he was not telling the truth, because the brigade had not been exposed to artillery fire that day, although the musketry fire was brisk and we were forced back by the advance of the Confederates, and lost heavily. The conduct of the officer created a deal of comment in the regiment and ugly rumors reached him. The surgeon of the regiment had great faith in the officer's bravery and, declaring that he was sound physically and mentally, urged that nothing be said about his conduct. I recovered from my wounds and rejoined my regiment, but did not see the officer mentioned under fire again until the Wilderness fighting. We were formed in four lines of battle and our line was the last, or the one next to the last, from the front. We were pushing forward and marching obliquely, which soon brought us within range of bullets, yet we were comparatively safe.

BRACE UP OLD MAN.

"While halting I had an opportunity to speak to him. As a friend, I said: 'Brace up now, and keep your position along with the regiment. You know the talk about Gettysburg, and you have a chance now to show the people at home that you are a brave man. Nerve yourself up to it. Make up your mind to go on.' He said he was all right and would go through. We pushed along further to the front, coming under heavier fire and seeing many wounded carried to the rear. Happening to glance around I saw the officer some distance from me, standing behind a tree with his pistol drawn. I didn't see him again until after I was wounded and carried to the rear. Then he told me that it was no use to try any more, because he could not go further than he had gone. I urged him to rejoin his regiment, but nothing could induce him to move; he had made up his mind to resign and go home. He was allowed to resign.

"Now," continued General Coey, "I will tell you the sequel. The surgeon of the regiment who was a warm friend of the officer and also my friend and confidant, was greatly perplexed. The officer was so well balanced mentally and physically that he could not account for his desertion from duty. It caused him to make a special study of the case as his family physician after the war was over. Some four or five years later I met the doctor, and he seemed to have a weight lifted from his mind because he had discovered in a surgical operation that there was some injury or defect in the officer's spine that affected the brain and rendered him mentally irresponsible when under undue excitement."

BAPTIZED AT BETHEL.

H. K. McJunkin, who went to the front with Knapp's Pittsburg battery, received his baptism of fire at Bethel. When asked to describe the sensation produced when under fire first, he said: "I can't describe it because it is indescribable. The natural desire to live which exists in all breasts causes self-preservation to be the first thought. In a measure the discipline of military life stifles that feeling. One may be nervously agitated and still control his mind and be able to render more service than another who manifests no feeling. The test of the man often comes before getting in the fight in the struggle to nerve himself up to the task. It is the fear of disgrace and of being called a coward that does the most to make a man stand up under fire. The natural inclination is to run away and save himself."

"How do you account for a man displaying bravery in one battle and running away from danger in another?"

"I can't account for it fully. The army records show many instances of this kind. Officers of high rank, conspicuous for bravery, have been displaced for cowardice and afterward become distinguished for courage."

"Did you have men in your company that could not go into battle whether they wanted to or not?"

"Yes. I knew one man who was physically incapable of doing anything. He could neither go forward nor back—was, in fact, limp and helpless."

PREMONITION OF DEATH.

Colonel Clarke, now of General Dimond's staff, was baptized at Perrysville. The shock of battle came without preliminary skirmishing. At daylight the enemy was in striking distance and struck hard.

"What was the first sensation?"

"I thought it was another surprise drill and hardly realized the situation until our line was broken and our battery taken by a charge of the Confederates. As near as I can recollect there was a tingling sensation all over my body and my legs seemed to be giving way. I recollect the shouting to rally and recapture the battery, which we did. I went in the battle swearing vigorously, although I never was what they call a profane man."

"What do you think of premonitions of being killed in battle?"

"That's hard to answer. There was a young fellow—a boy of 17—of whom I was very fond killed at Perrysville. I saw him lying on his face a short distance in the rear, and went to him and asked what was the matter. He said he was sick and I spoke pleasantly to him, telling him to come forward with the company and he would feel better. We advanced to a position nearer the enemy, and were lying down just under the crest of the hill to get shelter from a hot fire of the musketry. I saw the boy again some distance to the rear and told him he must get up and join the company. He said he couldn't, and I told him that he must do so. He said he would be killed if he moved, but I remonstrated until he rose up and started forward. He had hardly gained his feet when a bullet pierced his head and killed him instantly."

A CONFEDERATE SOLDIER'S BAPTISM.

Captain Charles D. Wheat, who served in the Forty-ninth Virginia of the Confederate Army—Extra Billy Smith's regiment—was baptized at the first battle of Manassas. In reply to the question as to how he stood the first shock he said: "I confess that it was pride and fear of being called a coward that made me stand the racket. I went all through the fighting till the close of the war, and never went into battle without experiencing the same sensation of fear."

"Did you ever see men who could not stand the ordeal, that is to say men unable to move and absolutely overcome by terror?"

"I cannot recall to mind now an individual instance. I have seen men demoralized wholly beyond control and running away like sheep without apparent reason. There were two regiments of dandy young fellows in our brigade. They were outfitted in such handsome style that we called them the Bandbox Regiment. In the first battle they broke and ran like sheep. In the absence of Mahone, Extra Billy Smith was commanding the brigade. He was a man of indomitable will and great bravery, and rode among them shooting right and left at the runaways. Failing to rally them, he lost his temper, and, shaking his fist at the fugitives, shouted: 'Run, run, run, you blankety blank big blank scoundrels! I hope the Yankees will kill every son of you!'

"The same regiments afterward stood fire like old veterans in the most trying places and gained high commendation for gallantry. I have known men of prominence, privates, non-commissioned and commissioned officers to resort to every device short of outright desertion in the face of the enemy to avoid going into battle. I knew one officer who appeared to be dumb under fire. He was always found in his proper place, but never uttered a word of command or an exclamation of joy or fright. I have seen men act hysterically while fighting desperately. They seemed to have lost control of the nervous system."

A HARD STRUGGLE TO CONQUER FRIGHT.

Colonel W. R. Smedberg was first under fire at Gaines' Mills, and served until he lost his leg at the Wilderness. He never went into a battle without feeling a sense of fear.

"Did you ever see a man completely paralyzed by fright?"

"Yes, I knew a young man who was so terror-stricken that he could do nothing but cry. I knew an officer of the regular army who could not stand the ordeal of a battle, and I call him a brave man for this reason. In the first battle he did not behave as a good soldier. He was dismissed from the service, but made up his mind that he would conquer his fear and thus redeem himself from the stigma of cowardice. He was given a chance to enter the service again with the rank of Lieutenant, although he had held a Captain's commission at the time of going into battle first. In the second engagement he nerved himself to the task of going in, but the strain was too heavy for him, and he broke down again in the presence of his fellow-officers. After this he retired from the service, confessing that he could not stand fire. He was a brave man because he tried in the face of death the second time to overcome his weakness."

D. L. Smoot, ex-District Attorney, who served in Kemper's Alexandria Light Battery of the Confederate army, says he received the first fire from the "Gentlemen in Blue" at Vienna Station on July 18, 1861, near Manassas. He served throughout the war, being taken prisoner three days before General Lee's surrender. When asked if it had come under his own observation that some officers and men who had proved themselves good fighters in several engagements had not, in other contests, unexpectedly failed in their duty and shirked out of battle, he replied in the affirmative.

"How do you account for it?" was the next question.

"It's the fault of the stomach. I cannot account for it in any other way. Some of the bravest men have been known to break all to pieces with nervous alarm."

The writer, who served in the ranks, knew of one officer in an Iowa regiment who was wounded at the battle of Pea Ridge and promoted for bravery and coolness at Vicksburg, who broke down utterly at Lookout Mountain. A rumor was spread that his supply of alcoholic stimulant was exhausted during the night, and there being no way to get whisky "above the clouds" he lost his nerve. In view of the officer's former gallant behavior he was not court-martialed, but was permitted to resign and go home. There was something so frowning and terrible about Lookout Mountain that the view from the valley of the Tennessee did not inspire much hope of success in the attack. The fight on the sides of the mountain was only a prolonged skirmish compared with the next day's battle at Missionary Ridge.

Another instance of a soldier making a desperate effort to overcome fear is recalled by the writer of this article. The man referred to was a Sergeant when the company went to the front, but lost his chevron for bad conduct. He could not go into a battle. It was simply a physical impossibility. He confessed his chagrin at the taunts of cowardice at Pea Ridge, and resolved to redeem himself at Vicksburg, but again failed there. Still he had friends who believed that his sickness just before going forward to battle was not feigned and they did not turn against him. The night before the battle of Lookout Mountain orders were received to "march and fight" at 6 o'clock the next morning. The order was something unusual, the previous custom having been to simply announce the hour of marching if any order at all was deemed necessary. The man in question went forward with the regiment until a line was formed and a section of artillery placed near the company. The regiment was then halted in a position comparatively free from danger and rested there an hour or more. As the firing grew brisker and the lines of battle were disclosed the man was taken deathly sick. Everything was done by his comrades to relieve him and brace him up, but he was pale, limp and nerveless. It was no use; he couldn't hold up his head. He lay there on the little knoll near the artillery when the infantry line was advanced. He never had an opportunity to try another battle. A worse fate was reserved for him, for he was captured a few months later while on detached duty guarding a crossing of the Tennessee river, and taken to Andersonville prison. There he remained until the war was about over. He came out alive, but never recovered his health.

It is pride that makes a man stand up to the rack. At Vicksburg, when the ordeal was very trying, General Williamson announced to the Iowa soldiers of his command, that every man found skulking would be published in the Des Moines *Register*. This address to the men brought to the front a number of stragglers.

When the next war comes journalism will be so far advanced that the *Examiner* will have instantaneous photographs of every man of the National Guard of California in action.

(This article appeared in the San Francisco Examiner *on Sunday, 29 April 1888, p. 10. Given Bierce's interest in the subjects of bravery and cowardice at this time, his ongoing tendency to discuss aspects of the Civil War in his columns, and his reputation at the* Examiner *as its specialist on war matters, he is a prime*

candidate for the authorship of this piece. Bierce did not sign all his extra contributions to the paper beyond his "Prattle" columns. The fact that this piece quotes so extensively from exchange items is another reason Bierce might have been reluctant to sign his name to it. But Bierce did have firsthand experience in the military campaigns around Chattanooga and Lookout Mountain, and the last sentence of the article is characteristic of Bierce's continual ridiculing of the California National Guard.)

◄ APPENDIX C ►

THE FORTUNE OF WAR.
How a French Gunner Was Made to Wreck His Home.
[Youth's Companion.]

THE STORY IS TOLD in a French newspaper of Pierre Barlat, an humble laborer, who lived at Sevres, near Paris, with his wife Jeanne and their three children. Industrious, frugal, knowing nothing of the wine shop, Pierre saved his spare money, working harder and harder, and at last bought the tiny cottage in which he and his wife lived. It was a tiny cottage indeed; built of stones, however, with tiled roof, standing amidst shrubs and covered with clematis, it always attracted the eye of the traveler on the left as he crossed the Sevres bridge. Pierre and Jeanne scrimped and saved until the little cottage was paid for, and made a feast when it was all done to celebrate their ownership. A landed proprietor, to be sure, does not mind an occasional expenditure to entertain his friends.

All this Pierre and Jeanne had accomplished just before the war of 1870 with Germany broke out. The conscription fell upon Pierre, who, moreover, was an old soldier and belonged to the reserves. A gunner he had been, famous for his skill in hitting a mark with a shell.

Sevres had fallen into the hands of the Germans, but the French guns were pounding away at them from the fort on Mont Valerien. Pierre Barlat was a gunner at that fort, and was standing one wintry day by his gun, when General Noel, the commander, came up and leveled his field-glass at the Sevres bridge.

"Gunner!" said he sharply, without looking at Pierre.

"General?" said Pierre, respectfully, giving the military salute.

"Do you see the Sevres bridge over there?"

"I see it very well, sir."

"And that little shanty there, in a thicket of shrubs, at the left.["]

"I see it, sir," said Pierre, turning pale.

"It's a nest of Prussians. Try it with a shell, my man."

Pierre turned paler still, and, in spite of the cold wind that made the officers shiver in their great coats, one might have seen big drops of sweat standing on his forehead; but nobody noticed the gunner's emotion. He sighted his piece deliberately, carefully—then fired it.

The officers, with their glasses, marked the effect of the shot after the smoke had cleared away.

"Well hit, my man! well hit!" exclaimed the General, looking at Pierre, with a smile. "The cottage couldn't have been very solid. It is completely smashed now.["]

He was surprised to see a great tear running down each of the gunner's cheeks.

"What's the matter, man?" the General asked rather roughly.

"Pardon me, General," said Pierre, recovering himself. "It was my house; everything I had in the world!"

(This exchange item from Youth's Companion *appeared in the San Francisco* Examiner, *Sunday, 23 October 1887, p. 9, col. 4. It bears a strong resemblance to "The Affair at Coulter's Notch," published in the Examiner on 20 October 1889, p. 9.)*

❈   APPENDIX D   ❧

HADES IN TROUBLE.
An Authentic Description of Ancient Pandemonium.

SATAN'S BAD MISTAKE.
How Dissension First Crept Into the Happy Home of the Devil.

"**D**ID YOU RING, your Highness?"

"Put on some coals and stir up the fire; it's getting cold enough to freeze."

"Yes, your Satanic Majesty."

"Anything going on outside?"

"Nothing to speak of, your Highness."

"What are all the little devils doing?"

"Very little, your Excellency. They gape and yawn and stretch themselves and look rather blue. Some are aimlessly playing skittles, others are sorrowfully dawdling over mumbly-peg, divers couples maunder feebly over progressive euchre, while liquor solaces, in a measure, a few sad and forlorn spirits—"

"Stop! Stop! Stop! In pity's sake, stop! Time," burst out Moloch, rousing from the luxurious couch on which he lay extended, "Make an end. Existence is tedious enough without listening to a catalogue of the woes of others. Are there no contests, no broils to arouse the slumbering senses?"

"None, your Excellency."

Satan gaped and stretched himself. "Time," he said, slowly, "this has gone far enough. A little monotony goes a great way, even here. You must make a change, or you'll lose your place. You understand, Time, change all this or you'll lost your place."

"Yes, your Satanic Majesty."

"Or we'll have you up, Time," put in Moloch, "and see if we cannot find some diversion in your antics. Not that we'll kill you, Time," he added, with a smile, as the old servitor looked at him askance. "You furnish a great deal more entertainment than any of your predecessors, but if you hope to retain your place change this wearying round of monotony."

Time bowed humbly. "An't please your lordship, there's a wandering minstrel without—"

"Was that the strange noise we heard a short while since?" interrupted Satan, idly swinging his leg against the couch.

"Yes, your Satanic Majesty."

"Well?"

"An't please your Majesty, he's a poor, lone, wandering devil, and he came to the gates turning the crank of what he calls an organ, and he asked for hospitality and I took him in, as your Majesty has ordered that none shall be turned from your gates."

"Quite right! But why ain't he playing? Can he offer us any amusement?"

"Please, your Highness, he's touching up the deviled-ham and chicken. He says he's been wandering about chaos for I don't know how long, and to see him at the deviled-ham and wine you'd think he'd been lost in chaos twice as long. I cannot recommend his instrument for harmony, but the chances are he may be able to narrate something interesting about his travels. He must have seen much and learned more of that great unknown. Assuredly he has learned the good qualities of deviled-ham and wine." And old Time nodded sagely as he pictured the stranger making devastating inroads on his prime edibles and drinkables.

"Have him brought in," proposed Belial. "He may serve to while away a few moments. Anything—anything to mix with this dullness."

"Show the fellow in, Time," ordered Satan, "and let him bring his organ."

Time backed to the heavy curtains and disappeared.

The next moment he reappeared, followed by a devil, whose noble form and lofty bearing only seemed magnified by his coarse and well-worn habiliments.

Satan, Moloch, Mammon and Belial did not even glance up as the stranger entered the gorgeous apartment and deposited his instrument on the floor, but seeking new positions on their couches, they wearily waited for him to attempt their amusement.

Time whispered this in his ear and withdrew.

"Potentates and Princes," he began, "thy servant has been wandering [these] many seasons in chaos—chaos, that wilderness of hubbub and despair. To beguile the tedium of my unhappy way, I cast about for some instrument to interrupt the din by occasionally whispering in my ear some note of harmony. This mel—music—box was the result." He tapped it fondly and went on hesitatingly. "It—it may not be much, I confess, but considering the place, the means and the expanse I was striving to enliven, it was doing a—er—something. I will first offer a melody very familiar to your Majesties."

Thereupon he seized the crank, and giving it a few vigorous turns, he warmed himself and the instrument, and what might be mistaken for "Give the Devil his Due" began to wail forth.

But hardly had the first strains of the frightful discord broke the air of that quiet apartment than Moloch jumped to his feet with a roar. "Time! Time!" he shouted, banging on the gong, "seize the wretched wanderer and kick him into chaos again!"

The stranger drew himself up proudly, folded his arms composedly and [calmly] regarded the storming Moloch. "Kick?" was all he vouchsafed, very quietly.

Moloch started towards him, but as his blazing eyes fell upon that noble brow and regal bearing, he paused, gazed and stammered, "Wha—what! Beelzebub, as I'm a sinner!"

"What!" shouted the recumbent majesties, "Beelzebub!" and leaping to their feet they rushed towards the minstrel and fervently wrung his hands.

"Welcome, welcome home, our long lost brother. Time, bring in the wine!"

"Steady, steady, brethren," cried Beelzebub, embracing them heartily and rapidly.

"Where have you been? What have you been doing?" demanded Satan as they reseated themselves on the couches. "Ah, you were right, quite right, as you always are, in embarking on adventures to avoid the inactivity of this place, for I swear nothing can surpass it. We have scarcely moved since you left; we've simply lain stagnant. You'll conceive what it has been in that time when I tell you that that bit of rage just shown by Moloch is all that has stirred him since you left. Nothing can be drearier than our existence. But how has it been with you? Bless my eyes! I feel quite animated, even with the sight of you."

Beelzebub smiled, bowed and quaffed a beaker of wine.

"Bad as this place may seem to you, believe me, there is a worse place—chaos. I've been wandering, swimming, wading, sliding, creeping, floating, climbing, walking, flying, sinking and rolling over, under, around and through its bogs, sands, marshes, rocks, pits and cliffs, tossed in a universal hubbub. Had I not been animated with the labor of trying to escape that dreadful place I shudder to think what might have become of me. Behold your instrument," and he pointed to the hand organ, "consider that I turned it and to it for cheer, and you will form some idea of my dolorous wanderings."

"You must have met with misfortune indeed," confessed Satan.

"Stupid as this place has been we couldn't stand that. But didn't you find anything novel, see anything interesting, or hear of anything marvelous? You're not the one to do all that plodding without some profit."

"Ah!" said the traveler, his face lighting at the compliment and the [remembrance], "that did I."

The audience gazed at him with renewed attention.

"Do you remember," he asked, "that fable, legend, tradition, rumor, tale, prophecy or what you will, of a new race of beings? I know people are always inventing new devils, but this is an old, old story."

"Ha!" exclaimed Satan, "you don't mean that story of the devil with a tail and cloven feet, and long pointed ears, incased in flaming red cloth at $2 a yard and always appearing and disappearing in red fire, popping up from below at unexpected moments and—"

"Hold on," protested Beelzebub, laughing, "you are ornamenting him with all the fantastic attributes that have ever been conceived. But imagine him plain and unadorned and you mention the one I mean. I've seen him!"

"Seen him! Never! It cannot be!"

"I have, though!"

"Then he's a fact?"

"Yes, he sits under a fig tree on a spherical lump of clay down there on the borders of chaos and he's well worth seeing."

"Then it's really so," exclaimed Satan recovering from his surprise. "Has he cloven feet and does he wear a flaming red dress at $2 a yard, and how does he wiggle his tail?"

"Has he got a spear on the end of it, like the stories say?" put in Moloch. "I've seen pictures of him with a spear on the end of it.

"About all you've heard is nonsense," explained Beelzebub, smiling. "Whoever invented the tales about him drew immensely on their imagination, and those who have repeated them have lengthened and adorned the tails. No; the most you have heard is pure fabrication with a fiber of truth to hold the yarn."

"Describe him then; what is he like?" demanded Satan.

"As near like us in form as you can imagine."

"How many are there?" asked Moloch.

"Two, when I left; a man and a woman. Adam and Eve."

"Woman!" echoed Belial, rubbing his hands. "So she—was she—why, the deuce, couldn't you bring her away with you anyway?"

"I thought of doing a good many things as I contemplated them strolling about. You'll give me credit for knowing a little, won't you?" and he looked at the group interrogatively.

"Oh, a great deal, a great deal!" they hastened to protest.

"Well, then," he continued, "I thought it best to leave them where they are. I studied the species rather carefully, and between us, they have senses lying dormant in their natures that I don't think it would be prudent to awaken, least of all cultivate."

"Yes," urged the eager Belial, "but consider they might serve to liven up this peaceful, slow-going place."

Beelzebub shook his head slowly and said: "You think this place devoid of interest, slow, somniferous; believe me, with all its dullness it is far preferable to the world outside. Rouse yourselves, infuse life into your slothful bodies! Brethren, I have explored chaos and the places adjacent, and I've returned to take up my quarters here, contented. Sheol is good enough for me."

"Yes, yes," protested Belial, rather impatiently, "it's all well enough to talk like that when you have been wandering about, visiting worlds and interviewing strange people, but consider we've been rusting here in the meanwhile. Now, if we only had that new man and woman to amuse us, life might be bearable. I feel a particular desire to go after that woman."

"And I the man," declared Satan.

"Take my advice and leave them alone," urged Beelzebub. "This is a quiet uneventful place, I know, but mark my words, if you bring those creatures here and let their instincts develop the place will grow too hot to hold us."

"But only one woman!" protested Belial. "Surely one woman can't turn the place topsey turvey."

Beelzebub shrugged his shoulders, seeing the futility of further opposition. "I see you have made up your minds," he said, "and it's useless resisting, but I warn you that the result will be disastrous. As your brother I will stand by you in the consequences, but I affirm firmly and emphatically that I will not stir to bring them here. The fact is I've had enough of them already."

"We'll venture it alone then," replied Satan, rising and stretching himself.

And seizing the hand organ he flung it over his shoulder and disappeared through the curtains.

While the worthies were dubiously speculating on the favorable outcome of this venture, Mammon bethought of calling to their assistance a new art of prognosticating as practiced by inventive Time. The old servitor was accordingly summoned.

"Time," explained Beelzebub, "Mammon tells us that in addition to your many merits you are an excellent medium, a seer, a revealer of the future. Use your arts and tell us what will be the result of Satan's exploit."

The old man bowed, shivered and shook, and rolled his eyes, but before they could ascertain what ailed him, he began to speak: "I see a queer place and a queer creature, with long wavy hair, decorated with plumes. It must be—yes, it is—a woman. She is rubbing red ochre stripes on her arms. Now she sits down and begins to braid her hair. She braids, she rubs a little ochre off one arm, she changes a few feathers in her hair, and steadfastly contemplates a tree opposite. She gazes, fondly, hungrily. It must be the tree she is looking at; no, it is the fruit. I cannot tell from this distance whether it is an apple, or a peach, or—"

"No matter," put in Belial, impatiently.

"Ha! a snake appears. It cogitates. Wonderful! It speaks. The woman looks inspired. She starts to leave. The snake places a detaining coil about her waist and whispers something. The woman blushes and answers bashfully—"

"Time, no levity," put in Beelzebub, sharply.

"They converse quite amiably," went on the rapt medium, not heeding. "Aha! the snake impales the fruit of the tree on the tip of his tail and politely presents it to the blushing woman. She smells it, hesitatingly. The serpent squeezes her, smiles and says something. The woman takes a nip. The snake chuckles and digs her in the ribs with his tail. Ha! it was so sudden the woman bit her tongue. She bolts the fruit. The serpent tries to apologize and attempts to chuck her under the chin. She resents his advancing tail. She grabs a stick and makes a cut at him. The serpent vanishes in the brush and—bless me! it's—"

"What!"

"Satan! He seems rather crestfallen. He thinks deeply and sadly. He shakes his head and sighs. I see him go out the garden gates and carefully close them after him. He takes out a card and writes on it, 'Satan, Sheol,' and puts it in his pocket. He picks up a stick and takes the road marked 'Chaos.'"

"What does that mean?" demanded Belial.

"Methinks the card is to insure his identity should he be lost; the address signifies he is returning home."

"Without the man and woman!" exclaimed Belial.

"So it seems."

"Impossible! Time, you're a fraud. You don't know anything about the future unless it is told you. Go out and polish up your glass and con the cards till you can give us a better test than that."

Old Time withdrew, while the potentates, influenced in spite of themselves by his revelations, fell to their old occupation of disconsolately tossing on the couches while they impatiently awaited the return of the crestfallen Satan.

* * * * *

Beelzebub, Moloch, Mammon and Belial lay extended upon luxuriant couches in the great chamber of Pandemonium, impatiently awaiting the return of Satan, who had been absent a long time on his extraordinary mission of bring Adam and Eve to Sheol.

"But why should he remain silent so long, Beelzebub? Surely he must have succeeded by this time," and Belial shook his head rather hopelessly.

"How long has he been gone?" asked Mammon, after a pause.

Beelzebub concentrated his noble brow in thought.

"An't please your lordships," came from Time, as he protruded his head between the curtains.

"Time," interrupted Beelzebub, "how long is it since our worthy brother departed for the earth?"

"Please your lordships, I have trimmed my beard to the ninth number and—"

"So long!" exclaimed Belial. "Then certainly something wrong has happened."

"An't please your Majesties, there is one without, a peculiar sort of devil, who says he bears a message from his Satanic Majesty."

"From Satan! Show him in instantly." And the four worthies sprang from their couches, impatient to greet the courier.

In another moment the curtains parted and their eyes fell upon a comely youth, bearing all the outward semblance of themselves; yet at a second glance he seemed unlike, wanting both the power of physique and loftiness of look that distinguished the people of peaceful Pandemonium from the inhabitants of Earth e'er that unfortunate connection was brought about that destroyed the peace of one and the simplicity of the other.

"From whence come you?" demanded Beelzebub, closely scrutinizing the messenger.

"From the Earth and my—Satan."

"And thy message!"

"Is here," and he touched a scroll in his girdle, "for him who is Beelzebub."

"I am he," replied his interrogator.

The youth extended his scroll and Beelzebub untwisting the thong, proceeded to unroll and read, while his brothers gathered closer with the liveliest interest.

—Beelzebub and Brothers ALL—GREETING: This to thee in mine jeopardy. Rouse thee, my brothers, in the morning. Don thy warlike gear; take on the ingenuity to plan great deeds; fling our standards to the breeze, and with martial blasts awake the peaceful. Beelzebub, brighten thou thy wisdom; wake, wake, my Moloch, stir thy spleen and prepare to vent thy rage; Mammon, sharpen thy greed and whet thy avarice; furbish thou thy most insinuating graces, Belial, for I thy fellow, thy brother always, am in deep distress, and call unto thee for aid.

As was thou knowest. Through Chaos I took my devious way, nor did the confusion deter me aught. The organ of discords lies buried in the deepest pit thereof, and there wound up adds discord to the horrid din. Unto the Earth I come. I seek the man and find the woman of whom Beelzebub spake. Like him I blush and grow confused, oh, brothers, and like him, now knowing, I much disprove their transfer to our peaceful home and destroying that which late I knew not how to appreciate and enjoy. My eyes are opened and I see and testify unto you and bear witness that Beelzebub, our brother, was right in opposing the introduction of this couple to peaceful Pandemonium. Yea, and moreover, he was warranted in the exercise of force to prevent what I now perceive is a consequence most dire. But we, who knew not, knew not what we did. The ignorant may overcome the wise for a moment, but folly betrays him e'er the struggle is done.

But how is it with me, oh, my brothers? In truth, I am in much perplexity and extremity, and with contrite voice call upon you to come forth and rescue me from this man and woman. Woman! Belial, simple one, thou knowest not for what thou cravest. If thou art as steadfast in thy delusion, come, for the peace of thy brother come and take her away. For the man I will say nothing. Suffice it that he has initiated me into ways and practices that I fear will work much disturbance and more grief if introduced into our happy home.

Beelzebub, when late thou passed this way there were but two; now there are many, and do not you, my brothers, make the greatest haste to my assistance, there will be many more. The evils grow apace. Delay not, I beseech you for my own safety and for the security of yourselves. For since my eyes have gathered new light I can easily conceive that these creatures, big with their swelling boldness and rampant in their newly awakened senses, may make a descent upon our happy home and bring you all here to pander to their insatiable greed for amusement.

This will be handed you by my eldest—brethren, I blush myself—whom after much diligence and craft I have succeeded in dispatching on this mission that his life at least may be taken away from this wicked place. Take him in, educate and foster him that he may in time forget the place of his birth and know only the peace of our happy home.

From this infer as you can how I am situate; describe it in detail. I cannot, nor have I the courage to let you learn even a part. Question not my offspring, I beseech you. And further I pray that nought of what I have here set down may be hinted to those poor devils sighing around you with the dolefulness of their position. Come to me quickly, my brothers, once behold my plight and you shall pity, forgive and help me.

Of these words take especial note, and in your preparations hold them constantly before you: the woman and man of whom Beelzebub learned—oh, so little—and their daughters and sons are something far out of the ordinary. Be not exalted in your own valor, nor deem my rescue a trifling matter; for surely, and I speak after much experience and forethought, you will be called upon to exercise your greatest and most subtle powers.

Again, and of the utmost importance: Should I be not discernible on your approach, do not hearken with trusting ears to the words of her who will call herself Eve, or mayhap my mother-in-law, or mayhap my aunt, or mayhap anything that a ready wit may conceive, for her craft passeth our simple understanding. When she speaks, no matter how or why or where, brethren, be on your guard, your stoutest guard.

But come you as indifferent travelers or, better, mongers of new things, and on the crest of opportunity I will be borne to your arms. Till the moment is ripe I will communicate with you privily. It is best, as you will see.

Again I tell you that my relief can be compassed only by the exercise of the greatest wisdom and perseverance.

Come to thy lorn brother in his misfortune and come in they greatest power, lest we all be undone.

Thy forlorn, penitent and wistful,

SATAN.

Believe not, I beseech you, the wicked stories you may

hear concerning me. These people tarnish everything with which they have to do, nor will the reputations of the best escape their vilifications. Believe me, my dear brethren, contrition and tribulation have very much chastened and refined the one whom you esteemed so highly as

S.

Beelzebub heaved a heavy sigh. "As I thought," he murmured, and slowly rolled the scroll, pondering deeply.

Moloch, Mammon and Belial stood lost in wonder while the stranger curiously contemplated them. It was his voice that finally broke the silence.

"He told me to say that he couldn't portray the faintest semblance of his wretched position and feelings in any writing. Then he said to me, kind of white and gulpy-like, 'Nick,' said he, 'just do your greatest, my boy, to get them to come to my help; they'll fix you up soft for my sake.' 'Twixt you me I think the old man was coming uncommonly soft himself. He always does when he talks about his old home. Ah, I see you keep the cheerful here—good custom. If you don't mind I'll try a little bracer. That chaos is about the rockiest section I ever traversed."

"Oh, do you drink?" said Beelzebub. "Certainly, help yourself. Time, attend to the wants of the young man." But the young man was already liberally attending to his own wants.

"He seems to be at home," whispered Belial, as they covertly glanced at the expert traveler.

"Fine stock you keep," he volunteered, after sampling all there was in sight. "Seem to be rather downily fixed here, too. I think I'll like the place after I get acquainted. I'm to stay, I suppose, you know?"

"So Satan says; his word is law here."

"The deuce it is!" replied the youth, grinning. "They'd like to hear that on earth. How Eve would smile! I must drop the folks a line and tell them. They'll enjoy the joke. Who's the ancient individual?"

"Time, who looks after our pleasures."

"Chief Keeper of Pleasures, eh? Egad! I must cultivate his acquaintance, sure. Must know a good deal about 'em from his looks. Good time! Who're the others?"

"Moloch, famed for his strength—"

"He *is* a trifle muscular; more so than my uncle Cain, I should say. I'd like to see them in a little scrap. I suppose you have some lovely set-tos here occasionally? I saw some fine material as I came through the place."

"No," admitted Beelzebub, becoming somewhat puzzled. "The fact is we have very few amusements here. Pandemonium, as you must have observed, is very quiet. Doubtless you will be able to teach us many new games and tell us much of interest. You have—"

"Games! interest! Well, I should say so! I can tell you more tales while a lamb's bleating than you can rake together in all that infernal chaos. You got the king-pin when you got me. I can give the others on earth all the points of the game and then double discount them. Why! didn't you ever hear tell of me, Nick[?] But who's the one here who gathers the glittering spoils and rakes the tumbling futures?"

"Mammon, there, evinces great foresight in calculating chances and prophesying the future."

"He does, eh! Well, Mr. Mammon, I'd just like to try the stuff that's in you, the first chance we get. Pleased to know you, anyhow. But who's the other fellow? I like his looks and style," and Nick good-naturedly extended his hand.

"Belial, who is grace and affability. He has the art of ingratiating himself with all."

"I knew you were a flower. You and I will get on famously together, I'll be bound. And now, if it ain't forcing the custom of the place too much, and just to give our friendship a good send-off, suppose we—er—well, I don't know what you call it in this royal abode—but, drink, you know?"

"Call Time!" spoke up Belial, cheerily, who felt he had found his soul's companion. "Time, replenish the beakers!"

"Call Time, is it?" laughed the young man, betraying strong signs of his introduction to the cordials of sheol. "Ay, call Time, with a will," and he flung himself on the most luxurious couch. "Call Time, and I'll tell you fellows the latest and rummiest yarns on Earth; they'll make your hair curl, I'll stake a stack. You're rather high here, but you ought to see us at home. Can you make a cobbler yet?"

The potentates looked at one another inquiringly and dumbly shook their heads.

"No! Well, of course you can mix a cocktail?"

Again the dumb look of pitiful ignorance.

"What! Not mix a cocktail! Well, this place does need shaking up. You've got lots to learn yet. Fine things, both of 'em. I'll rattle the cups for you on the next round and turn you out some titillations."

He seized the beaker and swallowed the contents in great gulps; as he set it down on the little stand and patronizingly regarded the Princes slowly draining their beverages, he muttered to himself: "Never heard of cocktail! Suffering Satan, what kind of place is this you have sent me to?"

"You fellows are really fixed down here, but I don't suppose you know it," he went on, volubly, as his nervous eye glanced admiringly over the luxurious furnishings of the apartment. "So Satan rules this roost!" and he smiled. "I don't wonder he looks so glum now. I suppose you know things have changed a good bit with him?"

Beelzebub nodded gravely, and touched the scroll. "So this letter would seem to imply."

The other laughed boisterously. "Oh, that's nothing, nothing at all! I can tell you more in three breaths than that could if it was trebled. And smash me, but I'll do it! Of course, Satan won[']t like it; he's my dad, I know, but, then, I couldn't help it. You seem to be pretty good fellows if you are his brothers. Once more to our fortune," and he seized the refilled beaker.

"Pretty heady stuff," he remarked, as he set it down. Stays with one, eh? Like Aggie, she—"

"She!" exclaimed Belial, starting. "A woman?"

"Woman! Well, I should say so! The flower of the lot; red hair, gray eyes and such a figure! Oh, shake me! I'm going to bring her here first chance I get. My eye! but she'll liven up this old slow-going place for you."

"Entrancing is she?" queried Belial, thoroughly aroused.

"Entrancing? She's a stunner! A regular out and outer! I wanted to bring her with me. But, whew! the dander that dad got into when I mentioned it. Mad! I never dreamed he had so much fire in him. I thought the peaceful old curmudgeon was really going to try and lick me right where I stood. 'Take that woman to Pandemonium,' he screamed, 'and I'll—I'll—and I'm blest if he wasn't so mad he really couldn't speak. I believe the honest old fellow really swore. If he ever lost his temper like that 'fore I was born, I don't wonder he's got such a bad reputation."

"[I]s his reputation so bad, then?" inquired Beelzebub.

"Beastly!" replied the eldest son of his father. "To tell the truth, though, I never saw him do anything out of the way. But you see, he seems to have begun somehow with a bad name and it sticks to him. I've heard lots of folks ask how such an innocent, harmless old gent could be such a great villain. Then he's a poor sort of devil all by himself, and humanity kind of looks down on him as being a little out of his regular way. Fact is, they wouldn't tolerate him if he hadn't married into the family long ago, and got a little respectable foothold to hang to. He's my dad, I know," the speaker added, with a hiccough, "but that don't seem to help him much."

"But surely," said Beelzebub, "these people must respect his great attributes, his noble character, his lordly standing."

Nick smiled benignantly. "Go try 't yourself," he said; "'f you think any devil's goin' t' hog our earth an' beat us you're much mistaken. Here, Time, gimme some wine. Good ole boy. Who's your father?"

"But this story you were about telling us," suggested Belial, mildly, "about the—"

"Oh, you want late scan'ls. I've got 'em all. Heard that one about Zel'y? Course you haven't. I forgot. But I'll tell you a better one 'bout Eve—'s 'bout Satan, too."

"What, our brother!" exclaimed Belial.

"Same feller. When he first come to earth, met Eve. Say, when d'ye eat in this place, anyway?"

"But what happened when he met Eve?" persisted Belial, earnestly.

"Oh, that's ole story. Tell you bimeby. I'm sleepy. Chaos too much f'r me; tired; call me s-u-p-p-'r," and the wearied traveler rolled over in a sound sleep.

The tears started to Belial's eyes as he muttered, "I'll find out what happened when Satan met Eve if I have to go to the earth."

The potentates gazed upon the slumbering figure with troubled and anxious faces.

"Well," finally remarked Moloch, breaking the silence, "if this is Satan's eldest, what must his youngest be?"

"I wonder if this is the fruit of his great mission?" hazarded Mammon.

"Of course not!" replied Belial. "He was to bring two—a man and a woman. There's no woman yet."

"It seems he has changed his plans," Beelzebub suggested.

"Not to this extent," protested Beelzebub. "I never dreamed he had changed them to this extent."

"Well, it seems he has," went on Belial, eagerly, "and naught remains for us but to act as his letter prays. We must go to his assistance."

"We must go to his assistance," they all assented.

"And see these strange people."

"And punish them for ill-treating him."

"And bring our Satan home."

"And act a guard about sheol to prevent their ingress."

And leaving the wearied Nick buried in slumber they went and summoned their hosts, and carefully following the injunctions of the letter, they sped toward the earth to the rescue of the much-persecuted Satan.

A careful and diligent historian, whose reputation for veracity is unimpeachable, has shown in a work in which the brilliancy of argument has only been surpassed by the felicity of expression that the mission of this gallant host was far, very far, from being a success.

B.

⊰ NOTES ⊱

Introduction

1. Because the main emphasis in this book is on Bierce's thought and art, I have not attempted to discuss the tangential but also important topic of his influence on other authors. Demonstrably, in his own time he influenced Stephen Crane, Frank Norris, George Washington Cable, H. L. Mencken, and George Sterling. Decades later, he directly influenced at least Ernest Hemingway in America, Ryunosuke Akutagawa in Japan, Jorge Borges and Julio Cortázar in Argentina, Carlos Fuentes in Mexico, and William Golding in England. It is quite possible that his stories broke the trail for the stark realism of Jack London and others. One or more of his stories ("Killed at Resaca" is a likely candidate) might have made it easier for William Dean Howells, who knew and praised his work, to write "Editha." It is less likely that he had much, if any impact, on Mark Twain; they did not like each other. Nevertheless, the two authors had a great deal in common, and the time may come when both are read more for their similarities than their differences.

2. "I confess that I should like to see some of my 'damn good-natured friends,' who are always prating of my 'obscurity,' in order, apparently, to pose as 'discoverers of genius,' gently rebuked." From Bierce's letter to Walter Neale, 18 April 1911. Quoted by permission of the Berg Collection, New York Public Library.

3. Lee Clark Mitchell, in the *Columbia Literary History of the United States,* incredibly dismisses Bierce with only three or four sentences in a section that erroneously

pigeonholes him as a naturalist and determinist. See his "Naturalism and Languages of Determinism," ibid., edited by Emory Elliott (New York: Columbia University Press, 1988), 533. Although Harry T. Levin, in the earlier *Literary History of the United States,* also miscast him as a bohemian and trotted out the stale clichés that Bierce was Kafkaesque, Freudian, misanthropic, grimly facetious, and ghoulish, he at least devoted several pages to him and respectfully acknowledged Bierce's unique power. See his "The Discovery of Bohemia," ibid., 3d ed., edited by Robert Spiller et al. (Macmillan: New York, 1963), 1068–70.

4. From the time William Dean Howells selected "An Occurrence at Owl Creek Bridge" for his prestigious 1920 anthology, *The Modern Great American Short Stories* (New York: Boni and Liveright), most collections of "great" short stories have included some Bierce story, usually "Owl Creek." It is a rare college anthology of short stories that does not continue this tradition.

5. Wilson Follett, "Bierce in His Brilliant Obscurity," *New York Times Book Review,* 11 October 1936, 2, 32.

6. Adolphe de Castro, *Portrait of Ambrose Bierce* (New York: Century, 1929), xi.

7. Jay Martin, "Ambrose Bierce," *The Comic Imagination in American Literature,* ed. Louis D. Rubin Jr. (New Brunswick, N.J.: Rutgers University Press, 1973), 195–205.

8. Harry Lynn Sheller, "The Satire of Ambrose Bierce: Its Objects, Forms, Device, and Possible Origins" (Ph.D. diss., University of Southern California, 1945), 457.

9. Eric Partridge, "Ambrose Bierce," *London Mercury* 16, no. 96 (October 1927): 630.

10. Much the same defense for Bierce against the charge of misanthropy can be made as that which Jonathan Swift proposed for himself. In his 29 September 1725 letter to Alexander Pope alluding to his forthcoming *Gulliver's Travels,* Swift wrote:

> I have ever hated all Nations professions and Communityes and all my love is towards individualls for instance I hate the tribe of Lawyers, but I love Councellor such a one, Judge such a one for so with Physicians (I will not Speak of my own Trade) Soldiers, English, Scotch, French; and the rest but principally I hate and detest that animal called man, although I hartily love John, Peter, Thomas and so forth. this is the system upon which I have governed my self many years . . . and so I shall go on till I have done with them I have got Materials Towards a Treatis [*Gulliver's Travels*] proving the falsity of that Definition *animal rationale* [a rational animal]; and to show that it should only be *rationis capax* [capable of reason]. Upon this great foundation of Misanthropy

> (though not Timons manner) The whole building of my Travells
> is erected: And I never will have peace of mind till all honest
> men are of my Opinion.

The parenthetical qualification distinguishing himself from Timon is further elucidated in his 26 November 1725 letter to Pope when Swift explains, "I tell you after all that I do not hate Mankind, it is vous autres [you others] who hate them because you would have them reasonable Animals, and are Angry for being disappointed." See *Correspondence of Jonathan Swift*, ed. Harold Williams, vol. 3, 1724–1731 (Oxford: Clarendon Press, 1963), 103, 118.

11. de Castro, *Portrait of Ambrose Bierce;* C. Hartley Grattan, *Bitter Bierce: A Mystery of American Letters* (Garden City, N.Y.: Doubleday, Doran, 1929); Walter Neale, *Life of Ambrose Bierce* (New York: Neale, 1929); and Carey McWilliams, *Ambrose Bierce: A Biography* (N.p.: Archon, 1967).

12. McWilliams himself admits, in his introduction to the 1967 edition of his biography of Bierce, that he underestimated the literary quality of Bierce's stories. Even so, his comments on them often have value from the perspectives of biography and literary history.

13. I have not included the novel, *The Monk and the Hangman's Daughter,* in my purview mainly because the book is a translation from German, and Bierce's role in it was more editorial than substantive, nor have I included the prose satires that Joshi and Schultz collect and competently discuss in *The Fall of the Republic and Other Political Satires* (Knoxville: University of Tennessee Press, 2000).

Chapter 1

1. Carey McWilliams, *Ambrose Bierce: A Biography* (N.p.: Archon, 1967), 21.

2. Paul Fatout, *Ambrose Bierce, The Devil's Lexicographer* (Norman: University of Oklahoma Press, 1956), 9, 13, 16. McWilliams's *Biography* lists Bierce as being one of nine children (21). Fatout is followed here both because his biography is more recent and because he adequately documents this point. Unless there are compelling reasons to go to other biographical sources, however, McWilliams will ordinarily be used because, all in all, the revised edition of his book is still the most accurate, comprehensive, and thorough of all Bierce biographies, and also one of the best critical studies.

3. Copies of both this and the preceding letter of 13 February 1876 can be found in the M. E. Grenander Papers in the library of the State University of New York, Albany.

4. McWilliams, *Biography,* 24.

5. Fatout, *Devil's Lexicographer,* 25.

6. Edmund Wilson, *Patriotic Gore: Studies in the Literature of the American Civil War* (New York: Oxford University Press, 1962).

7. General W. B. Hazen, *A Narrative of Military Service* (Boston, 1885), 265 n. 1.

8. McWilliams, *Biography*, 6.

9. See Fatout, *Devil's Lexicographer*, chapter 3, especially pp. 39–40, 47, 48, 57–58, and McWilliams, *Biography*, chapters 2 and 3. For a reliable record of Bierce's Civil War experiences and the official assessments of him as a soldier, see also Napier Wilt, "Ambrose Bierce and the Civil War," *American Literature* 1, no. 3 (November 1929): 260–85. Roy Morris Jr., *Ambrose Bierce: Alone in Bad Company* (New York: Oxford, 1995), is at his best in his Civil War chapters and valuably expands the context of the information available on Bierce's war experiences.

10. "'Way Down in Alabam,'" *The Collected Works of Ambrose Bierce*, 12 vols. (New York: Neale, 1909–12), I, 328. Hereinafter cited parenthetically as "CW," followed by the volume number in roman numerals, and the page number in arabic numerals. Where items can be dated, the date will follow in square brackets.

11. McWilliams quotes a revealing Bierce comment from the 2 September 1881 issue of the *Wasp*: "I have marked the frontiersman's terror-stricken hordes throng tumultuous into the forts before the delusive whoops of a dozen lurking braves. I have observed his burly carcass scuttling to the rear of the soldiers he defames, and kicked back into position by the officers he insults. I have seen his scruffy scalp lifted by the hands of squaws, the while he pleaded for his worthless life, his undischarged weapon fallen from his trembling hands. And I have always coveted the privilege of a shot at him myself" (*Biography*, 74).

12. Ibid., 81.

13. Ibid., 85.

14. *San Francisco Examiner*, 3 November 1889, 6. Hereinafter cited parenthetically as "E."

15. McWilliams, *Biography*, 83. Bierce and Twain were more than acquaintances but less than friends. They probably met each other in the small literary world of San Francisco when Twain returned there for a few months in 1868, and they associated with each other when both were in England at the same time, 1872–74. They later became estranged, Bierce making sour comments in his journalistic articles about Twain, and Twain using his influence to undermine Bierce (see Grenander, "'Five Blushes, Ten Shudders and a Vomit': Mark Twain on Ambrose Bierce's *Nuggets and Dust*," *American Literary Realism* 17, no. 2 [autumn 1984]: 169–79) and damning Bierce with faint recognition in his *Library of Humor* (1888). How much of this mutual enmity was professional jealousy and how much personal antipathy is yet to be determined. Nevertheless, Bierce could not fail to recognize Twain's skill at wit and hoax and understand, at the very least, that Twain had set the bar for competitors, of whom he was one.

16. Davis wrote a noteworthy obituary for Bierce in the newspaper he published in San Francisco during the Panama-Pacific International Exposition of 1915. Davis concluded: "He was regarded by many as a cynical and morose man and

had many bitter enemies but the writer cherished a friendship of forty years with Ambrose Bierce and ever found him a lovable and companionable man of the sunniest possible disposition. He always had the courage of his convictions and his word was his bond. He hated sham and spent a lifetime puncturing hypocrisy and humbug. He spoke the truth and knew how to speak it grammatically" (*Forty-Nine Camp Appeal*, 1 January 1915).

17. Future scholarship would do well to explore Bierce's connections with the Sagebrush school of writers of Nevada and California, and those associated with it. Bierce by his own testimony visited the mining communities of Nevada, and Sagebrush writers often visited the San Francisco area, and some lived there for extended periods of time. In addition to Bierce's connections to Twain, De Quille, and Davis, correspondence from Joe Goodman to Bierce, as well as the fact that they published in the same issues of the *Examiner*, suggests yet another connection.

18. Reprinted in Ernest Jerome Hopkins, ed., *The Ambrose Bierce Satanic Reader* (Garden City, N.Y.: Doubleday, 1968), 170.

19. The untitled account was collected and republished in *The Fiend's Delight* (1873), 120–21, and is included here as Appendix A because of the difficulty of accessing that book.

20. "The Haunted Valley," *Overland Monthly* 7, no. 1 (July 1871): 88–95.

21. McWilliams, *Biography*, 148.

22. M. E. Grenander has established that *Nuggets and Dust* came out in 1873 instead of 1872, as previously believed. See "Ambrose Bierce and Charles Warren Stoddard: Some Unpublished Correspondence," *Huntington Library Quarterly* 23, no. 3 (May 1960): 265 n. 18.

23. Van Wyck Brooks, *The Confident Years: 1885–1915* (New York, 1952), 204.

24. The original text of this letter is in the Huntington Library of San Marino, California.

25. "Working for an Empress," *Wasp*, 23 December 1882, 826. See also CW, I, 349–59.

26. *The Lantern* 1 (18 May 1874): 2.

27. For a general overview of *Fun*, see Edward Stuart Lauterbach, "*Fun* and Its Contributors: The Literary History of a Victorian Humor Magazine" (Ph.D. diss., University of Illinois, Urbana, 1961).

28. McWilliams, *Biography*, 109.

29. Useful extracts from Bierce's *Alta California* travel letters have been reproduced in *A Sole Survivor: Bits of Autobiography*, ed. S. T. Joshi and David E. Schultz (Knoxville: University of Tennessee Press, 1998), 106–24.

30. One strong example occurs in his "Prattle" column in the *New York Journal* of 10 December 1900 (reprinted in my edition of *Skepticism and Dissent: Selected Journalism, 1898–1901*, by Ambrose Bierce, rev. ed. [Ann Arbor, Mich.:

UMI Research Press, 1986], 273–75), where Bierce argues against includ-ing Great Britain in the control of a transisthmian canal.

31. Joshi and Schultz, eds., *Sole Survivor,* 107.

32. Charles Farrar Browne ("Artemus Ward") died in England in 1867. Date, set-ting, and circumstances of the piece all make it impossible for Bierce to have met him in real life.

33. I am indebted to the diligence and generosity of S. T. Joshi and David E. Schultz for generously sharing with me their discoveries of Bierce's contributions to the *London Sketch-Book,* which they found too late to include in their *Ambrose Bierce: An Annotated Bibliography of Primary Sources* (Westport, Conn.: Greenwood, 1999).

34. M. E. Grenander, in her *Book Collector* article, establishes that although the pub-lication date of *Tales* is 1891, it was "manufactured" in 1891 but not released until 1892.

35. See Paul Fatout, *Ambrose Bierce and the Black Hills* (Norman: University of Okla-homa Press, 1956).

36. These and others have been collected in S. T. Joshi and David E. Schultz's *The Fall of the Republic and Other Political Satires* (Knoxville: University of Tennessee Press, 2000). See also my "Two Impossible Dreams: Ambrose Bierce on Utopia and America," *Huntington Library Quarterly* 44, no. 4 (autumn 1981): 283–92.

37. For the history of *The Devil's Dictionary,* see the introduction (especially pp. xvi–xvii) to David E. Schultz and S. T. Joshi's excellent edition, *The Unabridged Devil's Dictionary* (Athens: University of Georgia Press, 2000).

38. The historical background and an analysis of the story is to be found in G. Thomas Couser, "Writing the Civil War: Ambrose Bierce's 'Jupiter Doke, Brigadier-General,'" *Studies in American Fiction* 18, no. 1 (spring 1990): 87–98.

39. "A Thumb-Nail Sketch," CW, XII, 305.

40. McWilliams, *Biography,* 174.

41. *Wasp,* 14 July 1883. Also quoted in McWilliams, *Biography,* 45.

42. McWilliams, *Biography,* 188–89.

43. Ibid., 193.

44. A scrapbook of clippings of reviews from America and abroad, apparently com-missioned by Bierce, is in the Bierce collection of the Library of Congress. One of the most memorable is an undated one from the *Transvaal Weekly Illustrated:* "It may take you half an hour to read one of [Bierce's] stories, but if you have read it carefully and aright you are months older when you finish it."

45. For details see Frank Monaghan, "Ambrose Bierce and the Authorship of *The Monk and the Hangman's Daughter,*" *American Literature* 2, no. 4 (January 1931): 337–49.

46. See Daniel Lindley, *Ambrose Bierce Takes on the Railroad: The Journalist as Muckraker and Cynic* (Westport, Conn.: Praeger, 1999).

47. Much of his journalism from 1898 to 1901 is collected in my annotated edition, *Skepticism and Dissent.*

48. The *Collected Works* represent only a fraction of his total output, especially of his weekly "Prattle" columns, much of which is available only in the microfilm files of the *Examiner*. Moreover, his principle of selection was somewhat arbitrary. While certain of his works, such as most of his stories, were included, other stories were not and some of his best nonfiction prose pieces were left out. In a letter to Herman Scheffauer in July 1903, Bierce explains that he wanted his book of poetry, *Shapes of Clay*, to represent his work at its average and that because he felt it would be dishonest to republish only his best work, he included "trivialia" in it. Unfortunately, he seems to have retained that belief when he prepared the *Collected Works*, and many trivial "Little Johnny" dialect pieces crowded out much better works. Additionally, Bierce's dating of pieces in the *Collected Works* is often incorrect. His long essays, especially, are often conflations of shorter pieces written years apart and the dates for those reconstituted pieces can be very misleading.

49. *The Letters of Ambrose Bierce*, ed. Bertha Clark Pope (San Francisco: The Book Club of California, 1922), 196–97.

Chapter 2

1. *The Letters of Ambrose Bierce*, ed. Bertha Clark Pope (San Francisco: The Book Club of California, 1922), 204. The quotation comes from an unaddressed and undated letter fragment whose original Schultz and Joshi have not been able to locate. On the basis of internal evidence, it can probably be dated to 1902, when Bierce was anticipating a trip to his old battlefield sites, including the West Virginia ones, or to 1903, when he made the trip. He uses similar wording in a number of letters from 1902 and 1903. Schultz speculates that the letter from which the fragment came might have been addressed to his friend George Sterling.

2. Bierce retained a lifelong horror of suffering and mutilation. In his 22 December 1911 letter (in the Huntington Library collection) to his editor S. O. Howes about the death of their mutual friend Percival Pollard after brain surgery, Bierce wrote: "I *was* sorry that you could not be in Baltimore on Tuesday, but now I am not sorry. You would hardly care to have in memory the image of Pollard that I must carry for life. You'd not have recognized the handiwork of death. Poor Percy! he must have suffered horribly to become like *that*."

3. Helen Bierce, "Ambrose Bierce at Home," *American Mercury* 30, no. 120 (December 1933): 458.

4. Even so sensitive a reader as Stephen Cushman is ambivalent about this passage, admiring its accuracy and power but nevertheless misinterpreting Bierce's effort to distance himself from its horror as "cruel sarcasm" (*Bloody Promenade: Reflections on a Civil War Battle* [Charlottesville: University Press of Virginia, 1999], 157–58).

5. In the "Prattle" of 5 July 1891, Bierce recalls events from the Civil War that made him an advocate of mercy killing: "Scores of times it has been my unhappy lot to deny the piteous appeals of helpless fellow creatures, comrades of the battle field, for that supreme and precious gift which by a simple movement of the arm I was able and willing to bestow—the simple gift of death."

6. "Owl Creek" is discussed in full in chapter 6.

7. The gruesomeness of the engagement is recounted in horrifying detail in Roy Morris Jr.'s *Ambrose Bierce: Alone in Bad Company* (New York: Oxford, 1995), 83–86. General O. O. Howard continued to reap honors in his long career, and Howard University, in Washington, D.C., is named after him. Bierce, however, never ceased to remind "Prattle" readers of Howard's criminal incompetence at Pickett's Mill and denounced him whenever the opportunity presented itself.

8. Carey McWilliams, *Ambrose Bierce: A Biography* (N.p.: Archon, 1967), 53.

9. E, 11 March 1900, 26. As pointed out above, the *Collected Works* arbitrarily omits some of Bierce's best prose. Bierce also made editorial changes in some *Examiner* items he later included in the *Collected Works*. In order, therefore, to call attention to the importance of uncollected material from Bierce's journalism, to reconstruct fully and accurately the background of his stories, and to use an original text, I have made extensive use of the *San Francisco Examiner* and other periodicals and journals for which he wrote. When compelling reasons obtain, I cite the original texts in preference to those of *Collected Works*.

10. Bierce took a liberal view toward the defeated Confederates. He assumed that most of them had fought for what they had thought to be right, and he was willing to let bygones be bygones. He was especially angered, therefore, at the self-righteous superpatriotism of such militiamen as General E. S. Salomon who were notoriously unforgiving and who, in the name of the Union, practiced petty bigotry. In "To E. S. Salomon," (CW, V, 62–64), Bierce satirized him for his ex post facto chauvinism. In "The Confederate Flags" (CW, IV, 335–37) (but first published in the *Examiner* of 26 June 1887), Bierce asks that captured Confederate battle flags be returned to the units that requested them. From the chiding tone of the first line, "Tut, tut, give back the flags," the poem increases in seriousness and concludes that insurrection might be right or wrong, but that an honest and honorable man, though he had been an enemy, was more to be respected than a servile ally who had pledged his "manhood in advance / To blind submission."

11. McWilliams, *Biography*, 53.

12. The original letter is in the library of the University of Cincinnati.

13. H. L. Mencken, *Prejudices: Sixth Series* (New York: Knopf, 1927), 260–61.

14. In the *Examiner* of 29 April 1888, p. 10, is a long article on fear and bravery in battle entitled "The Baptism of Fire." Although it is unsigned, I assign it to Bierce on the basis of internal evidence (see Appendix B). Analyzing a number of specific "case histories," it deals with considerable complexity and sensitivity

with the issue of distinguishing the reality of either bravery or cowardice from their appearances. If my assignment is correct, the article is a remarkable insight into the workings of Bierce's mind as he was writing his powerful war stories. Also of interest is an answer Bierce wrote in the "Prattle" of 31 May 1894 to a correspondent who had apparently raised the question of cowardice in relation to a story, probably "One Officer, One Man," which had been collected in *Can Such Things Be?* (1893): "'Ned.' Thank you. Observe that the inexperienced officer committed suicide because, from many symptoms, he *thought* himself cowardly. It is nowhere intimated that he was." Here, again, Bierce distinguishes the *appearance* of heroism or fear from its essence.

15. George Sterling, introduction to *In the Midst of Life* by Ambrose Bierce (New York: Modern Library, 1927), i–ii.
16. Leroy J. Nations, "Ambrose Bierce: The Gray Wolf of American Letters," *South Atlantic Quarterly* 25, no. 3 (July 1926): 259.
17. Belknap Long, introduction to *Portrait of Ambrose Bierce* by Adolphe de Castro (New York: Century, 1929), 14.
18. J. Milton Sloluck [Ambrose Bierce], introduction to *Nuggets and Dust* (London: n.d. [1873]), vi.
19. For fuller discussion of "A Tough Tussle," see chapter 4.
20. The original letter is in the Berg Collection of the New York Public Library.
21. Ibid.
22. "Nature as a Reformer," *Cosmopolitan* 45, no. 1 (June 1908): [1].
23. McWilliams, *Biography*, 62–63.
24. Vincent Starrett, *Buried Caesars* (Chicago: Covici-McGee, 1923), 60.

Chapter 3

1. A shorter version of this chapter, published with my permission as a chapter from a projected book (which became this), appeared in *Critical Essays on Ambrose Bierce,* ed. Cathy N. Davidson (Boston: G. K. Hall, 1982), 136–49.
2. The original letter is in the Berg Collection of the New York Public Library. Bierce's *Devil's Dictionary* definitions of "romance" and "reason" are additional testimonies to the appeal of the first and distrust of the second. Further discussion of the issue of Bierce and sentiment will occur in the next chapter.
3. See *Argonaut* 2, no. 9 (9 March 1878): 9. A liberal attitude toward the Chinese is also present in "The Haunted Valley," which appeared in the *Overland Monthly* in 1871. In the *Wasp* of 24 March 1882, Bierce aligned himself with the abolitionist sentiment toward blacks. His later attitude becomes more complicated, as he sometimes ridiculed their aspirations to equality as being impractical, but the thrust of his remarks was never that they were inferior but

that society was simply not prepared to treat them as equals. On the contrary, he repeatedly praised the performance of black troops in the Civil War.

4. Bierce was outraged by the federal government's reluctance to infringe upon the sovereignty of a Southern state by demanding the release of some Italian nationals from what he considered arbitrary imprisonment. The Italians were released, however, before the incident reached more serious proportions.

5. One of Bierce's 1904 epigrams distinguishes his cynicism from the popular conception of it: "A cheap and easy cynicism rails at everything. The master of the art accomplishes the formidable task of discrimination."

6. The original letter is in the Berg Collection of the New York Public Library.

7. Item no. 5, "The Manual of Epictetus," *The Stoic and Epicurean Philosophers,* ed. Whitney J. Oates (New York: Modern Library, 1957), 469. Hereinafter referred to parenthetically as "Epictetus."

8. The implications of the temptation to read Bierce's Civil War stories as more or less all autobiographical is exposed by examining the background of "The Affair at Coulter's Notch." In all probability, the direct inspiration for the tale came to Bierce from his reading of a narrative of the Franco-Prussian war in his own paper, the *San Francisco Examiner,* two years before he published "Coulter's Notch." The source narrative, "The Fortune of War," is identified and reproduced for the first time as Appendix C in this book. Pairing it with "Coulter's Notch" dramatically illustrates that Bierce could conform even his war stories to his imagination, and that some ideas for plots, as well as the stories' philosophical content, came to him from his reading. Lest the impression be given that Bierce's tales sprang from single sources, it is important to acknowledge that his mind was apparently made receptive to "The Fortune of War" by other readings and experiences that made a lasting impression on him. In the "Prattle" of 1 March 1891, for example, he recounted two anecdotes that also have a bearing on "Coulter's Notch." One was a report that when Stonewall Jackson was a young artillery officer in the Mexican War, he was ordered "to fire into a certain street of a city. He did so, killing at every discharge women and children. Later in life he was asked if his conscience approved the act. 'Certainly,' he replied; 'your question should be addressed to the officer who gave me the order.'" The other was an item about the battle of Shiloh. A Federal artillery officer was ordered to fire on a column of troops. The officer recognized the troops as Union and so informed the general, but the general said he was mistaken and told him to obey orders. The officer promptly opened fire enthusiastically and caused heavy casualties to the column. Afterward, he made himself comfortable and lit his pipe. "When obeying orders it was his habit to obey them in letter and in spirit." Obviously, these two anecdotes (which do not imply agreement with the easy silencing of conscience) are contrapuntal to "Coulter's Notch" and represent a different direction his story might have taken.

9. Meditation no. 31, "Meditations, Book VI," *The Stoic and Epicurean Philosophers*, 530. Hereinafter referred to parenthetically as "Marcus Aurelius."

10. See chapter 6 for a fuller discussion of the story.

11. "The Social Unrest," *Cosmopolitan* 41, no. 3 (July 1906): 301. This article was a transcription of a debate between Bierce and Robert Hunter and Morris Hillquit. Hunter and Hillquit leaned toward socialism to varying degrees; Bierce opposed their views. The debate was inconclusive. Its main merit, apart from the sensationalism upon which Hearst publications thrived, was in its giving three public figures an opportunity of extemporaneously applying their respective philosophies to the issue noted in the title.

12. The original letter to Nellie (Vore) Sickler, 17 April 1913, is in the Bancroft Library, University of California, Berkeley.

13. The original letter is in the Berg Collection of the New York Public Library.

14. Adolphe de Castro, "Ambrose Bierce as He Really Was: An Intimate Account of His Life and Death," *American Parade*, October 1926, 32.

15. Carey McWilliams, introduction to *The Devil's Dictionary* by Ambrose Bierce (New York: Hill and Wang, 1961), xi–xii.

16. A transcript of this letter is in the M. E. Grenander Papers in the library of the State University of New York, Albany.

17. Joseph W. Slade, "'Putting You in the Papers': Ambrose Bierce's Letters to Edwin Markham," *Prospects* 1 (1975): 350.

18. A transcript of this letter is in the Bancroft Library, University of California, Berkeley.

19. The original letter is in the Alderman Library of the University of Virginia.

20. Quoted by Harry Lynn Sheller in "The Satire of Ambrose Bierce: Its Objects, Forms, Device, and Possible Origins" (Ph.D. diss., University of Southern California, 1945), 417, from *The Argonaut*, 9 March 1878.

21. Ibid., 438–40, 443–44, 448.

22. Sheller observed that Bierce never seriously imitated anyone. He was ready and eager to learn from the great intellects and artists of the past, but his creative genius adapted to its own purposes the suggestions and thoughts Bierce selected from them (ibid., 434).

23. Like many other authors, Bierce occasionally gives his characters names that suggest significant traits about them. The similarity of "Brayle" to "Braille" may be a clue to Bierce's characterization of Brayle as a man of feeling but not of sight.

24. La Rochefoucauld, maxim no. 220, *Maxims*, translated with an introduction by L. W. Tancock (Baltimore, Md.: Penguin, 1959), 62. Hereinafter referred to parenthetically as "Maxims."

25. Bierce's difficulty with accepting the philosophical sufficiency of individual maxims should be a warning against trying to infer his beliefs from the definitions of *The Devil's Dictionary*. The nature of maxims requires them to be memorable as well as pithy. Their writers, therefore, are often compelled to sacrifice

qualification for the sake of literary condensation, and the results are overstatements, striking in their simplification but reductionistic and canted for effect. The cumulative effect of Stoic epigrams at least cohered into a philosophical system, whereas those of La Rochefoucauld fall short, and the wittily irreverent definitions of *The Devil's Dictionary* do not even attempt to represent adequately the complexity of Bierce's thought. For that reason, his epigrams, with their searching ironies, are somewhat better, and the larger literary unit of individual short stories better yet, but the fullest treatment of his deepest and most characteristic philosophical positions can be found only in the interrelationships present in the corpus of his short stories written between 1887 and 1893.

Chapter 4

1. I say "unmistakably" because the entire tenor and drift of Bierce's remarks in his reply to "F. H. L." clearly indicates that "F. H. L." had questioned Bierce about a theory he had advanced in the previous week's "Prattle," by way of attacking "these little fellows, the so-called realists." A selection from that "Prattle" follows (E, 22 May 1892, 6; previously quoted in part in chapter 2):

    > In short, he to whom life is not picturesque, enchanting, terrible, astonishing, is denied the gift and faculty divine, and being no poet can write no prose. . . . He has not a speaking acquaintance with Nature . . . and can no more find

    > Her secret meaning in her deeds

    > than he or any other strolling idiot can discern and expound the immutable law underlying coincidence. . . .

    > Probability? Nothing is so improbable as what is true. It is the unexpected that occurs; but that is not saying enough; it is also the unlikely—one might almost say the impossible. . . .

    > Fiction has nothing to say to probability; the capable writer gives it not a moment's attention, except to make what is related *seem* probable in the reading—*seem* true. Suppose he relates the impossible; what then? Why, he has but passed over the line into the realm of romance, the kingdom of Scott, Defoe, Hawthorne, Beckford and the authors of the Arabian Nights—the land of the poets, the home of all that is good and lasting in the literature of the imagination.

    There can be no doubt that Bierce is here expressing one of his major critical tenets. The passage is reprinted in CW, X, 247–48, and is echoed in the *Devil's Dictionary* definition of "romance."

2. Fred Lewis Pattee, *The Development of the American Short Story* (New York: Harper, 1923), 302–3, 305. M. E. Grenander took a similar position in her dissertation when she applied the following observation to Bierce: "There were several pit-falls writers working in these forms [serious art forms of the tragic, the terrible, and the ghostly] might fall into. Probably the most serious was the danger that the artist would overshoot his mark and produce shock rather than legitimate artistic effects. Thus he must be careful not to attain the illusion of reality, which would cause pain" ("The Critical Theories of Ambrose Bierce" [Ph.D. diss., University of Chicago, 1948], 69). My disagreement with this position centers on the phrase "legitimate aesthetic effects." I certainly concede that Bierce op-pugned careless or self-indulgent overwriting that shocked readers unnecessarily or unintentionally, but I maintain that Bierce regarded shock as a legitimate aes-thetic effect when used purposefully and with control, and he not infrequently used it deliberately to cause discomfort.

3. Frederic Taber Cooper, "Ambrose Bierce," *Some Contemporary Americans* (New York: Henry Holt, 1911), 347.

4. M. E. Grenander, "Bierce's Turn of the Screw: Tales of Ironical Terror," *Western Humanities Review* 11, no. 31 (summer 1957): 258.

5. Ibid., 259.

6. Ibid. Although Grenander applies this insight only to lesser stories, such as "The Man and the Snake," its relevance to "An Occurrence at Owl Creek Bridge" will be demonstrated in chapter 6.

7. The last page of *The Fiend's Delight* (1873) has a picture of a donkey above the following quotation ascribed to Swift: "For my own part, I must confess to bear a very singular respect to this animal, by whom I take human nature to be most admirably held forth in all its qualities as well as operations; and, therefore, whatever in my small reading occurs concerning this, our fellow creature, I do never fail to set it down by way of commonplace; and when I have occasion to write upon human reason, politics, eloquence or knowledge, I lay my memoran-dums before me, and insert them with a wonderful facility of application." See also CW, I, 87. The full title of the Gulliverian narrative that begins on this page is "The Land Beyond the Blow / (After the method of Swift, who followed Lu-cian, and was himself followed by Voltaire and many others)."

8. Pattee, *American Short Story*, 306.

9. See above, chapter 2, 32.

10. CW, III, 254. The story originally appeared in *Cosmopolitan* 40, no. 5 (March 1906): 544–45. In CW, the following footnote is attached to the title: "Rough notes of this tale were found among the papers of the late Leigh Bierce. It is printed here with such revision only as the author himself might have made in transcription." The relative role of Bierce in the composition of this story is problematical. I regard this story as a legitimate inclusion in Bierce's canon both from the point of view of its relevance to his personal and artistic life and from

the point of view of craftsmanship. The story was not almost finished when it came into his hands; he developed it from *"rough* notes."

11. Carey McWilliams, *Ambrose Bierce: A Biography* (N.p.: Archon, 1967), 38–39. This charge was made in the original, 1929 edition of his biography and still appears in the text. McWilliams reversed himself on this matter, however, in the introduction to the reissued edition.

12. Robert Littell, "Bitter Bierce," *New Republic* 40, no. 515 (15 October 1924): 177.

13. Vincent Starrett, *Buried Caesars* (Chicago: Covici-McGee, 1923), 60.

14. Paul Fatout, *Devil's Lexicographer* (Norman: University of Oklahoma Press, 89.

15. An early manifestation of this line of argument (but still perpetuated by inertia) is in Bailey Millard, "Personal Memories of Ambrose Bierce," *Bookman* 40 (February, 1915): 655–56. "He [Bierce] prided himself upon being ruled wholly by intellect, never by emotion. But being, after all, human, he could not successfully live up to his vaunt, and occasionally we see him lapsing into tender passages in spite of himself." Millard's word "lapse" implies that Bierce abandoned reason in order to be tender. Although Millard intends to be favorable to Bierce—and is more so than most biographical critics—he posits an "either reason or tenderness" dichotomy that, in failing to take account of the organic, contrapuntal interrelationship of the two, precludes the possibility of tragedy in Bierce's stories and admits only pathos.

16. Percy Boynton, "Ambrose Bierce," *More Contemporary Americans* (Chicago: University of Chicago Press, 1927), 81.

17. I have adopted the term "rationalistic protagonist" from C. Hartley Grattan, *Bitter Bierce: A Mystery of American Letters* (Garden City, N.Y.: Doubleday, 1929), 161–62. In a discussion of Bierce's handling of ghost stories, Grattan uses the term and briefly relates it to them. I have expanded it far beyond his implications, however, and bear responsibility for the particular way I use it in this book.

18. Carey McWilliams, introduction to *Bierce and the Poe Hoax* by Carroll D. Hall (San Francisco: The Book Club of California, 1934), v.

19. Bierce perhaps implies a commentary of this sort of fiction in his *Devil's Dictionary* definition of "story": "A narrative, commonly untrue." One of the examples appended to the definition is an anecdote about W. C. Morrow, with this introduction: "Mr. W. C. Morrow, who used to live in San Jose, California, was addicted to writing ghost stories which made the reader feel as if a stream of lizards, fresh from the ice, were streaking it up his back and hiding in his hair."

20. The most compelling evidence to counter the position that Bierce took seriously his own writings on supernatural occurrences comes from Bierce himself in an admission he made in a 1901 "Prattle": "One day I got a letter from the secretary of the Society for Psychical Research. He explained that the society was greatly interested in these remarkable occurrences and would be pleased to have further particulars, with such corroborative evidence as I might be willing to

take the trouble to supply. I could have supplied the further particulars easily enough, but the corroborative evidence—that is where I was weak. Whether the society, doing the best it knew how without my assistance, published the narratives in its official records, or sadly excluded them as the work of one unworthy of belief, I have never sought to know." See my *Skepticism and Dissent: Selected Journalism, 1898–1901,* by Ambrose Bierce, rev. ed. (Ann Arbor, Mich.: UMI Research Press, 1986), 285.

21. E, 30 September 1888, 9. The subtitle does not occur in later editions of the story, including the first edition of *Tales of Soldiers and Civilians.* This is one of Bierce's war stories that seem to be based upon autobiography. The genesis of the story is related in "A Cold Night," one of four short tales grouped under the heading of "Bodies of the Dead" (E, 22 April 1888, 9). Considerably less complete than "A Tough Tussle," it is simply a recollection of an unusual reflex action noticed in a Confederate corpse. After a cold night, it was found with its knees hunched up near its breast, the hands inside the jacket, the head reclining against the collar bone, the posture of "one suffering from intense cold."

22. This point is supported by a "Prattle" column dated two weeks later (E, 14 October 1888, 4). In it, Bierce defended some passengers who had jumped from a careening cable car and had incurred injuries while the ones who had stayed aboard, too petrified to move, ironically were not hurt. He told of a similar occurrence in his own life—a boat collision—in which he had been injured while acting rationally, while others, rooted to the spot by fear, were unhurt. His conclusion is: "It will not do to judge the wisdom of an act in the light of the matured event; an act is wise or unwise the moment it is decided on and according to the light which the person making the decision then had. That which is most probable is not always that which occurs, but it is always that upon whose occurrence it is wisest to calculate." In short, even with careful reasoning, humans had best resign themselves to a certain number of misfortunes.

23. "It [the sword] was, in fact, Byring's own." This line does not occur in the *Examiner* original text. Its addition to the story removes the possibility that one of the Confederate raiders who had charged by had killed Byring with a captured Federal sword. This change, in turn, forces the reader to accept one of only two conclusions: that Byring had killed himself, or that the corpse killed him.

24. Like reports of live burial, accounts of humans being hypnotized by snakes, sometimes with fatal effects, appeared with some frequency in newspapers of the period. The *Examiner* of 5 May 1889, for instance, ran a three-column illustrated story entitled "Catalina: The Horror of Sleeping in a Chamber with a Boa Constrictor" that has some similarity to "The Man and the Snake." Although it is not here claimed that "Catalina" was the source of Bierce's tale, he could hardly not have been aware of the popular interest in the topic.

25. Marcus Klein, "San Francisco and Her Hateful Ambrose Bierce," *Hudson Review* 7, no. 3 (autumn 1954): 403.

26. Ambrose Bierce, introduction to *The Woman Who Lost Him* by Josephine Mc-Crackin (Pasadena, Calif.: George Wharton James, 1913).

Chapter 5

1. A possible reason for Bierce's abstention from dialect is given in a later "Prattle" column. In it, he denounced James Whitcomb Riley, Joel Chandler Harris, Mary Murfree, Mary Wilkins, and their "school" on the ground that their dialect "is not true dialect; it is simply English as spoken by none but ignorant people, and written, not by themselves, for they do not write, but by those to whom ignorance is attractive and seems picturesque" (E, 13 September 1896, 6). However mistaken, although ingenious, this argument might be, given Bierce's emphasis on precision and his fear of falling into maudlin sentimentalism, this comment says more about him than it does about dialect. Why he continued for most of his life to write the abominable "Little Johnny" sketches in the dialect of a very young boy from a rural background is probably a question that can never be answered definitively. He did not use the sketches to say anything of depth, and I suspect that he derived a perverse pleasure out of contemplating that readers seemed to like them.

2. Bierce's willingness to come to the defense of the Chinese has been previously mentioned. Bret Harte also took their side in some of his writings, the most famous example of which is the poem "Plain Language from Truthful James" (1870).

3. A parallel tendency in Bierce to concern himself with universals is noted, in another connection, by Carey McWilliams: "He elevated sandlotism to universal significance; he magnified it out of all proportion to scale or significance" (*Ambrose Bierce: A Biography* [N.p.: Archon, 1967], 135). Between this observation and Bierce's criticism of writers who use dialect, a reason for Bierce's discontinuance of the local color tradition can be surmised. His sense of the limited development possible of his characters Gopher and Whisky Jo. must have discouraged him from further experiment.

4. While I do not intend to suggest a direct influence by the use of this quotation, I think it is certain that Bierce studied Pope closely. In a "Prattle" column in which he discusses some of his own verse, he says "The influence of the 'Queen Anne's men' and of the greatest of them is obvious enough in these extracts, but for my part, I wish it were more obvious in the work of more men" (E, 31 January 1892, 6). Except for the clue that he frequently used the heroic couplet, the reference to the "greatest" of the Queen Anne's men is somewhat ambiguous in this context. A clearer idea of his esteem for Swift and Pope appears in his article "The Passing of Satire," in which he says, "If we had to-day an Aristo-

phanes, a Jonathan Swift or an Alexander Pope, he would indubitably be put into a comfortable prison with all sanitary advantages" (CW, X, 283–84).

5. In the *Examiner* version (29 July 1888, 9), the word "consistency" is used in place of "pitiless perfection" in the last line, and the word "one" is italicized. The stronger term in the CW version can be explained as compensation for the deletion of several clues from the earlier part of the story.

6. "I never felt so brave in all my life. I rode a hundred yards in advance, prepared to expostulate single handed with the victorious enemy at whatever point I might encounter him. I dashed forward through every open space into every suspicious looking wood and spurred to the crest of every hill, exposing myself recklessly to draw the Confederate fire and disclose their position. I told the commander of the relief column that he need not throw out any advance guard as a precaution against the ambuscade—I would myself act in that perilous capacity, and by driving in the rebel skirmishers gain time for him to form his line of battle in case I should not be numerically strong enough to scoop on the entire opposition at one wild dash. I begged him, however, to recover my body if I fell" (McWilliams, *Biography*, 45). McWilliams quotes this from the *Wasp*, 14 July 1883.

7. McWilliams, *Biography*, 45.

8. In the CW version, the word "Historical" is deleted, thus heightening the illusion of immediacy by not reminding the reader that the action supposedly took place in the past. The *Examiner* text will be followed in this discussion because it is more revealing than that of the revised CW.

9. The initial capitalization of "Commander" suggests an abstract or allegorical dimension; revision reduced the term to all lowercase characters. The CW version (II, 58–70) also replaces the image of a "river" parted by a rock to the less pointed "tide waves."

10. M. E. Grenander and I have a significant difference of interpretation on this story. She considers my dissertation's reading of it "based on the assumption that the story in the *Collected Works* [II, 15–26] is merely a revision of the original *Examiner* one." See her *Ambrose Bierce* (New York: Twayne, 1972), 128–30. The argument in my dissertation, as it is here, is *not* that the CW version is "merely" a revision of the E version, but that knowing about E helps us understand the CW version, which I have always regarded as superior in control and economy. She and I decidedly disagree on our understanding of the story. She finds a hopeful note in its ending. After making his "terrible moral choice," she maintains, Carter "has the mind and heart to make it and to endure and live with it" (130). There is no evidence whatsoever in the text that projects this postincident conclusion. She also maintains that E was "radically revised" to become CW (128). This is not so. Bierce made a few important changes (I've listed most of them) and some minor, stylistic changes, but by no stretch of language can the story be said to have been radically revised. It was

tightened up, made less obvious, but not altered in direction. I have considerably expanded my discussion of this story herein to make this clearer.

11. E, 14 April 1889, 8. The story is subtitled "An Incident of the Civil War" in the *Examiner* version, but this was deleted from the CW version, as was a reference in the second section to the incident's having happened "a quarter of a century ago." By removing specific references that would closely tie his stories to specific times, places, and events, and by making his tales more general, Bierce reveals his inclination toward allegory. The word "incident" is, of course, a noncommittal understatement, just as "affair" in "The Affair at Coulter's Notch" and "occurrence" in "An Occurrence at Owl Creek Bridge" would prove to be.

12. In "One of the Missing" (1888), Bierce also likens its soldier protagonist Jerome Searing to a rat. Even Searing is "perfectly conscious of his rathood."

13. Because of the obvious human interest involved, anecdotes of such incidents were frequently circulated among newspapers during the Civil War. One such, from the *Sacramento Daily Union*, 2 June 1862, 8:3, is about the battle of Pittsburg Landing, the prelude to Shiloh, and claims to have been "related by an eye and ear witness": "Two Kentucky regiments met face to face, and fought each other with terrible resolution, and it happened that one of the Federal soldiers wounded and captured his brother, and after handing him back, began firing at a man near a tree, when the captured brother called to him and said: 'Don't shoot there any more—that's father!'"

14. "Peace, be still" is from Mark 4:39. Although the quote is literally appropriate, its context forms a completely ironic contrast to Carter's situation.

Chapter 6

1. Letter from Crane to Richard Harding Davis. *Stephen Crane: Letters*, ed. R. V. Stallman and Lillian Gilkes (New York: New York University, 1960), 139–40 n. 94.

2. Bierce's manipulation of topography and the railroad is detailed in David M. Owens, "Bierce and Biography: The Location of Owl Creek Bridge," *American Literary Realism* 26 (spring 1994): 82–89. Years later, Hemingway also altered topography in "The Big Two-Hearted River" to keep the name of the river.

3. Sam Davis, *Short Stories* (San Francisco: Golden Era, 1886), 96.

4. In the "Prattle" of 14 February 1892 (rev. "The Chair of Little Ease," CW, XI, 365–66), Bierce objected vigorously to the claim of physicians that a man executed by electricity suffered no pain. "The physicians know nothing about it; for anything they know to the contrary, death by electricity may be the most frightful torment that it is possible for any of nature's forces or processes to produce. The agony may be not only inconceivably great, but to the sufferer it may seem to endure for a period inconceivably long. . . . Through what unnatural

exaltation of the senses may not the moment of its [death by electricity] accomplishing be commuted into unthinkable cycles of time?" Even though this comment was written more than a year after the publication of "Owl Creek" and addresses electrocution and not hanging, it nevertheless reflects Bierce's ongoing interest in how a moment of "real time" might be translated by a moribund mind into perceptions of stretched time.

5. In other essays, I have argued that not only did Mark Twain, for example (who began his literary career in Nevada with colleagues of the Sagebrush School), use the hoax in his major works of literature but that hoaxes are in fact at the heart of them. See, for example, "The 'Poor Players' of *Huckleberry Finn*," *Papers of the Michigan Academy* 53 (1968): 291–31; "*A Connecticut Yankee:* A Serious Hoax," *Essays in Arts and Sciences* 19 (May 1990): 28–44; and "The Trickster God in *Roughing It*," *Thalia* 18, no. 1–2 (1998): 21–30 repr. in Jeanne Campbell Reesman, ed., *Trickster Lives: Culture and Myth in American Fiction* (Athens: University of Georgia Press, 2001), 84–96. The history of the literary hoax is long and distinguished and includes such outstanding works by Bierce's model Swift as "A Modest Proposal" and, perhaps, *Gulliver's Travels*.

6. This phrase and the previous quotation come from chapter 14 of Coleridge's *Biographia Literaria*.

7. Roy Morris Jr. suggests that Farquhar could have evaded military service on the basis of the "Twenty Negro Law," which exempted slave owners from active service if they had more than twenty slaves on their property (*Ambrose Bierce: Alone in Bad Company* [New York: Oxford, 1995], 217). Even if Bierce was aware of this law, he also would have known that many slave owners waived this right in order to serve. In any case, Farquhar's civilian status does not befit such a supposedly ardent patriot—as he wishes to think himself.

8. In "One Officer, One Man" (originally titled "A Coward" [1889]), the protagonist Capt. Graffenreid also is impatient at being posted behind the lines, away from the fields of Death or Glory. He gets his wish to go to the front, and there he finds death, but not glory.

9. Bierce here again involves readers in a practical demonstration of the limits of reason, showing how truth sometimes cannot be determined except in retrospect.

10. Bierce was fully aware that he was manipulating grammar. The earlier story, "A Son of the Gods," was originally subtitled "A Study in the Historical Present Tense."

11. According to a recent dissertation by Donald Blume, Bierce apparently knew that there may be as much as a fifteen-minute interval between the fatal snapping of the neck in a hanging and the moment of medical death ("Ambrose Bierce's Civilians and Soldiers in Context: A Critical Study" [Ph.D. diss., Florida State University, 2000], chapter 14). Therefore, Blume argues, there was enough time for Farquhar to imagine his entire fantasy. But the fantasy precedes

the breaking of the neck. Furthermore, the text conjoins immediately the blow on the neck, the blinding light and loud sound (probably the neck snapping), then darkness and silence, so it does not appear that Bierce, even if he did have this knowledge, applied it in the story. In this respect the Sam Davis story seems closer to the mark, with its emphasis on the blazing mind making use of the instant between the start of the fall and the breaking of the neck. This construction has the added advantage of continuing the process of mental acceleration and the consequent stretching out of time begun before Farquhar dropped. And it is supported by the story's last line, in which death is implied by a still swinging body.

12. F. J. Logan, "The Wry Seriousness of 'Owl Creek Bridge,'" *American Literary Realism* 10, no. 2 (spring 1977): 101–13. Logan, however, apparently mixed two of Zeno's paradoxes: that of Achilles pursuing a tortoise and that of an arrow in flight. For the sake of literal accuracy, I have reverted to the first and more pertinent one.

13. Thomas Beer, *The Mauve Decade* (New York: Vintage, 1961), 64. Evidence of the unreliability of Beer's formerly respected and influential "scholarship" is presented in the exposé by Stanley Wertheim and Paul Sorrentino, "Thomas Beer: The Clay Feet of Stephen Crane Biography," *American Literary Realism* 22, no. 3 (spring 1990): 2–16.

Chapter 7

1. Neither Swift nor Poe, for example, two authors Bierce obviously admired and emulated, was highly regarded by most nineteenth-century critics. All three writers were considered somewhat aberrant, because their subject matter and style were too outré for the times and were thought to be projections of their abnormal personalities.

2. Carey McWilliams, *Ambrose Bierce: A Biography* (N.p.: Archon, 1967), 200. See also Sam Davis's compliment of Bierce's disposition in chapter 1, n. 9.

3. See my article "'A Strange Adventure': The Story Behind a Bierce Tale," *American Literary Realism* 14, no. 1 (spring 1981): 70–76, for both the text of Morrow's sketch and my explanation of its significance.

4. "A Baby Tramp" may be read either as an ironic contrast to "The Little Story" (1874) or as an indication of a later change of heart by Bierce.

5. See Appendix D for the text, which at present is otherwise available only in my introduced edition of it, "'Hades in Trouble': A Rediscovered Story by Ambrose Bierce," *American Literary Realism* 25, no. 2 (winter 1993): 67–84.

6. S. T. Joshi and David E. Schultz's *The Fall of the Republic and Other Political Satires* (Knoxville: University of Tennessee Press, 2000), with notes and commentary, is

the most complete and competent compilation of these satires, many of which have been hitherto almost entirely overlooked.

7. From 1887 through 1889, Bierce subtitled his "Prattle" columns "A Record of Individual Opinion." In 1890, he modified the subtitle to "A Record of Transient Individual Opinion." In 1899, he sometimes retitled his columns "The Passing Show: A Record of Personal Opinion and Dissent." Still later, he occasionally titled his columns "The Curmudgeon Philosopher" and "The Bald Campaigner." Despite the self-disparagement, however, the columns serve as an almost Cassandraic and therefore valuable history of his time and place. It is inadequate to pigeonhole Bierce as a conservative, for some of his stands were ahead of his time. See Janet Francendese, "Ambrose Bierce as Journalist" (Ph.D. diss., New York University, 1977), for an excellent overview of some recurrent positions he advocated in his journalism, and my *Skepticism and Dissent* (Ann Arbor, Mich.: Delmas, 1980; rev. ed., Ann Arbor, Mich.: UMI Research Press, 1986) for an edition and analysis of his journalism of the period 1898–1901.

8. Edgar Lee Masters, "English Thornton," *Spoon River Anthology* (1916), ed. John E. Hallwas (Urbana: University of Illinois Press, 1992), 247:

> Here! You sons of the men
> Who fought with Washington at Valley Forge,
> And whipped Black Hawk at Starved Rock,
> Arise! Do battle with the descendants of those
> Who bought land in the loop when it was waste sand,
> And sold blankets and guns to the army of Grant,
> And sat in legislatures in the early days,
> Taking bribes from the railroads.
> Arise! Do battle with the fops and bluffs,
> The pretenders and figurantes of the society column
> And the yokel souls whose daughters marry counts;
> And the parasites on great ideas,
> And the noisy riders of great causes,
> And the heirs of ancient thefts.
> Arise! And make the city yours,
> And the State yours—
> You who are sons of the hardy yeomanry of the forties!
> By God! If you do not destroy these vermin
> My avenging ghost will wipe out
> Your city and your state. . . .

In his famous poem "Invocation" (E, 5 July 1888, repr. CW, IV, 34–39), Bierce uses a different form but anticipates the sentiment of "English Thornton."

9. The "Parenticide Club" tales constitute a unit in CW, VIII, 147–184.
10. C. Stuart Woodruff, *The Short Stories of Ambrose Bierce: A Study in Polarity* (Pittsburgh: University of Pittsburgh Press, 1964), 117; Roy Morris Jr., *Ambrose Bierce: Alone in Bad Company* (New York: Oxford, 1995), 191; Jay Martin, "Ambrose Bierce," *The Comic Imagination in American Literature,* ed. Louis D. Rubin Jr. (New Brunswick, N.J.: Rutgers University Press, 1973), 204–5; Cathy Davidson, foreword to *The Complete Short Stories of Ambrose Bierce,* comp. Ernest Jerome Hopkins (Lincoln: University of Nebraska Press, 1984), 3–4; M. E. Grenander, *Ambrose Bierce* (New York: Twayne, 1971), 131–32.
11. In an undated scrapbook clipping of one of Bierce's columns is the following relevant comment: "Sin is not at all dangerous to society; what does all the mischief is the sinner. Crime has no arms to thrust into the public treasury; no hands with which to cut a throat, no tongue to wreck a reputation withal. I would no more attack it than an isosceles triangle. . . . My chosen enemy must be something that has a skin for my switch, a head for my cudgel—something that can smart and ache."
12. Charles Dickens, of course, in such novels as *Oliver Twist* (1837–38) and *David Copperfield* (1849–50), was the era's most outspoken critic of mistreatment of children. In naming Dotheboys (lit. "kill" the boys) Hall in *Nicholas Nickleby* (1838–39), Dickens anticipated Bierce in being so daringly and sardonically direct.
13. Both stories show the influence of Poe; "The Widower Turmore," especially, incorporates details of plot obviously derived from "The Cask of Amontillado."
14. George Sherburn, "The Restoration and Eighteenth Century," *A Literary History of England,* ed. Albert C. Baugh (New York: Appleton-Century-Crofts, 1948), 860–61.
15. Carey McWilliams, introduction to *Bierce and the Poe Hoax,* by Carroll D. Hall (San Francisco: The Book Club of California, 1934), iii–vi. The very beginning of his career in his San Francisco Mint days was largely occupied with "devising literary mischiefs" with his friends. Bierce later disparaged his early work as lacking "literary sincerity," and confessed of his entire career that in it he was "addicted to trifling," but this self-depreciation is too sweeping and too harsh. Bierce, for example, disparaged all his journalism on the ground that only literature deserved praise and that his journalism was not literature.
16. *Argonaut,* 29 September 1877.
17. See Carroll D. Hall, *Bierce and the Poe Hoax.*
18. Cathy N. Davidson, *The Experimental Fictions of Ambrose Bierce: Structuring the Ineffable* (Lincoln: University of Nebraska Press, 1984), 103–14.
19. F. J. Logan is certainly correct when he observes that "a Bierce passage depends heavily for its success upon the strength and smooth articulation of its logical skeleton. The germ of most good Bierce passages is logical, and accretes about

it the other elements of prose, naturally, as it evolves" ("The Wry Seriousness of 'Owl Creek Bridge,'" *American Literary Realism* 10, no. 2 [spring 1977]: 135).

20. See the exchange between Franz Rottensteiner and E. F. Bleiler in *Science Fiction Studies* 15 (1988) on the story. Rottensteiner believes that Moxon's automaton contained a human man inside, probably a homosexual lover of Moxon (107–12, 388–90), whereas Bleiler maintains that it contained a woman, Moxon's mistress (386–88). Damon Knight is closer to the mark when he summarily sets aside both interpretations and ironically praises Bierce's "ingenuity in creating puzzles for unborn scholars" in *Science Fiction Studies* 16 (1989): 117.

21. I paraphrase here one of Bierce's statements in "The Social Unrest," a transcript of a debate between Bierce, Morris Hillquit, and Robert Hunter. Hillquit and Hunter leaned toward socialism; Bierce opposed their views.

22. *New York Journal*, 16 December 1900.

☙ BIBLIOGRAPHY ❧

Beer, Thomas. *The Mauve Decade.* New York: Vintage, 1961.

Berkove, Lawrence I. "Ambrose Bierce." *Updating the Literary West.* Sponsored by the Western Literature Association, 209–13. Fort Worth: Texas Christian University Press, 1997.

———. "Ambrose Bierce's Concern with Mind and Man." Ph.D. diss., University of Pennsylvania, 1962.

———. "Arms and the Man: Ambrose Bierce's Response to War." *Michigan Academician* 1, no. 1–2 (winter 1969): 21–30.

———. "*A Connecticut Yankee:* A Serious Hoax." *Essays in Arts and Sciences* 19 (May 1990): 28–44.

———. "'Hades in Trouble': A Rediscovered Story by Ambrose Bierce." *American Literary Realism* 25, no. 2 (winter 1993): 67–84.

———. "The Heart Has Its Reasons: Ambrose Bierce's Successful Failure at Philosophy." *Critical Essays on Ambrose Bierce,* edited by Cathy N. Davidson, 136–49. Boston: G. K. Hall, 1982.

———. "The Man with the Burning Pen: Ambrose Bierce as Journalist." *Journal of Popular Culture* 15, no. 2 (fall 1981): 34–40.

———. "The 'Poor Players' of *Huckleberry Finn.*" *Papers of the Michigan Academy* 53 (1968): 291–310.

———. "A Possible Influence of Bierce upon Cable." *Markham Review* 7 (spring 1978): 59–60.

———. "The Romantic Realism of Bierce and Norris." *Frank Norris Studies* 15 (spring 1993): 13–17.

————. "'A Strange Adventure': The Story behind a Bierce Tale." *American Literary Realism* 14, no. 1 (spring 1981): 70–76.

————. "The Trickster God in *Roughing It*." *Thalia* 18, no. 1–2 (1998): 21–30.

————. "Two Impossible Dreams: Ambrose Bierce on Utopia and America." *Huntington Library Quarterly* 44, no. 4 (autumn 1981): 283–92.

————, ed. *Skepticism and Dissent: Selected Journalism, 1898–1901,* by Ambrose Bierce. Ann Arbor, Mich.: Delmas, 1980; rev. ed., Ann Arbor, Mich.: UMI Research Press, 1986.

Bierce, Ambrose. *Can Such Things Be?* New York: Cassell, 1893.

————. *The Collected Works of Ambrose Bierce.* 12 vols. New York: Neale, 1909–12.

————. Introduction to *The Woman Who Lost Him,* by Josephine McCrackin. Pasadena, Calif.: George Wharton James, 1913.

————. "Nature as a Reformer." *Cosmopolitan* 45, no. 1 (June 1908): [1].

————. "The Social Unrest." *Cosmopolitan* 41, no. 3 (July 1906): 297–302.

————. *Tales of Soldiers and Civilians.* San Francisco: E. L. G. Steele, 1891 [1892].

Bierce, Helen. "Ambrose Bierce at Home." *American Mercury* 30, no. 120 (December 1933): 453–58.

Bleiler, E. F. "More on 'Moxon's Master.'" *Science-Fiction Studies* 15 (1998): 386–88.

Blume, Donald Thomas. "Ambrose Bierce's Civilians and Soldiers in Context: A Critical Study." Ph.D. diss., Florida State University, 2000.

Boynton, Percy. "Ambrose Bierce." *More Contemporary Americans.* Chicago: University of Chicago Press, 1927.

Brooks, Van Wyck. *The Confident Years: 1885–1915.* New York: Dutton, 1952.

Coleridge, Samuel Taylor. *Biographia Literaria,* edited by J. C. Metcalf. New York: Macmillan, 1926.

Cooper, Frederick Taber. "Ambrose Bierce." *Some American Story Tellers.* New York: Henry Holt, 1911.

Couser, G. Thomas. "Writing the Civil War: Ambrose Bierce's 'Jupiter Doke, Brigadier-General.'" *Studies in American Fiction* 18, no. 1 (spring 1990): 87–98.

Cushman, Stephen. *Bloody Promenade: Reflections on a Civil War Battle.* Charlottesville: University Press of Virginia, 1999.

Davidson, Cathy N., ed. *Critical Essays on Ambrose Bierce.* Boston: G. K. Hall, 1982.

————. *The Experimental Fictions of Ambrose Bierce: Structuring the Ineffable.* Lincoln: University of Nebraska Press, 1984.

————. Foreword to *The Complete Short Stories of Ambrose Bierce,* compiled by Ernest Jerome Hopkins. Lincoln: University of Nebraska Press, 1984.

Davis, Sam. *Short Stories.* San Francisco: Golden Era, 1886.

de Castro, Adolphe [Adolph Danziger]. "Ambrose Bierce as He Really Was: An Intimate Account of His Life and Death." *American Parade,* October 1926, 28–44.

————. *Portrait of Ambrose Bierce.* New York: Century, 1929.

Fatout, Paul. *Ambrose Bierce and the Black Hills.* Norman: University of Oklahoma Press, 1956.

————. *Ambrose Bierce, The Devil's Lexicographer.* Norman: University of Oklahoma Press, 1951.

Follett, Wilson. "Bierce in His Brilliant Obscurity." *New York Times Book Review,* 11 October 1936, 2, 32.

Francendese, Janet. "Ambrose Bierce as Journalist." Ph.D. diss., New York University, 1977.

Gale, Robert L. *An Ambrose Bierce Companion.* Westport, Conn.: Greenwood Press, 2001.

Grattan, C. Hartley. *Bitter Bierce: A Mystery of American Letters.* Garden City, N.Y.: Doubleday, Doran, 1929.

Grenander, M. E. *Ambrose Bierce.* Twayne's United States Author Series, no. 180. New York: Twayne, 1971.

————. "Ambrose Bierce and Charles Warren Stoddard: Some Unpublished Correspondence." *Huntington Library Quarterly* 23, no. 3 (May 1960): 261–92.

————. "Ambrose Bierce and *In the Midst of Life.*" *Book Collector* (autumn 1971): 321–31.

————. "Bierce's Turn of the Screw: Tales of Ironical Terror." *Western Humanities Review* 11, no. 31 (summer 1957): 257–64.

————. "The Critical Theories of Ambrose Bierce." Ph.D. diss., University of Chicago, 1948.

————. "Five Blushes, Ten Shudders and a Vomit." *American Literary Realism* 17, no. 2 (autumn 1984): 169–79.

Grile, Dod [Ambrose Bierce]. *Cobwebs from an Empty Skull.* London: Routledge, 1874.

————. *The Fiend's Delight.* London: Hotten, 1873.

————. *Nuggets and Dust Panned Out in California.* "Collected and Loosely Arranged by J. Milton Sloluck [Ambrose Bierce]." London: Chatto and Windus, 1872 [1873].

Hall, Carroll D. *Bierce and the Poe Hoax.* San Francisco: The Book Club of California, 1934.

Hazen, Gen. W. B. *A Narrative of Military Service.* Boston: Ticknor, 1885.

Hopkins, Ernest Jerome, ed. *The Ambrose Bierce Satanic Reader.* Garden City, N.Y.: Doubleday, 1968.

Howells, William Dean, comp. and ed. *The Modern Great American Short Stories.* New York: Boni and Liveright, 1920.

Joshi, S. T. *The Collected Fables of Ambrose Bierce.* Columbus: The Ohio State University Press, 2000.

Joshi, S. T., and David E. Schultz, eds. *Ambrose Bierce: An Annotated Bibliography of Primary Sources.* Westport, Conn.: Greenwood, 1999.

————. *The Fall of the Republic and Other Political Satires.* Knoxville: University of Tennessee Press, 2000.

————. *A Sole Survivor: Bits of Autobiography,* by Ambrose Bierce. Knoxville: University of Tennessee Press, 1998.

Klein, Marcus. "San Francisco and Her Hateful Ambrose Bierce." *Hudson Review* 7, no. 3 (autumn 1954): 392–407.

Knight, Damon. "'Moxon's Master' Again: The Definitive Solution." *Science-Fiction Studies* 16 (1989): 117.

La Rochefoucauld. *Maxims.* Translated with an introduction by L. W. Tancock. Baltimore, Md.: Penguin, 1959.

Lauterbach, Edward Stuart. "*Fun* and Its Contributors: The Literary History of a Victorian Humor Magazine." Ph.D. diss., University of Illinois, 1961.

Levin, Harry T. "The Discovery of Bohemia." *Literary History of the United States,* 3d ed., edited by Robert Spiller et al., 1065–79. New York: Macmillan, 1963.

Lindley, Daniel. *Ambrose Bierce Takes on the Railroad: The Journalist as Muckraker and Cynic.* Westport, Conn.: Praeger, 1999.

Littell, Robert. "Bitter Bierce." *New Republic* 40, no. 515 (15 October 1924): 177.

Logan, F. J. "The Wry Seriousness of 'Owl Creek Bridge.'" *American Literary Realism* 10, no. 2 (spring 1977): 101–13.

Long, Belknap. Introduction to *Portrait of Ambrose Bierce,* by Adolphe de Castro. New York: Century, 1929.

Martin, Jay. "Ambrose Bierce." *The Comic Imagination in American Literature,* edited by Louis D. Rubin Jr., 195–205. New Brunswick, N.J.: Rutgers University Press, 1973.

Masters, Edgar Lee. *Spoon River Anthology,* edited by John E. Hallwas. Urbana: University of Illinois Press, 1992.

McWilliams, Carey. *Ambrose Bierce: A Biography.* With a new introduction by author. N.p.: Archon, 1967.

———. Introduction to *Bierce and the Poe Hoax,* by Carroll D. Hall. San Francisco: The Book Club of California, 1934.

———. Introduction to *The Devil's Dictionary,* by Ambrose Bierce. New York: Hill and Wang, 1961.

Mencken, H. L. *Prejudices: Sixth Series.* New York: Knopf, 1927.

Millard, Bailey. "Personal Memories of Ambrose Bierce." *Bookman* 40 (February 1915): 653–58.

Mitchell, Lee Clark. "Naturalism and Languages of Determinism." *Columbia Literary History of the United States,* edited by Emory Elliott, 525–45. New York: Columbia University Press, 1988.

Monaghan, Frank. "Ambrose Bierce and the Authorship of *The Monk and the Hangman's Daughter.*" *American Literature* 2, no. 4 (January 1931): 337–49.

Morris, Roy, Jr. *Ambrose Bierce: Alone in Bad Company.* New York: Oxford, 1995.

Nations, Leroy. "Ambrose Bierce: The Gray Wolf of American Letters." *South Atlantic Quarterly* 25, no. 3 (July 1926): 253–68.

Neale, Walter. *Life of Ambrose Bierce.* New York: Neale, 1929.

Oates, Whitney J., ed. *The Stoic and Epicurean Philosophers.* New York: Modern Library, 1957.

Owens, David M. "Bierce and Biography: The Location of Owl Creek Bridge." *American Literary Realism* 26 (spring 1994): 82–89.

Partridge, Eric. "Ambrose Bierce." *London Mercury* 16, no. 96 (October 1927): 630.

Pattee, Fred Lewis. *The Development of the American Short Story.* New York: Harper, 1923.

Pope, Bertha Clark, ed., with memoir by George Sterling. *The Letters of Ambrose Bierce.* San Francisco: The Book Club of California, 1922.

Reesman, Jeanne Campbell, ed. *Trickster Lives: Culture and Myth in American Fiction.* Athens: University of Georgia Press, 2001.

Rottensteiner, Franz. "Who Was Really Moxon's Master?" *Science-Fiction Studies* 15 (1998): 107–12, 388–90.

Schultz, David E., and S. T. Joshi, eds. *The Unabridged Devil's Dictionary,* by Ambrose Bierce. Athens: University of Georgia Press, 2000.

Sheller, Harry Lynn. "The Satire of Ambrose Bierce." Ph.D. diss., University of Southern California, 1945.

Sherburn, George. "The Restoration and Eighteenth Century (1660–1789)." *A iterary History of England,* edited by Albert C. Baugh, 823–1108. New York: Appleton-Century-Crofts, 1948.

Slade, Joseph W. "'Putting You in the Papers': Ambrose Bierce's Letters to Edwin Markham." *Prospects* 1 (1975): 335–68.

Stallman, R. W., and Lillian Gilkes, eds. *Stephen Crane Letters.* New York: New York University Press, 1960.

Starrett, Vincent. *Buried Caesars.* Chicago: Covici-McGee, 1923.

Sterling, George. Introduction to *In the Midst of Life,* by Ambrose Bierce, i–xvi. New York: Modern Library, 1927.

Swift, Jonathan. *A Tale of a Tub.* Oxford: Basil Blackwell, 1957.

Wertheim, Stanley, and Paul Sorrentino. "Thomas Beer: The Clay Feet of Stephen Crane Biography." *American Literary Realism* 22, no. 3 (spring 1990): 2–16.

Williams, Harold, ed. *Correspondence of Jonathan Swift.* Vol. 3, 1724–1731. Oxford: Clarendon Press, 1963.

Wilson, Edmund. *Patriotic Gore: Studies in the Literature of the American Civil War.* New York: Oxford University Press, 1962.

Wilt, Napier. "Ambrose Bierce and the Civil War." *American Literature* 1, no. 3 (November 1929): 260–85.

Woodruff, Stuart C. *The Short Stories of Ambrose Bierce: A Study in Polarity.* Pittsburgh: University of Pittsburgh Press, 1964.

INDEX